D1542753

OFF THE BEATEN PATH®
KENTUCKY →

Help Us Keep This Guide Up to Date

We would love to hear from you concerning your experiences with this guide and how you feel it could be improved and kept up to date. Please send your comments and suggestions to:

editorial@GlobePequot.com

Thanks for your input, and happy travels!

NINTH EDITION

OFF THE BEATEN PATH®
KENTUCKY

A GUIDE TO UNIQUE PLACES

ZOÉ AYN STRECKER

Revised and Updated by

Jackie Scheckler Finch

travel

Guilford, Connecticut

All the information in this guidebook is subject to change. We recommend that you call ahead to obtain current information before traveling.

Text design: Linda R. Loiewski
Maps: Equator Graphics © Morris Book Publishing, LLC
Excerpt from "Outdoor Lore" reprinted with the permission of the estate of Nevyle Shackelford

ISSN 1535-8038
ISBN 978-0-7627-5137-2

Printed in the United States of America
10 9 8 7 6 5 4 3 2 1

To those Kentuckians who, with lots of love and humor, continue to guide me off the beaten path in all realms of life

To my kin and friends who help me discover the beauty of Kentucky. Thanks to my parents, Jack and Margaret Poynter, for instilling in me the desire to travel and showing me the heart of the Bluegrass State. Some of my happiest childhood memories are of visiting with my grandparents, aunts and uncles, and cousins in the Danville area. My sister Elaine and I always looked forward to staying with Aunt Doris and Uncle Walker Poynter in Danville and having fun with our cousins Joyce, Carolyn, Susie, Jeannie, and Jim Poynter.

Thanks to my daughter, Kelly Rose, for helping carry the load. A special remembrance to my husband, Bill Finch, whose spirit goes with me every step of the way through life's amazing journey.

—Jackie Sheckler Finch

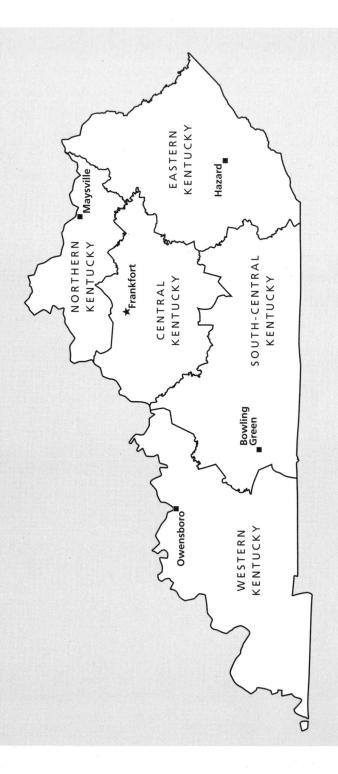

EASTERN KENTUCKY

Hazard

Maysville

NORTHERN KENTUCKY

Frankfort

CENTRAL KENTUCKY

SOUTH-CENTRAL KENTUCKY

Bowling Green

Owensboro

WESTERN KENTUCKY

Contents

Introduction

In an age when *Vive la difference!* is our cultural rallying cry, Kentucky should be a traveler's sheer delight. This 40,000-square-mile stretch of land is home to a greater variety of distinct cultures than any other rural state in the United States. Our landscapes vary wildly, our accents fluctuate county to county, and we're downright contradictory, always have been. This contradictory nature is a quality that is both enjoyable and educational for locals as well as inquisitive outsiders. Despite being a longtime victim of simplified stereotypes, the Commonwealth of Kentucky doesn't include a single "typical Kentuckian." Where the edges of Kentucky's cultures overlap, delightful contrasts abound. Where else can you find hitching posts for horse and buggy rigs in a Druther's fast-food parking lot? Where else do you hear English spoken with a heavy German lilt and a thick Southern twang? Or an Elizabethan dialect with a drawl?

Maybe the contradictions started with Daniel Boone (what didn't?), who was torn between settling the land he loved passionately and, not trusting his fellow pioneers, merging with the Native people who loved and adopted him. Maybe Kentucky's contradictory nature proved itself in bearing both Civil War presidents into the world within a year and fewer than 100 miles apart. The same waters that produce the world's smoothest bourbon and worst bootleg also sustained the life of Carrie Nation and continue to fill the teetotalers' baptismal fonts. Stereotypes of illiteracy are at loggerheads with a remarkable history of erudition and fine literary accomplishments, and the lack of national recognition for Kentucky's contributions to the high arts is suspect upon examination of the state's almost unequaled tradition of music, dance, and fine craft.

Then there's our geography, as erratic as Colorado's, yet older and more diverse in terms of flora and fauna. Vast, big-sky country dominates the western regions, where acre after fertile acre fan out, making a flat, Midwestern horizon, ending in swampland and rich arable bottomland by the banks of the great Mississippi and Ohio Rivers. Central and northern Kentucky ride on a high, fertile plateau, where game has always grazed and where livestock continue to make the region wealthy and world famous for equine and bovine bloodlines. Eastern Kentucky's lush mountains are well rounded with age, well supplied with precious seams of coal and iron ore, and laced with clear, beautiful streams. The south-central region has a touch of it all, including some of the world's most spectacular caverns.

In this book I'm just giving you leads to places that you may not have otherwise found. Your job is to immerse yourself and explore everything with fresh eyes and an open heart. The people here are so friendly, you'll get tired of smiling.

KENTUCKY TRAVEL AT A GLANCE

KENTUCKY TOURISM

Kentucky Department of Travel
Capital Plaza Tower 22nd Floor
500 Mero Street
Frankfort 40601
(800) 225–8747
www.kentuckytourism.com

REGIONAL AND LOCAL TOURISM OFFICES

Ashland Area Visitors Bureau
1509 Winchester Avenue
Ashland 41101
(800) 377–6249 or (606) 329–1007
www.visitashlandky.com

Bardstown-Nelson County Tourist and Convention Commission
One Court Square
Bardstown 40004
(800) 638–4877 or (502) 348–4877
www.visitbardstown.com

Berea Welcome Center
201 North Broadway
Berea 40403
(800) 598–5263 or (859) 986–2540
www.visitberea.com

Bowling Green–Warren County Tourism
352 Three Springs Road
Bowling Green 42104
(800) 326–7465 or (270) 782–0800
www.visitbgky.com

Carroll County Tourism and Convention Commission
515 Highland Street
P.O. Box 293
Carrollton 41008
(800) 325–4290 or (502) 732–7036
www.carrollcountyky.com

Cave City Tourism Center
502 Mammoth Cave Street
Box 518
Cave City 42127
(800) 346–8908 or (270) 773–3131
www.cavecity.com

Corbin Tourist Bureau
P.O. Box 956
Corbin 40701
(800) 528–7123 or (606) 528–8860

Danville–Boyle County Convention & Visitors Bureau
105 East Walnut Street
Danville 40422
(800) 755–0076 or (895) 236–7794
www.danvillekentucky.com

Elizabethtown Tourism & Convention Bureau
1030 North Mulberry Street
Elizabethtown 42701
(800) 437–0092 or (270) 765–2175
www.touretown.com

Frankfort Tourist Commission
100 Capital Avenue
Frankfort 40601
(800) 960–7200 or (502) 875–8687
www.visitfrankfort.com

Georgetown/Scott County Tourism
399 Outlet Center Drive
P.O. Box 825
Georgetown 40324
(888) 863–8600 or (502) 863–2547
www.georgetownky.com

Harlan Tourist and Convention Center
201 South Main Street
P.O. Box 489
Harlan 40831
(606) 573–4495
www.harlantourism.com

Harrodsburg/Mercer County Tourist Commission
P.O. Box 283
Harrodsburg 40330
(800) 355–9192 or (859) 734–2364
www.harrodsburgky.com

Henderson County Tourist Commission
101 North Water Street Suite B
Henderson 42420
(800) 648–3128 or (270) 826–3128
www.hendersonky.org

Hopkinsville–Christian County Convention and Visitors Bureau
2800 Fort Campbell Boulevard
P.O. Box 1382
Hopkinsville 42240
(800) 842–9959 or (270) 885–9096
www.visithopkinsville.com

Lexington Convention and Visitors Bureau
301 East Vine Street
Lexington 40507
(800) 845–3959 or (859) 233–7299
www.visitlex.com

Louisville and Jefferson County Information Center
301 South Fourth Street
Louisville 40202
(800) 792–5595 or (502) 584–2121
www.gotolouisville.com

Maysville-Mason County Convention & Visitors Bureau
201 East Third Street
Maysville 41056
(606) 564–6986
www.cityofmaysville.com

Morehead Tourism Commission
111 East First Street
Morehead 40351
(800) 654–1944 or (606) 780–4342
www.moreheadtourism.com

Murray Tourism Commission
805 North Twelfth Street
P.O. Box 190
Murray 42071
(800) 651–1603 or (270) 753–5171
www.tourmurray.com

Northern Kentucky Visitor Center
605 Philadelphia Street
Covington 41011
(800) STAY–NKY or (859) 655–4172
www.nkycvb.com

Owensboro–Daviess County Convention & Visitors Bureau
215 East Second Street
Owensboro 42303
(800) 489–1131 or (270) 926–1100
www.visitowensboro.com

Paducah–McCracken Convention & Visitors Bureau
128 Broadway Box 90
Paducah 42001
(800) 723–8224 or (270) 443–8784
www.paducah.travel

Paris–Bourbon County Chamber
720 High Street Suite 114
Paris 40361
(877) 868–8744 or (859) 987–8744
www.parisky.com

Richmond Tourism
345 Lancaster Avenue
Richmond 40475
(800) 866–3705 or (859) 626–8474
www.richmondkytourism.com

Somerset–Pulaski County Convention and Visitors Bureau
522 Ogden Street
P.O. Box 622
Somerset 42501
(800) 642–6287 or (606) 679–6394
www.lakecumberlandtourism.com

KENTUCKY TRAVEL AT A GLANCE

Winchester/Clark County Chamber
2 South Maple Street
Winchester 40391
(800) 298–9105 or (859) 744–0556
www.tourwinchester.com

Woodford County Chamber of Commerce
141 North Main Street Box 442
Versailles 40383
(859) 873–5122
www.woodfordchamber-ky.com

The pleasure of traveling in Kentucky begins with studying the map. Read the names of our towns and you'll begin to believe that Kentucky soil grows poets (and humorists) even better than tobacco: Bear Wallow, Horse Fly Holler, Cat Creek, Dog Town, Dogwalk, Dog Trot, Maddog, The Bark Yard, Monkey's Eyebrow, Possum Trot, Terrapin, Otterpond, Buzzard Roost, Pigeon Roost, Beaver Bottom, Beaver Lick, Rabbit Hash, Chicken Bristle, Chicken City, Ticktown, Scuffletown, Coiltown, Gold City, Future City, Sublimity City, Preacherville, Fearsville, Shuckville (population 7), Spottsville, Jugville, Blandsville, Pleasureville, Touristville, Wisdom, Beauty, Joy, Temperance, Poverty, Chance, Energy, Victory, Democrat, Republican, The Mouth, Mouth Card, Dimple, Nuckles, Shoulderblade, Big Bone, Back Bone, Wish Bone, Marrowbone, Cheap, Habit, Whynot, Pinchem Slyly, Mossy Bottom, Needmore, Sugartit, Hot Spot, Climax, Limp, Subtle, Geneva, Moscow, Bagdad, Warsaw, Paris, London, Athens, Versailles, Ninevah, Sinai, Buena Vista, Key West, Texas, Pittsburg, Omaha, Yosemite, Two Mile Town, Four Mile, Ten Mile, Halfway, Twenty-six, Seventy-six, Eighty-eight, Bachelor's Rest, Belcher, Brodhead, Oddville, Waddy, Wax, Dot, Empire, Embryo, Factory, Tidal Wave, Troublesome Creek, Vortex, Princess, Savage, Clutts, Decoy, Thousand Sticks, Gravel Switch, Quicksand, Halo, Moon, Static, Nonesuch, No Creek, Slickaway, Slap Out, Sideview, Nonchalanta, Fleming-Neon, Hi Hat, Go Forth, Alpha, Zula, Zoe, Zag, Zebulon, Zilpo, Yamacraw, Yeaddis, Yerkes, Uz (YOOzee), Wooton, Tyewhoppety, Kinniconic, Willailla, Whoopflarea, Symsonia, Smilax, Escondida, Cutshin, Cubage, Dongola, Nada, Nada (NAdee), Nebo, Slemp, Se Ree, Gee, Gad, Glo, Guy, Ono, Uno, Ino, Elba, Ulva, Ula, Ep, Eden, Devil's Fork, Paradise, Hell'n Back, Kingdome Come, Hell Fer Certain.

Kentucky Travel at a Glance

IN AN EMERGENCY

All regions of the state use the 911 emergency number. If you're involved in an accident, call (800) 222–5555, the emergency dispatcher's number for the Kentucky State Police.

CURRENT ROAD CONDITIONS

For prerecorded road reports call 511 when in-state, (800) RDREPORT from out of state.

A Few Facts about the Commonwealth

- **Capital:** Frankfort
- **Largest city:** Louisville, population approximately 1 million (metro area)
- **State bird:** Kentucky cardinal
- **State flower:** goldenrod
- **State fish:** Kentucky bass
- **State horse:** thoroughbred
- **State song:** "My Old Kentucky Home" by Stephen Collins Foster; written 1853
- **State bluegrass song:** "Blue Moon of Kentucky" by Bill Monroe; copyright 1947
- **Land area:** 39,732 square miles; rank, 37
- **Highest elevation:** 4,145 feet at Black Mountain
- **Lowest elevation:** 257 feet, near the Mississippi River in Fulton County

A Few of the Many Famous Kentuckians

- Bobbie Ann Mason, writer
- Cassius Marcellus Clay, abolitionist, ambassador to Russia
- Crystal Gayle, country singer
- Dwight Yoakam, country singer
- Gus Van Sant, award-winning movie director
- Harry Dean Stanton, actor
- Henry L. Faulkner, artist and poet
- James Bowie, Texas Ranger who designed the Bowie knife
- Jean Ritchie, folk singer/songwriter
- Johnny Depp, actor
- Kit Carson, agent for Native Americans
- Lee Majors, actor

- Loretta Lynn, country singer
- Muhammad Ali, boxer
- Ralph Eugene Meatyard, photographer
- Tom T. Hall, country singer
- Tom Cruise, actor
- Wendell Berry, writer

CENTRAL KENTUCKY

Like nowhere else in the world, central Kentucky seems to have been created for horses. For this we can thank the rocks. Water percolates through the limestone strata and brings phosphates into the soil that, in turn, enrich plants like bluegrass (actually green with a subtle blue tint), which give our thoroughbreds strong, lightweight bones—perfect for racing. The same water is the magic ingredient in this region's world famous bourbon whiskey.

Central Kentucky is also a kind of Mesopotamia of the South, a cradle of civilization west of the Allegheny Mountains. Modern buildings and businesses revolve around the region's direct links to the past. Antiques malls and bed-and-breakfasts in restored homes are ubiquitous in central Kentucky, and many of the humorous sites, like old country stores, are funny precisely because of their anachronisms. But there's nothing homogeneous about an area that can comfortably be home to everyone from Trappist monks to soul food chefs, jockeys, millionaires, Amish farmers, sculptors, and yoga teachers. And there's no chance you'll be bored exploring it all.

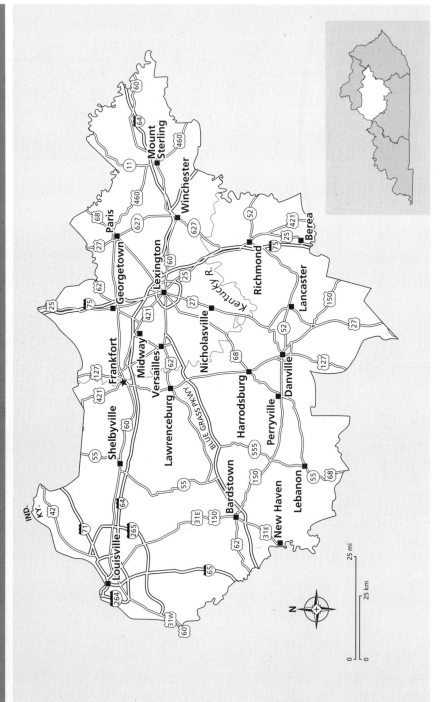

Bluegrass on the Rocks

Wherever there is bluegrass, there are horse farms. To get a good long look at some of the world's best-known horse farms, start in *Lexington*. Take a drive on Harrodsburg Road, Old Frankfort Pike, Iron Works Pike, Paris Pike, Danville Road, or Versailles Road. Many of these and the smaller lanes that weave through them make wonderful bicycling routes. The miles of wooden-plank fences are dizzying; these days most are sprayed with a black, creosote-based paint instead of the traditional white. Dotting the countryside are ostentatious mansions and lavish horse barns where handmade wainscoting and brass chandeliers are not unheard of.

Lexington is surrounded by hundreds of horse farms. The most famous are the thoroughbred farms, where the top racehorses in the world are bred, born, trained, and retired. Amid those gangly-legged foals you see romping in the fields in the spring may be a future Kentucky Derby—or Epsom or French Derby—winner.

AUTHOR'S FAVORITE PLACES IN CENTRAL KENTUCKY

Abbey of Gethsemani
New Haven
(502) 549–3117
www.monks.org

Actors Theatre
Louisville
(502) 584–1265 or (800) 428–5849
www.actorstheatre.org

American Printing House for the Blind
Louisville
(800) 223–1839
www.aph.org

Bernheim Forest Arboretum
Bardstown
(502) 543–2451
www.bernheim.org

Frasca Strecker Studio
Harrodsburg
(859) 734–5271

Harry C. Miller Lock Collection
Nicholasville
(859) 885–6041
www.lockmasters.com

Kentucky History Center
Frankfort
(502) 564–3016
www.history.ky.gov

Shaker Village of Pleasant Hill
Harrodsburg
(800) 734–5611
www.shakervillageky.org

21C Museum Hotel
Louisville
(502) 217–6300
www.21chotel.com

Weisenberger Mill
Midway
(859) 254–5282
www.weisenberger.com

Thoroughbreds are just one of many types of horse breeds raised on farms in and around Lexington. Standardbreds, American saddlebreds, draft horses, miniatures—all kinds of equines call Lexington home. Visitor policies on farms vary widely. There are several local tour companies. One is *Historic and Horse Farm Tours Inc.* (859–268–2906; www.horsefarmtours.com), which offers tours from April 1 through the end of October at the price of $32 per person in groups of four or more. The oldest tour company, *Blue Grass Tours* (859–252–5744; www.bluegrass tours.com), offers horse farm tours at $30 for adults and $20 for kids twelve and under. An excellent option for independent types is the tour of the stallion division of *Three Chimneys* (859–873–7053), located on Old Frankfort Pike between Lexington and Midway. Here you'll see 1997 Kentucky Derby and Preakness winner Silver Charm and other racing champions. Tours are offered strictly by appointment. Call (859) 873–7053 for reservations and directions to the farm. Also check www.threechimneys.com or write to P.O. Box 114, Midway 40307.

The best way to find out which farms are currently open is to call or stop by the *Lexington Convention and Visitors Bureau* (859–233–7299 or 800–845–3959; www.visitlex.com), which keeps updated information. The bureau is in downtown Lexington at 301 East Vine Street. There's no admission charge to tour individual farms, but keep in mind that it's traditional to tip the groom who shows you around, at least $5 to $10.

While you're at the visitor center, pick up a free copy of the *Lexington Walk and Bluegrass Country Driving Tour* guide, which directs your attention to specific histories while you absorb horse-farm aesthetics. The visitor center also offers special guides on more than a dozen topics of special interest, from antiques stores to area museums.

The *Kentucky Horse Park* (859–233–4303 or 800–678–8813), located a few miles north of downtown on Iron Works Pike, is not off the beaten path in any sense, but it is a great place to see all kinds of real horses, from thoroughbreds to rare breeds. There are some lesser-known aspects of this 1,032-acre park. Everybody stops at the Man o' War statue and grave, but take time also to visit the grave of Isaac Murphy. Here's a reminder of the important and largely unheralded role African Americans played in the early days of thoroughbred racing. Fourteen of the 15 riders in the first Kentucky Derby were black. Murphy, born in Lexington in 1861, remains the all-time most winning jockey, achieving victory in 44 percent of his races.

The Kentucky Horse Park is an educational center as well as a tourist attraction. So in addition to watching the films and looking at the antique carriages and other exhibits in the museum, be sure to walk through the Big Barn. You might find future horse trainers or veterinarians hard at work or meet some members of the Mustang Troop, Lexington inner-city youngsters who come to the park to care for once-wild western mustangs. The Mustang Troop rode in the 1997 Presidential Inaugural Parade.

Horses have been a favorite subject of artists, and the William G. Kenton Gallery, part of the park's *International Museum of the Horse,* is host to fascinating exhibits from around the globe. Something interesting is always on display, so don't skip over the gallery. Also be aware that the International Museum of the Horse is undergoing renovations and a building extension that are expected to be completed by 2012.

The Kentucky Horse Park is open from 9 A.M. to 5 P.M. daily from midMarch through October and from 9 A.M. to 5 P.M. Wednesday through Sunday, November through March. There are many special shows and events

Jot 'Em Down

Stop by the **Jot 'Em Down Store** at the intersection of Iron Works Pike and Russell Cave Road. Once called Terrell's Grocery, this little store has long been a favorite hangout for horse-farm employees. Founder Robert Terrell remembered the late 1930s, when his father and uncle listened for 15 minutes every night to a radio show called Lum and Abner, a comedic series about two store owners much like themselves. Lum was tall and savvy, while Abner was short, dim-witted, and funny. The fictional characters ran a grocery called the Jot 'Em Down Store in Pine Ridge, Arkansas. The Terrells' customers got into the habit of calling them Lum and Abner and began adopting character names from the show, like Mousie and Grandpappy Spears. Once when the real Lum and Abner were in Lexington buying horses, they heard about the tradition at Terrell's Grocery, so they dropped in for a visit, bringing with them a sign that read Jot 'Em Down Store. The rest is history. Come by for sandwiches and beers and you will meet Robert Terrell II ("Robey"), who has run the store since his father's death in 1998.

throughout the year. Admission is $15 spring through fall, $9 in winter (www
.kyhorsepark.com).

To experience other important aspects of Kentucky's equine industry, go
to the races or one of the big sales. In late April through May and in late September and early October, standardbred horses race at the **Red Mile Harness
Track** (859–255–0752), the second oldest harness-racing track in the U.S.,
located off South Broadway, just a few blocks from the downtown business
district. Great trotters and pacers have been racing this track and provoking
bets since 1875. Tattersalls Sales holds a variety of standardbred auctions at the
track throughout the year (www.theredmile.com).

Across the street from the Red Mile at 711 Red Mile Road (859–252–3481)
is a small riding apparel store called **Le Cheval Ltd.** Paige Kahn tailors custom-
made riding apparel for clients from coast to coast. The store is open weekdays
and Saturday mornings. Even if you're not in the market for a $1,500 riding
suit, the fine designs are worth seeing (www.lechevalltd.net).

About 43 percent of all the thoroughbred horses sold in North America
are sold at public horse sales in Kentucky. And the most prestigious horse sale
in the world is the July Selected Yearling Sale at **Keeneland Race Course**
(4201 Versailles Road; 859–254–3412 or 800–456–3412) in Lexington. This sale
dates to 1943, and the horses sold must meet high bloodline and conformation
standards. The bidders are an impressive group, too. From sheiks and film stars to international business moguls
and Texas cowboys, you just never know who you'll see at the Keeneland
sales pavilion. But you can bet that they will have one thing in common: the
means and the desire to spend big bucks on horses. You don't have to be a
millionaire just to watch the sales from the pavilion lobby or to walk through
the barns while the horses are being shown to potential buyers. It's a fascinating and surreal experience. Additional sales are held at Keeneland in January,
September, and November.

trueblue

In 1789 there were more horses
than people in Lexington.

Race meets at Keeneland are brief (just three weeks in April and three
weeks in October), but they usually attract the top echelon of the thoroughbred world. The spring meet includes the Blue Grass Stakes, an important preparatory race to the Kentucky Derby. The atmosphere is relaxed and genteel
(until 1997, the track didn't even have a public address system), and this is
one of the few tracks in North America where the public is allowed access to
the barn areas. Keeneland is worth a visit at any time of year. The old stone
buildings and grounds are lovely, and at the track's training center, you can

catch early morning workouts year-round. Plan to have breakfast at the track kitchen. For more information check www.keeneland.com.

If you are driving from downtown Lexington out to Keeneland, you'll be on Versailles Road (or Route 60). About halfway out of town, watch the right-hand side of the road for ***Bondurant's Pharmacy*** (1465 Village Drive, 859–254–8852), a working drug store inside a 1974 building the shape of a giant mortar and pestle, a traditional image used on pharmacy signs for hundreds of years. When a building mimics an object or an animal, in this case an image of its function, it is known as mimetic architecture, or a "duck." Bondurant's has been included on many national lists of and programs about wacky architecture as roadside attractions. The fact that you can walk inside does have its allure. Other examples of mimetic architecture in Kentucky include the Wigwam Village in Horse Cave (page 157) and the Mother Goose House in Hazard (page 97). There's something essentially American in using such cartoonish, "hey-look-at-that" buildings to boost business and put a silly smile on our faces. So, stop by for some saline solution.

Lexington boasts plenty of beautiful mansions, many dating to the early 1800s. One of the historic houses open for tour is ***The Hunt-Morgan House*** (201 North Mill Street; 859–233–3290). This lovely Federal-style brick house was built in 1814 by John Wesley Hunt, an early Lexington entrepreneur believed to be Kentucky's first millionaire. Later residents included Thomas Hunt Morgan, who won a Nobel Prize for medicine in 1933. Civil War buffs will be interested in the collection of uniforms, weapons, pictures, and other items relating to its most flamboyant occupant, Confederate general John Hunt Morgan. The escapades of Morgan and his "Morgan's Raiders" are recounted to this day in many a Kentucky community. Tour guides tell visitors that Morgan is reputed to have ridden his horse into the front hall of the house, kissed his mother, and galloped out the back door, with Union troops in hot pursuit. Morgan must have had a thing about riding his horse in the house, because there's a similar story attached to a house Morgan and his troops occupied in Lebanon, Kentucky.

trueblue

Kentucky has more than 1,500 miles of marked hiking trails.

Tours of the house are offered hourly Wednesday through Friday from 1 to 5 P.M., Saturday from 10 A.M. to 4 P.M., and Sunday from 1 to 5 P.M. (www.nps .gov/history/nR/travel/lexington/hun.htm). If you like old houses, you'll enjoy strolling in the surrounding Gratz Park neighborhood, Lexington's most posh address in the early 1800s. For more information on historic buildings call The Bluegrass Trust at (859) 253–0362.

Several of the historic Lexington homes operate as bed-and-breakfasts. The five guest rooms at *A True Inn* (467 West Second Street; 859–252–6166 or 800–374–6151; www.atrueinn.com) are named for historic Lexingtonians, from statesman Henry Clay and First Lady Mary Todd Lincoln to Belle Brezing, the city's most famous madam (thought to be the inspiration for the Belle Watling character in *Gone with the Wind*). The inn itself, an 1843 Romanesque-style brick house, is named for owners Bobby and Beverly True. Rates range from $149 to 199 per night.

Consider a man who was a jewelry designer known to drape diamond necklaces around the stubby red neck of his dachshund, Ernie, then send the dog out to model them for potential clients who were sunbathing by the swimming pool at the Bel Air Hotel. Try to imagine what kind of museum such a man would build. When you give up, take a drive west from downtown on the Old Frankfort Pike to the *Headley-Whitney Museum* (859–255–6653; www.headley-whitney.org). Originally, the late George W. Headley III established the space at his home to privately display his jewel collection, but in 1968 he and his wife opened the place to the public. Headley died in 1985, but the legacy of his museum continued. In the dramatic setting of the Jewel Room, visitors could once marvel at Headley's unusual jeweled boxes and bibelots, ranging from a ruby-encrusted abalone horse head to a scene of the moon landing in semiprecious stones. Unfortunately, in a sensational 1994 heist, burglars made off with many of the pieces. Since the robbery, the museum has increased its focus on fine decorative arts and features changing exhibits of clothing, textiles, and furniture. There are still many Headley creations on display, loaned by private owners, and if you need further evidence of his eccentricity, you need only step into the Shell Grotto—an entire room encrusted with thousands of seashells. The museum is open from 10 A.M. to 5 P.M. Tuesday through Friday, and from noon to 5 P.M. Saturday and Sunday. It's closed in January. Recently established as a Smithsonian Affiliate, the museum also hosts temporary exhibits that change every three months; these exhibits focus on the categories of decorative arts and historic fine art. The grounds are elegant for picnicking. Old Frankfort Pike is a great place for biking; part of it is an official National Scenic Byway.

true blue

Transylvania University in Lexington was the first university west of the Alleghenies.

For more art, the Lexington Art League has its offices and a small gallery in a strange, castellated 1852 Gothic villa in downtown Lexington, one of five designed by the architect A. J. Davis. The exhibitions at the *Loudoun House* provide a taste of the work of some visual artists in the area. A national juried exhibition every January called (and featuring) *The Nude* is the most popular event. Two alternate galleries run by the Art League are The Project Space, a space within the Loudoun House used for installation art projects, and the MetroLex Gallery off-site at 301 East Main Street in the atrium of the National City Bank Building. From downtown go north on North Broadway and turn right (east) on Loudon Avenue, then bear left when you reach a V in the road. Turn right onto Castlewood Drive. Hours are Tuesday through Sunday 1 to 4 P.M. (859–254–7024, www.lexingtonartleague.org).

Two artists who can almost always be found at work in the studio are Erika Strecker and Tony Higdon, a married couple of blacksmiths/sculptors. The public is welcome to stop by their gallery and studio, **Higdon-Strecker Studio,** on the edge of downtown Lexington, at 610 West Third Street near its intersection with Newtown Pike. Erika designs and builds tables, benches, sculpture, garden accessories—such as gates and trellises—and lighting fixtures, which often include hand-blown glass shades. Tony specializes in innovative architectural metalwork, like railings, balconies, furniture, fire screens, kitchen hoods, vanities, lighting, and furniture. Both use a variety of techniques that range from traditional blacksmithing with a hammer, forge, and anvil to sleek fabrication with high-tech equipment. Whatever the combination of techniques, every piece made by these artists is unique and hand-made at a high level of craftsmanship—a welcome respite in this world of mass production. The work in their gallery is for sale, but also serves to help visitors see the range of possibilities in terms of materials and forms. Commissions are welcome. The gallery is open between 9 A.M. and 5 P.M. Monday through Friday or by appointment. Call (859) 396–7118 for more information. To see portfolio images, take a look at www.ironhorseforge.com and www.erikastrecker.com.

Despite being central Kentucky's second-largest tourist attraction (the largest is the Kentucky Horse Park), Lexington children's museum, the **Explorium,** is something of a hidden treasure. It is hidden to adults because we might assume it's not for us. Think again. I found myself replanning the design of my shower stall after playing in the "bubble area," where you stand in a funny little booth and pull a giant vertical bubble completely around you, while watching it all in a fun-house mirror. Being confronted with "kid" information is also humbling. The ever-changing display areas range from cultural exhibitions about the Ukraine to a hands-on exhibit about how animation works. One educational area is a walk-through human heart, a series of sculpted and painted plaster chambers representing ventricles and auricles, all vibrating to the constant beat of our most powerful muscle. This megaheart was designed (and made, in part) by medical illustrator Rick Gersony. This museum is an all-day treat at the price of $6 per person; children under one admitted free. Hours are 10 A.M. to 5 P.M. Tuesday through Saturday, and 1 to 5 P.M. Sunday. The museum is located downtown, in Victorian Square, a complex of renovated 19th-century commercial buildings at the corner of Vine and Broadway. Call (859) 258–3253 for more information (www.explorium.com). If you have kids, be sure to call or stop by the *Lexington Children's Theatre* at 418 West Short Street, also by Victorian Square. Get a schedule of plays and special events at (859) 254–4546, www.lctonstage.org.

Lexington is Kentucky's second-largest city, so there are all manner of eateries and shops, but there are a few special places, oddballs, or old standbys that you don't want to miss. *Flag Fork Herb Farm Gift Shop,* at 900 North Broadway (859–233–7381), has transplanted a little bit of country into the city. In 1994 Mike and Carrie Creech moved their gardens from a farm in rural Franklin County to Lexington. Behind the shop, a 1790s carriage house, are large herb, perennial, and everlasting gardens. The shop carries live plants, dried herbs, jellies, potpourri, and handmade soaps. Hours are 10 A.M. to 4 P.M. Tuesday through Saturday and until 6 P.M. on Thursday. You can have lunch at *The Garden Cafe*, which overlooks the bird-feeding garden. Cafe hours are 11 A.M. to 2 P.M. for lunch Wednesday through Saturday. Call (859) 252–6837 for reservations.

The *Atomic Cafe* (859–254–1969), located in an old corner building near downtown at 265 North Limestone (across Third Street from Transylvania University), is definitely a hot place to eat. Guinness on tap and a huge basket of spicy sweet-potato chips are reasons enough to go. The whole menu is Caribbean, ranging from a savory chicken pot pie to spicy lime shrimp. In good weather there's outdoor patio seating. Indoors, the cafe tends to be loud and lively. Island murals cover the walls from floor to ceiling. Dinner only, Tuesday through Saturday.

The Dame: Lexington's Live Music Hall (367 East Main Street, 859–231–7263) really and truly is Lexington's primary venue for live music six nights a week. Perhaps the beauty of a town the size of Lexington is that a place like this has to be diverse to survive—they stage big-name nationally known acts as well as every local and regional band worth hearing. Their Web site, www .dameky.com, is great, not due to fancy graphics, but due to the way band information is presented by fan affiliation. Never heard of the Swells? Well, their fan base overlaps with that of Django Reinhardt, the Squirrel Nut Zippers, and Billie Holliday. Okay, not for you. How about Hair Police, whose fans also groove to Wolf Eyes, Black Dice, and Lightning Bolt. Even better than association, you can listen to a track and go to the band's Web site. Ticket prices are so reasonable that you're encouraged to experiment. Show times vary. The Dame also hosts special events like the Lexington Mardi Gras celebration, a local filmmakers showcase, open mic nights, and so forth.

Just blocks away is the **Kentucky Theater** (214 East Main, 859–231–7924, www.kentuckytheater.com), a true living treasure of the city and an architectural gem to boot. The main theater was built in 1922 in Italian Renaissance style, complete with highly ornamental ceiling and massive velvet stage curtain. In 1929 the adjacent State Theater was built in a Spanish style—clouds are painted on the dreamy blue sky ceiling. A fire in 1987 nearly condemned the buildings. But ten years later a restored Kentucky was open to the delighted and now faithful public. There is also an ongoing effort to fully restore the theater's original Wultitzer Organ. It's a real pleasure to see a film or a concert in the space, but what makes the theater a living treasure is its devotion to showing art films, documentaries, animated shorts, and midnight flicks, like *The Rocky Horror Picture Show* or *Eraserhead*. Monday nights are devoted to the live taping of the *Woodsongs Old-Time Radio Hours,* an internationally syndicated live folk music program the public is welcome to attend and become the live audience at a price of usually only $6.50, except for special shows (www.woodsongs.com). Several times a year look for fabulous concerts organized by the Troubadour Concert Series—big names in the theater's gorgeous, almost intimate setting (www.troubashow.com).

Ashland, the Henry Clay Estate was originally the home and 600-acre farm of Henry Clay, 19th-century statesman (U.S. Senator, Speaker of the House of Representatives, Secretary of State, peace commissioner, and presidential candidate). The Italianate mansion itself

trueblue

Kentucky became the 15th state in 1792.

has the status of a National Historic Landmark and is worth the $7 tour. The most interesting room is an octagonal library with a vaulted, domed ceiling, reportedly designed by Benjamin Latrobe, who also designed the U.S. Capitol in Washington, D.C. Even if you choose not to go indoors, the serpentine paths through the grounds and handsome gardens are a pleasure to walk. Clay named the place Ashland because the estate grounds were, and still are, covered with majestic old ash trees. The gardens are formal, 18th-century parterre style, and are lovingly maintained by the Garden Club of Lexington. You can also get a box lunch (seasonally) at the **Ginkgo Tree,** open from 11 A.M. to 4 P.M. daily late April through October, weather permitting. The garden is open dawn to dusk daily, year-round. House tours are given from 10 A.M. to 4 P.M. Monday through Saturday and from 1 to 4 P.M. Sunday. The house is closed in

January and on Monday, November through March. Ashland is located at 120 Sycamore Road, off Richmond Road. Call (859) 266–8581 or visit www.henry clay.org for more information.

When **Alfalfa Restaurant** opened in the early 1970s, it was probably one of thousands of health-food cooperatives that operated on limited budgets and lots of heart. It has survived and flourished as one of Lexington's most cherished eateries. Although it is not purely vegetarian, the restaurant has always catered to the vegetarian and health-conscious population. Whole grains, vivid flavors, internationally inspired recipes, potent desserts, imported beers, and cinnamon coffee keep us coming back. There's live music nightly by your table, ranging from jazz flute to Irish bouzouki. Alfalfa is located at 141 East Main, next door to the Downtown Arts Center. Hours are 11 A.M. to 2 P.M. Monday through Saturday, and for dinner from 5:30 to 10 P.M. Wednesday and Thursday, and 5:30 to 11 P.M. Friday and Saturday, and 9 A.M. to 2 P.M. for a beloved Sunday brunch. Call (859) 253–0014 for specials and information.

Located near the campus of the University of Kentucky, **Joe Bologna's** (859–252–4933; www.joebolognas.com) has been a favorite Lexington hangout since the early 1970s, and not just for students. In the early 1990s it moved across the street from its original location to a restored church building at 120 West Maxwell Street—the bar is sacrilegiously located right where the altar used to be, and televisions are everywhere. Joe B's is the place to go for pizza and other Italian dishes. You must order the famous breadsticks, served in a sinful pool of garlic butter. For a dinner that's a bit more expensive, but much more Italian, try **Giuseppe's Ristorante Italiano.** Go south out of town on Nicholasville Road 1/2 mile beyond Man o' War, and look for the sign on the left. A great wine list dominated by Chianti is featured. Call (859) 272–4269 for reservations, a recommended practice or visit www.giuseppeslexington.com.

Almost directly across Nicholasville Road is the **Waveland State Historic Site** (859–272–3611), a grand Greek Revival mansion that was built in 1847 by Joseph Bryan, the grandnephew of Daniel Boone. Guided tours cost $7 and are offered year-round (except January when it is closed), Monday through Saturday between 10 A.M. and 5 P.M. and on Sunday from 1 to 5 P.M. You'll see all aspects of life on an antebellum plantation, from the smokehouse and icehouse to the servants' quarters and some remarkable period furnishings. The most intriguing object is a hickory ladderback chair that originally came from the home of Daniel Boone's parents in Pennsylvania. The chair was tied to the side of a packhorse in 1779 to make a seat for two-year-old Rebecca Boone Grant, Daniel's niece, as her family traveled to Kentucky from North Carolina. The building underwent an extensive renovation in 2000 and is in excellent condition.

Although **Raven Run Nature Sanctuary** (5888 Jacks Creek Road, 859–272–6105) is just outside of town, it has the ability to make you feel as if you're deep in Appalachian wilderness. From downtown take Richmond Road (also Main Street) east out of town and turn right onto Highway 25 (across from Jacobson Park). Go approximately 3½ miles to Jack's Creek Pike and turn right (at Judy Ray's Grocery Store). Go about 5½ miles on Jack's Creek Pike, and Raven Run is located on the left. A large chain-link fence and a sign mark the entrance. The sanctuary's 470 acres include a perfect little piece of the region's most dramatic geologic feature—the Kentucky River limestone palisades—and the remarkable diversity of native wild plant species unique to it. Raven Run is open daily year-round (except for major holidays) for hiking along its 8 miles of trails. Just sign in at the nature center and bring your own water. Along the trails you'll discover remnants of 19th-century structures like stone chimneys.

The sanctuary's nature center has a number of hands-on exhibits that kids will love. Make sure to ask about current programs, which include sessions on the life cycles and identification of butterflies and dragonflies, bird watching, tree-identification, night hikes to view nocturnal animals and learn owl calls, map and compass navigations, and so forth. Spend some time there and you'll see why Lexingtonians, especially children, love their nature sanctuary.

The other natural area owned by the Lexington Fayette County Urban Government, Parks and Recreation Department, is **McConnell Springs** (416 Rebmann Lane). It's not near town, it's in town, a 26-acre pocket of preserved natural space inside an industrial area just inside New Circle Road. To get there, get onto Old Frankfort Pike and watch for signs on the south side. It's open daily from 9 A.M. to 5 P.M. year-round. There are two miles of very well-maintained hiking trails that wind through farmland with stone fences and wooded areas, and past several unusual natural springs. The site was first settled in 1775 by William McConnell and is said to be the site where Lexington was named. A gunpowder mill here supplied powder for the war of 1812. After the mill closed, the land changed hands five times, finally coming to the Cahill family. The stone foundation at the farm site once supported a large 1920s-era dairy barn. In 1958 the land was sold to the Central Rock company, which tore down the buildings and started mining rock and gravel. The Friends of McConnell Springs bought the land in 1994 and conserved it as a natural area.

The most amazing features of the preserve are the two springs. The waters of the Blue Hole emerge from underground through the limestone bedrock from a wide area of southwest Lexington. The name comes from the prismatic blue effects caused by its unusual depth of 15 feet into a conical basin filled by the springs. The Boils get their name from the energetic surging of water into the spring after heavy rains. The pressure is great enough that the fountainlike columns may reach two feet tall. The Boils are cold, with an average temperature of 55 degrees Fahrenheit. Both the Boils and the Blue Hole are artesian springs—wells or springs that force water to the surface due to subsurface pressures.

When the waters reach the final sink, they disappear underground into a cavelike formation for a third of a mile before surfacing again at Preston's Cave and eventually reaching Elkhorn Creek. An exposed window like the Final Sink is characteristic of the Karst topography that underlies much of this area. Sinkholes are also a common feature of Karst systems, formed when surface soil is carried away from below as cracks in the limestone bedrock enlarge. A major evolution of the Final Sink took place just after the property was acquired. Part of the soil bank at the back right of the main sinking point collapsed and formed a deep, vertically walled shaft. This new sink began to enlarge rapidly and threatened some of the trees overlooking the sink. Measures were taken to stop or slow the erosion, but, as many local farms can attest, the natural processes of the springs always win.

The other superstars of the site are the majestic 250-year-old bur oak trees dating from the era before much human intervention when the bluegrass region was predominantly an open savannah, open fields of thick native grasses with a few interspersed trees. You can occasionally get the sense of a savannah on some of the older horse farms where ancient trees dot pasture. Imagine large cats like cougars lounging on massive branches and waiting for a herd of elk or deer to stop for shade.

trueblue

The Vest-Lindsay Home in Frankfort was the boyhood home of U.S. Senator George Graham Vest, credited with the immortal phrase "Dog is man's best friend."

For an unusually intimate look at the workaday world of thoroughbred training, plan to tour *The Thoroughbred Center* (now owned by Keeneland Race Course), 3380 Paris Pike. From downtown Lexington take North Broadway out of town, which becomes Paris Pike (or U.S. Highways 68 and 27). After a few miles, look for the horse center on your right. Since 1969, when this business was started, it has been one of the most prestigious privately owned thoroughbred training centers in the world. More than 1,100 stalls are leased to individual horse owners, who supply their own trainers and riders.

The tour takes you through a barn, by the rail where you can talk to a trainer, and into the sales pavilion, where you'll be amazed at the complexity of yet another aspect of the business—horse sales. Tours take one and a half hours and cost $10 for adults, $5 for children. They're given at 9 A.M.,

10:30 A.M., and 1 P.M., Monday through Friday, plus on Saturday April through October. November 1 through March 31, only the 9 A.M. tour is available (or by appointment). Call ahead because tour space is limited (859–293–1853; www.thethoroughbredcenter.com). Either before or after the tour, stop by the extensive tack shop, where you may luck into an opportunity to watch leather workers in action.

From The Thoroughbred Center, drive north to Paris along US 68, "Paris Pike" as it's known locally. This beautiful route represents an innovative approach to highway planning. With numerous accidents along its narrow, curving path, this busy road had a deadly reputation, but it was also lined by mature trees, dry-laid rock fences, and some of the area's finest horse farms. Highway planners and preservationists battled for years over how to improve the road without destroying its character. Their compromise is a four-lane highway that runs through carefully preserved scenic setbacks; the rock fences were moved and rebuilt.

If a hearty meal is what you have in mind, try *Campbell's Restaurant.* This friendly, family-owned spot has been open since the 1960s. The menu includes a little bit of everything, from prime rib to seafood, all prepared with a gourmet touch. Campbell's serves lunch Monday through Friday and dinner Monday through Saturday. Reservations are suggested for groups of more than four; call (859) 987–5164 or go to www.campbellsinparis.com.

Campbell's would have had a serious competitor in the late 18th century when the *Duncan Tavern,* at 323 High Street, was in its heyday. Major Joseph Duncan built the huge inn out of native limestone on this spot in 1788, four

Freedom and the Spirit of Invention

On the corner of Tenth and Vine Streets is a bronze historical marker recognizing the birthplace of Garrett Morgan, African-American inventor of the tri-color traffic signal, forerunner of the present traffic light, and a gas mask design that became the basis for one used during World War I. Among his many awards was the first grand prize of the Second International Exposition of Safety and Sanitation in 1914. In addition to the highway marker, there is a permanent exhibit on Garrett Morgan on display at the Hopewell Museum, 800 Pleasant Street (see page 16).

Also recognized on the marker is Morgan's childhood school, Branch School, located in the neighborhood of Claysville, adjacent to the marker. Claysville was one of the early black settlements that sprang up after the Civil War when newly emancipated slaves needed a place to live, work, and structure their lives as free citizens. Garrett Morgan's maternal grandfather, Rev. Garrett Reed, was one of the early settlers in the little community.

years before Kentucky was a state. Everything else in town was built of logs, so the tavern was an eye-catcher as well as a social catchall. Originally there was a ballroom, a bar, a billiards room, dining rooms, kitchens, and bedrooms. Daniel Boone slept there. So did frontiersman Simon Kenton.

Today the Duncan Tavern and Anne Duncan House is a historic site owned by the Kentucky Society of the Daughters of the American Revolution (DAR), which has acquired enough period furniture and significant artifacts to fill the huge building gracefully. Much of the original large furniture was built on-site. Its tradition as a tavern is maintained by keeping it active as a party place: People can rent the Duncan Tavern for parties and receptions. The DAR hosts small events in the original dining room and serves meals on a long, cherry, boardinghouse-style table, valued at $30,000. The tavern has recently been renovated. Normally the tavern and genealogy library are open to visitors Tuesday through Saturday from 10 A.M. to noon and from 1 to 4 P.M. Tours are given Tuesday through Saturday at 1:30 P.M. Admission to the tavern is $8; the genealogy library is $15. Call (859) 987–1788 or visit www.kentuckydar.org/duncantavern.htm for more details.

Learn about area history at the **Hopewell Museum** (859–987–7274; www.hopewellmuseum.org), in a proud little building at the corner of Eighth and Pleasant Streets. Admission is free, and hours are Wednesday through Saturday from noon to 5 P.M. and Sunday from 2 to 4 P.M. Closed in January. Just up the street is the **Nannine Clay Wallis Arboretum,** 616 Pleasant Street, at the headquarters of the Garden Club of Kentucky (859–987–6158). A "study guide" for tree identification is available. Admission is free, and hours are Monday through Saturday from 10 A.M. to 6 P.M. and Sunday from noon to 6 P.M.

Bourbon County has more than 85 horse farms, but very few allow visitors. One exception is **Claiborne Farm,** home and burial place of the celebrated Triple Crown winner Secretariat, which generously welcomes visitors by appointment only. Call (859) 233–4252 or (859) 987–2330 or visit www.claibornefarm.com. From downtown Paris go south on Highway 627 (also called Winchester Road) beyond the edge of town. Watch for the farm entrance on your left.

Cane Ridge Meeting House Shrine is the site of some powerful events and the source of some wild stories. Follow Main Street (US 68) north from downtown Paris and go east on U.S. Highway 460 to Highway 537 North. Take the latter for 5.4 miles and look left (north) for the shrine. Said to be the largest one-room log structure in North America, the church is impressive.

Two events make this church significant. The first was the Cane Ridge Revival, which took place August 6–12, 1801. It was the nation's largest revival during a period of big ones. Between 20,000 and 30,000 people attended. Preachers stood on platforms, stumps, and hay bales all over the fields talking simultaneously to thousands of people for seven days and six nights. As the story goes, women's hair stood straight out and crackled like fire; people spoke in tongues, shook, danced, laughed, and sang, and were moved every which way by the Holy Spirit. The excitement ended when the food ran out. The second event occurred in 1804 when Cane Ridge preacher Barton Warren Stone led the people away from the Presbyterian Church and started a new movement that became the Christian Church (Disciples of Christ), the denomination that now owns and manages the shrine. In 1957 an enormous limestone superstructure was erected to protect the log church. Later a museum was built nearby. From April through October the whole place is open Monday through Saturday from 9 A.M. to 5 P.M. and from 1 to 5 P.M. on Sunday. Donations are encouraged. Call (859) 987–5350 or go to www.caneridge.org.

Roll up your sleeves and choose your own produce at either of these two Paris area farms. Call ahead to see what's ripe and to ask whether you should bring your own containers. **Reed Valley,** 239 Lail Lane (859–987–6480), features blueberries, blackberries, nectarines, raspberries, peaches, pears, and apples. And **Marshalls' Strawberries,** 325 Austerlitz Road (859–987–6502), features—guess what—strawberries.

Downtown **Georgetown** is chock-full of history. It's also a good place for a walk. Pick up a **Walk Through Time** tour brochure from the Georgetown Tourism office (399 Outlet Center Drive) or at various locations around town, and take a stroll along this pretty Main Street where architecture spans

Sentenced to a New Life

One building you can't overlook in downtown Georgetown is the *Old Scott County Jail Complex* at Main and Water Streets. When it was built in 1892, this massive Victorian-style building was acclaimed as the "jewel" of Kentucky jails and offered the latest amenities, such as electric lights and indoor plumbing. A hundred years later, when the county built a new Justice Center, the old jail seemed archaic and gloomy inside by modern standards. Some wanted to tear it down, but a small group of local citizens and artists thought this former jewel might be creatively recut. Since the late 1990s, Scott County Arts Consortium has been working to transform the historic jail and attached jailer's house for use as a community arts and cultural center. By applying for grants, soliciting memberships and donations from local citizens, sponsoring art shows, house tours, suppers, silent auctions, and locally famous bake sales (the group includes some awesome cooks), they've overcome the naysayers and put a new copper roof on the jailer's house, renovated the porch, and developed a phased plan to rehabilitate the structure. If you'd like to find out more about this project (or those bake sales), call the consortium's director, Barbara Strippelhoff, at (502) 863–0909 or check www.scottcountyarts.org or wwww.artsandculturalcenter.org.

more than 200 years, and many buildings have interesting legend and lore attached—such as the statue of justice on the courthouse that is rumored to come to life and roam the streets every Halloween! One local collector of such lore is Kay Vincent, who with her sister Barbara Hoffman owns **Bohannons' Books With a Past,** 152 East Main Street (502–863–3003; www.bookswith-apast.net). Bohannons' is a good place to browse for reasonably priced reading material and friendly conversation. The shop carries used titles as well as new books of regional and local interest. Hours are 10 A.M. to 5 P.M., Monday through Saturday. **Fava's Restaurant,** established in 1910 on East Main Street (502–863–4383), is a true diner in the old style (which are fast becoming extinct in Kentucky), where you can eat breakfast, lunch, or dinner between 6:30 A.M. and 9 P.M. from Monday through Saturday. Or, have three o'clock coffee and argue local issues with politicians and merchants.

If you're interested in antiques, look in any direction. In a state as obsessed with old stuff as Kentucky, any town that dares call itself the Antiques Capital of Kentucky better be able to back up that claim with something substantial. Georgetown does, with five malls all within easy walking distance of the courthouse. If it's old, you probably can find it at the **Central Kentucky Antique Mall,** or the **Georgetown Antique Mall.** A list of antiques dealers is available at www.georgetownky.com/shop.html. Just west of Georgetown Antique Mall on Main Street is **Heirlooms and Gretchen's** (502–863–2538) www .heirloomsandgretchens.com, where the Heirloom crew does picture framing, custom leaded- and stained-glass work, and what they call "family heirloom bears." Say your grandmother had a fur coat, but moths have damaged it over the years. You can take what's left to Heirloom's, and they'll transform it into lovable Mama, Papa, or Baby bears.

The old buildings on Georgetown's Main Street have seen other changes in recent years. When the post office moved from Main and Mulberry to a new suburban building, many residents were concerned about the fate of the stately limestone building that had housed the post office since the early 1900s. They were thrilled when the county purchased the building as a home for the **Georgetown and Scott County Museum.** The museum features a variety of displays about local history, from bourbon to ballpoints, with special programs on local history every month. The marble-floored lobby of the post office has been left pretty much intact. Museum hours are 9 A.M. to 4 P.M. Monday through Friday, 10 A.M. to 4 P.M. Saturday. Admission is free. Call (502) 863–6201 or visit www.georgetownky.com/attrac.html.

From downtown Georgetown take US 25 North out of town and watch for signs to **Cardome Centre** (502–863–1575; www.cardomecenter.com), a property that has played a significant role in Kentucky history for hundreds of years. After having been a major hunting ground for Choctaw, Mingo, and Shawnee Indians, it was one of the first areas deeded and settled west of the mountains. It was home to a number of early prominent white families during the 1800s, including James F. Robinson, a Kentucky governor, who gave the place its name, Cardome, after the Latin phrase *cara domus,* or "dear home." The Sisters of Visitation, a cloistered sect, bought Cardome in 1896 and ran an academy there until 1969. Now Cardome belongs to the city of Georgetown and operates as an educational center and historic site, open for self-guided tours Monday through Friday from 8 A.M. to 4 P.M. Or, take a guided tour by appointment. Visitors can walk through the original academy and monastery buildings as well as a science classroom and a "dream house," where the senior girls were finally allowed to have outside visitors and even to smoke. Cardome's pride and joy is the school chapel, which features some gorgeous woodwork, Romanesque vaulted ceilings, stained-glass windows, and a classic bell tower. The whole property can be rented for

Moonshine and Wood Carvings

You'd better sit down for this one: The father of bourbon whiskey was a Baptist preacher. According to legend, the good Reverend Elijah Craig ran a distillery, a hemp rope walk, and a paper mill (the first in the state). A fire swept through a building where barrels were being stored, and being something of a tightwad, Reverend Craig decided to put new corn whiskey into the charred barrels despite the damage. The color of the whiskey changed, the flavor mellowed, and a tradition was born. Eventually this new sour mash was named bourbon because large quantities were made in nearby Bourbon County. Baptists, don't despair. In the late 18th century, Baptists were not as concerned with temperance. Drunkenness among preachers was prohibited, but drinking was not. In fact, clergy often were paid in whiskey. Gambling, dancing, and going to barbecues, on the other hand, were considered serious crimes.

Elijah Craig's sundry enterprises were all built near the **Royal Spring,** a steady water source gurgling up from under a huge bed of limestone, discovered in 1774. Georgetown was built around the spring, and the city still gets its water from it. A small park around the spring is the site of an 1874 log cabin built by a former slave, Milton Leach, and a 1997 wooden statue of Elijah Craig by Georgetown artist Sandy Schu. This is no typical wood carving; it was created using a chainsaw from a tree still rooted in the park grounds. Other examples of Schu's noisy yet surprisingly detailed work can be seen throughout the area. He created the buffalo on display at Cardome Centre, north of downtown. His 20-foot eagle inspires golfers at the 12th hole of Kearney Hill Links golf course in Lexington. For more information about Royal Spring and other Georgetown attractions, call **Scott County Tourism** at (502) 863–2547 or go to www.georgetownky.com.

huge company picnics, or smaller areas can be used for weddings, seminars, meetings, and so forth.

Adjacent to Cardome is an unusual work in progress, "the official Kentucky-Japan Friendship Garden," *Yuko-En on the Elkhorn.* The garden was envisioned by members of the Scott Education and Community Foundation as a way to commemorate the 10th anniversary of the sister city relationship between Georgetown and Taharo-cho, Japan. Plants and rock native to Kentucky are used in accordance with Japanese gardening principals. So, in place of bamboo, there is a large grove of native cane. The spare Zen rock garden employs large pieces of naturally sculpted Kentucky limestone. In the Savannah Gardens, there are upper and lower waterfalls cascading down natural limestone outcrops into reflecting pools lined with walls built like central Kentucky's famous dry-laid stone fences. The high canopy of American maple trees hovers almost protectively over the delicate little Japanese maple in the Stroll Garden in which the land has been resculpted to represent the rolling bluegrass region in miniature. Visitors are welcome to stroll through this unique landscaping gem anytime year-round. There are six acres to explore—by Japanese standards, that's almost endless. The address is 700 Cincinnati Pike. For more information call Scott County Education and Community Foundation at (502) 863–8039. Visit www.yuko-en.com. Guided tours can be organized around various topics—Japanese culture, the Elkhorn Creek corridor, or wildlife conservation. There are ongoing programs for regional students in environmental education.

While a Japanese garden may be a new idea in Georgetown and Scott County, growing things certainly isn't. Across US 25 from Cardome is *Bi-Water Farm* (502–863–3676; www.biwaterfarm.com), one of a bumper crop of Scott County farm markets. Bi-Water, run by the Fister family, features flowers and herbs as well as homegrown vegetables. The farm's Autumnfest runs several weekends in the fall with hayrides, a corn maze, and other family activities. On Newtown Pike, look for *Evans Farm Orchard* (502–863–2255; www .evansorchard.com), which features a petting zoo and tomatoes, squash, and other hot-weather veggies in the summer and dozens of apple varieties in late summer through fall. *Amerson Farm Orchard* (502–863–3799; www .amersonfarms.com) on the U.S. Highway 62 bypass also features vegetables and apples along with delicious apple cider slushies. So, summer through fall, this is a great place to load up on farm-fresh food. All are open on weekends; weekday hours vary.

Through all of its varied projects since 1989, *Shooting Star Nursery* is accomplishing the goals of educating people about preserving the world's biodiversity and promoting renaturalization in Kentucky and elsewhere. The nursery itself supplies more than 3,000 species of nursery-propagated native plants for gardening, landscaping, and restoring damaged lands such as strip mines and tired farmland. The nursery's botanists spend lots of energy doing consultation for those involved in ecological restoration and education. (See, for example, the native prairie grassland plantings at the Shaker Village at Pleasant Hill on page 24.) Their Web site, www.shootingstarnursery.com, is in itself an excellent resource. It explains that natural landscaping provides lost habitat and protects natural resources, but also that it is extremely important not to dig plants from the wild as the practice further endangers native species. Descriptions are thorough and the photos are lovely. You can, for example, order a collection of plants that form a native perennial hummingbird garden, complete with suggested landscaping layout. Or order enough native grass and wildflower seed to restore an entire farm to its pre-1700 botanical condition. Plants described on the Web site can be mail-ordered directly from Shooting Star. Otherwise you are welcome to visit the nursery by appointment. They are open to the public on a drop-in basis for retail sales twice a year, in May and September. Call (502) 867–7979 or (866) 405–7979 or check the Web site for exact dates and times. To get there, take US 460 out of Georgetown to the west (3.7 miles from the Interstate 75 exit) and watch for Soards Road on the left-hand side. The nursery is on the left. The address is 160 Soards Road, Georgetown.

One of the best-selling family sedans in America, the Camry, as well as Avalon sedans and Sienna minivans, are made in Georgetown at ***Toyota Motor Manufacturing, Kentucky, Inc.,*** on Cherry Blossom Way (exit 129 from I–75). Hourlong guided tours of the plant are given at 10 A.M., noon, and 2 P.M. Monday through Friday, with an additional tour at 6 P.M. on Thursday, by reservation. Call (800) 866–4485. No shorts, cameras, purses, or children under first grade are allowed. You'll don a hard hat and safety goggles and ride an electric tram through the stamping, body weld, and assembly areas of the plant. The plant is a big—about eight million square feet under roof—bright, and noisy place, all the more mind-boggling when you consider that nearly 400,000 vehicles and 500,000 engines are made here each year. Plant tours usually get booked far in advance, but you can stop by and look at the cars and manufacturing exhibits at the visitor center any time between 10 A.M. and 4 P.M. Monday through Friday (www.toyotageorgetown.com).

In the Beginning

In the beginning there was ***Harrodsburg.***

A friend of mine swears that it takes a Harrodsburg resident, in any conversation, less than four minutes to bring up the fact that the genesis of the

American West is Harrodsburg, Kentucky. On June 16, 1774, James Harrod and his company took a great leap of faith and of foot when they chose to settle the fertile strip of land between the Kentucky and Salt Rivers, the "Big Spring"—more than 250 miles of wilderness and mountains away from the nearest Anglo-Saxon settlement to the east.

Today Harrodsburg sports a full reproduction of the 1775 fort in the **Old Fort Harrod State Park,** at the intersection of U.S. Highways 68 and 127, a good place to begin your exploration of one of the state's significant historic areas. (Oddly, the reproduction fort is not exactly sited where the original stood.) Inside the park's entrance is the **Mansion Museum,** featuring Civil War artifacts, and the **Lincoln Marriage Shrine,** a redbrick building that protects the log chapel where Abraham Lincoln's parents "got hitched." Inside the fort's walls, people in period costumes demonstrate pioneer crafts during the summer. The fort is open to the public year-round, and from March 16 to November 30 the museum is also open. Hours vary by season. Admission is $5 for adults and $3 for kids. Call (859) 734–3314 or visit http://parks.ky.gov/findparks/recparks/fh. For general information on Harrodsburg, check www.harrodsburgky.com.

Follow Chiles Street south to Kentucky's first row house, circa 1800, known as **Morgan Row,** after the builder Joseph Morgan. The street is named after Morgan's son-in-law, John Chiles, who ran a famous tavern on the site. In front of Morgan Row, Uncle Will of Wildwood, a prominent Mercer County farmer, is said to have been cited for speeding in his one-horse buggy. When Uncle Will went to pay his ticket, he paid double the amount, telling the clerk in a voice loud enough for the whole courthouse to hear, "I'm paying you double 'cause I plan to leave the way I came." Today Morgan Row houses, among other things, the **Harrodsburg Historical Society Museum** and office (859–734–5985; www.rootsweb.com/~kymercer/hhs/).

Soooooeyyy!!!

If you leave town going northeast on US 68, toward Lexington, you will pass my alma mater, Harrodsburg High School, affectionately known as "Hog Town." This nickname harks back to the late 1820s, when hogs outnumbered county residents two to one, and on the hill where the school stands now were huge hog corrals, sales rings, and auction blocks that served the whole region. Our official high school sports mascot was a pioneer with a coonskin cap, but our proud rallying cry was *Soooooo-eyyy!!!* (Self-deprecating humor is healthy, especially for the adolescent soul.)

Another of Harrodsburg's claims to fame is ***The Beaumont Inn.*** The massive brick Greek Revival building, constructed in 1845, was once a finishing school called the Greenville Institute, then Daughter's College, and later Beaumont College. It was converted into an inn in 1919 by Annie Bell Goddard and her husband, Glave. The inn has remained in the family and is now managed by Annie Bell's great-grandson, Chuck Dedman. The dining room serves very traditional Kentucky-style meals that include dishes such as two-year-old cured country ham (smoked and cured by the proprietor himself), fried chicken, corn pudding, and Robert E. Lee Orange-Lemon Cake. Be ready for a feast! The antiques-filled sleeping quarters suggest the extravagance of the Old South, with a few modern conveniences. A swimming pool, tennis courts, and a gift shop are also on the premises. The newly added ***Old Owl Tavern*** has become a watering hole and features fine wines, spirits, and draft beer as well as more casual lunch and dinner menus. Reservations are advisable for meals and lodging. Closed late December though early March. Call (859) 734–3381 or (800) 352–3992 or visit www.beaumontinn.com.

Acting as a business-savvy alchemist, the city of Harrodsburg transformed an unsightly lot where an old building burned down in the first block of South Main Street into a city park, called ***Olde Towne Park,*** which includes a stage for civic events and a 14-foot-high by 35-foot-wide sculptural wall/water fountain designed and made by me, Zoé Strecker, your author with a double life. The fountain sculpture is a lyrical representation of the historic limestone palisades that line the Kentucky River on the eastern border of Mercer County. This work is made of nearly 700 large, high-fired ceramic tiles, all molded or directly sculpted by hand, featuring high-relief plants, vines, reptiles, and rocklike textures for the falling water to play over. For more information call (859) 734–6811.

The umbrella tables in the park by the fountain are very popular lunch spots. And if they're not too busy two doors down at ***La Fonda Restaurant,*** 121 South Main Street (859–734–0033), the waiters will actually serve your meal in the park. This little restaurant is very popular for its genuine Mexican dishes (the *chiles rellenos* are unusually good) for its reasonable prices, and, in a mostly dry or "moist" county, beer. You get the pleasant feeling that the chefs are making the food that they love. Open every day for lunch and dinner.

One of the most unique historical buildings in Mercer County is the ***Old Mud Meeting House,*** built in 1800 by members of the Dutch Reformed Church. As early as 1781 a group of Dutch settlers immigrated here and formed a community where they spoke Dutch and worshiped as they did in the Old World. The church they built became known as the Mud Meeting House because massive timber walls are chinked with clay, straw, twigs, roots, and gravel. The handsome structure, constructed "for the sole Benefit & use of the said Reformed Church forever," has long outlasted its little congregation. The church was restored to its original form in 1971. To visit the site, drive south from town on US 127 to the junction of US 68 (Moreland Avenue) and turn right. Follow US 68 until you reach Dry Branch Pike; turn left and look for the historical marker. Getting there can be confusing. Here's an even better idea: Call the Historical Society office at (859) 734–5985 to arrange a guided tour.

Shaker Village of Pleasant Hill is one of central Kentucky's most significant historic sites. It is located 8 miles east of Harrodsburg off US 68. The whole restored village is a museum featuring 30 original Shaker buildings and more than 2,700 acres of manicured farmland (about half of what the Shaker community farmed in its prime). "The United Society of Believers in Christ's Second Appearance" was originally founded by an English Quaker woman, Mother Ann Lee, who came to America in 1774 and claimed to be Christ incarnate (this time as a woman) to herald the millennium preceding the total destruction of Earth, as prophesied in the Book of Revelations. The most publicized doctrine of the sect was that Believers should remain pure by avoiding "the World" (non-Shakers) and all its ways, including the "disorderly" state of matrimony. Instead of procreating, the Shakers adopted orphans and received converts, who were plentiful during America's "Great Revival" period of Protestant faiths in the early 19th century. Shakers also avoided "the World" by remaining economically self-sufficient; their products were always of the highest quality, from seeds to silk, and continue to influence modern design. The Shakers' utopia at Pleasant Hill lasted more than 100 years, until the death of the village's last resident in 1923.

The village admission fee enables you to take a self-guided tour through the buildings, which, like Shaker furniture, are renowned for their graceful, functional aesthetic simplicity. (The song "Simple Gifts" is associated with the Shakers.) In recent years, this village has expanded its interpretation of historic farming techniques. Draft horses and oxen are used for traction in the gardens of heirloom vegetables and to power an impressive collection of period equipment. Blacksmithing, sorghum growing and making, and seed propagation and sales are among the agricultural practices demonstrated. Be sure to visit the interpretive center, where an excellent video and other exhibits provide insight into the Shakers and their tenure at Pleasant Hill. The village offers fine Southern dining and overnight accommodations in original buildings.

A recent and wonderful development at Shakertown is the system of trails for hiking, mountain biking, horseback riding, and Lampton Carriage travel. Ask at the lodging desk for a map pamphlet and gate keys. Some essential features of central Kentucky's geography, flora, fauna, and 19th-century history are made vividly accessible as you travel these trails. You'll see remnants of Shaker structures like bridges, dams, and mills for grinding flour, extracting flax seed oil, and fulling wool for textiles. The trails bring you close to some wonderful examples of the dry-stacked rock fence for which the area is famous. In the springtime the wildflowers are stunning, especially on the trails that wind into creek valleys. Two native grass and flower prairies have been reestablished on the property and although they are small, you will get a rare glimpse into how the landscape looked to native hunters and to Daniel Boone.

Horse enthusiasts are welcome to bring their trusty mounts with them on this vacation. Overnight equine guests may be boarded, for a small fee, in facilities with handsome paddocks and fully equipped stalls, with an available tack room while owners tuck themselves into village lodgings. Ask about special "Bed and Bridle" packages. Call (800) 734–5611 for more information, special programs, and reservations (www.shakervillageky.org).

The Shakers traded goods with "the World" in large part by river. The road built by the Shakers in 1861 still accesses one of the most spectacular stretches of the Kentucky River, known as ***The Palisades,*** where high Ordovician limestone bluffs change color with the time of day. Go east about ⅛ mile from Shakertown's entrance and turn right where a sign indicates RIVER EXCURSIONS. Shakertown offers one-hour trips on a paddle-wheel boat called *The Dixie Belle*. From the boat you have a perfect view of ***High Bridge,*** the first cantilever

trueblue

John A. Roebling, designer of the famous bridges in Cincinnati and Brooklyn, New York, also designed a suspension bridge for the Kentucky River at the site where High Bridge now stands. After the financial panic of 1857, the project was abandoned; his exquisite stone piers were torn down in 1929, never having been used.

bridge in the United States, a miracle of engineering at the time of its completion in 1877. High Bridge stretches 1,125 feet and stands 280 feet high; it is still the highest two-track railroad pass in North America.

For a dizzying view of High Bridge, follow US 68 east across from Shakertown, toward Lexington. The road begins to wind dramatically as it descends into the river gorge, crosses the Kentucky River on Brooklyn Bridge, and begins another curvy climb. At the top of the hill, take Highway 1268 into Wilmore, then turn right onto Highway 29 and drive to the little community of High Bridge. There are places to park so you can walk to the end of the underside of the criss-crossing bridge structure. Wait for a train. It's a goofy thrill to feel the frequent trains passing over your head. Notice too the

One Well-Used Cavern

Just behind High Bridge on the Jessamine County side is the mouth of a fabricated cavern that is as big as my farm—32 acres of limestone rooms, 130 feet underground. The 30-foot-high corridors were originally created by the Kentucky Stone company between 1900 and 1972 as it mined commercial-grade limestone. The Civil Defense Department has used the space for the storage of food and equipment during the bomb-shelter era, the Campbell Soup Company once filled the floors with loam and grew mushrooms for soup there, and local hearsay is that the secretive Free Masons continue to conduct rites in the unused, unlighted recesses of the mine. In 1979, when Bill Griffin bought the mine to use for underground commodity storage, engineers advised him to drain the water from an underground spring in order to control humidity. It was going to be a big expense. One day Mr. Griffin glibly commented to his daughter, "Well, why don't we just bottle the stuff and sell it off?" Everyone laughed, but by 1990 the family-run business, High Bridge Springwater, had sold over two million gallons of bottled spring water. It now dominates the local market as bottled water becomes increasingly common in households with unfiltered cisterns and in those with unsavory, chlorinated city water.

confluence of the Kentucky and Dix Rivers. The Kentucky is the big, usually brown, slow-moving river, while the Dix is often a clearer green. If you were down on the water, you'd also notice that the Dix River's water is much, much colder. Less than a mile away, the river is being released from the base of the Dix Dam, which forms Herrington Lake. Often, in the summer, the colliding air temperatures form a low, flat layer of fog, just 3 feet high, right over the water's surface, so that people in boats appear to be floating heads. Swimming in that 48-degree water can stop your heart.

Beginning at the Kentucky River and traveling north on US 68, turn west (or left) onto Highway 33 and follow the signs to *Irish Acres Antiques* (859–873–7235; www.irishacresgallery.com) in *Nonesuch* (population 343), a "downtown" composed of the smallest freestanding voting building you'll ever see and a cluster of houses, one of which has the greatest number and variety of purple martin houses known to humanity (the owner must be a frustrated urban housing planner). Irish Acres Antiques is a not-to-be-missed 32,000-square-foot antiques gallery and tearoom founded by Bonnie and Arch Hannigan and now run by their daughters Emilie and Jane. Two floors of what was once the Nonesuch School are gracefully crammed with antiques, which range from affordable early American primitives to pricey Asian art, 15th-century Chinese lacquered boxes, and 19th-century French country furniture. An ornate $38,000 French palace bed is among the treasures. Hours are 10 A.M. to 5 P.M. Tuesday through Saturday.

The old basement cafeteria has been converted into a whimsical, elegant tearoom called *The Glitz*. Amid a fantasia of lights, grapevines, iridescent paper, and silver cherubim, you can enjoy a lavish four-course meal for $19.95. It's a good place to take your time and not the best place to take your kids. Reservations are required. Lunch is served from 11 A.M. to 2 P.M., when the gallery is open. Gallery hours are 10 A.M. to 5 P.M. Tuesday through Saturday. Irish Acres and The Glitz are closed January through mid-March. They reopen on St. Patrick's Day (surprise!). Call (859) 873–6956.

Get back onto Highway 33, which winds through lush horse-farm country, to *Versailles* (pronounced ver-SALES). You can also get to Versailles by way of US 60 or 62, once one of the largest buffalo trails in the United States. From the landscaping and architecture in town, one senses an aura of the wealth and deliberate pace of the Old South. Downtown Versailles is full of well-preserved old Federal and Beaux Arts homes, beautiful churches, and antiques stores, one of which is the *Olde Towne Antique Mall,* with two floors of goodies at 161 Main Street (859–873–6326; www.oldetowneantiquemall.com).

At 199 South Main Street, the *Garden Deli* (859–879–1991; www.garden deli1991.com) is known for delicious pizza and excellent sandwiches. Hours are Monday through Saturday 11 A.M. to 8 P.M.

People come to Kentucky from all over the country to towns that were early settlements in search of information about their ancestors. Like the Mercer County Public Library in Harrodsburg (859–734–3680; www.mcplib.info), the *Woodford County Historic Society Museum* (859–873–6786) has an excellent library of genealogical data that is free and available for anyone's use. The museum is housed in what was formerly the Big Spring Church, circa 1819, at 121 Rose Hill. Hours are Tuesday through Saturday from 10 A.M. to 4 P.M.

For the toy train enthusiast, Versailles offers a once-in-a-lifetime opportunity to pore over the collection of Wanda and Winfrey Adkins, who have converted an old (1911–32) Louisville and Nashville (L&N) railroad station into the *Nostalgia Station Toy Train Museum,* located at 279 Depot Street, a one-way street on the east side of Main. The Adkinses, who do repairs and will find rare parts, can tell you just about anything there is to know about model trains and antique cast-iron and mechanized toys. Before meeting the Adkinses, I didn't realize that there are modern versions of the 1950s locomotives, boxcars, switches, coal cars, and crossing lights that we played with every Christmas. Wanda likes to point out a wind-up Mickey and Minnie Mouse hand-pump car, one of L&N's forgotten "cheap" toys from the 1930s, when the company was struggling, and a regular engine and coal car that cost at least $32. Hours are Wednesday through Saturday from 10 A.M. to 5 P.M. and Sunday from 1 to

5 P.M. Admission is $3.50. Call (859) 873–2497 for more information or www .bgrm.org/nostalgiastation.

For enthusiasts of full-size railroad artifacts, follow US 62 west to the ***Blue Grass Railroad Museum Inc.*** in Woodford County Park. On weekends from May through the end of October, you can take a 5½-mile train ride on the Old Louisville Southern Mainland through quintessential bluegrass country, including a hawk's view of the Kentucky River palisades, Wild Turkey Distilleries, and Young's High Bridge. The museum is an actual train car with historic railroad displays. A recent addition to the collection is an original L&N railroad bay-window caboose. From June 3 through October 29, Saturday and Sunday, trips are at 2 P.M. (arrive 15 minutes early). Admission is $10 for adults and $8 for kids. For special events, call (859) 873–2476 or (800) 755–2476 or visit www.bgrm.org.

Boyd Orchard, 1500 Pinckard Pike, Versailles (859–873–3097), is a farm where you can pick your own strawberries, apples, and pumpkins, each in its own season. The setting is lovely and practical. Call ahead to see what is ripe and what the current hours are.

"Here's to Old Kentucky, The state where I was born, Where the corn is full of kernels and the Colonel's full of corn" goes an old Kentucky toast. The abundant corn crops of early Kentucky settlers played an important role in the creation of bourbon whiskey, as did, undoubtedly, its appreciation by Southern gentlemen. When, how, and by whom bourbon was first made remains a matter of debate that may never be settled (Georgetown claims it was Baptist minister Elijah Craig; nearby Bourbon County credits Jacob Spears). There's no disagreement, however, that by the early 1800s whiskey making had evolved into a fine art in bluegrass country. Elijah Pepper started making whiskey near Versailles in 1797. In 1812, in search of a more abundant water supply, he moved his operation to a spot along Glenn's Creek. Today, whiskey is still made at the site of Pepper's early distillery, under the name ***Labrot & Graham, The Bourbon Homeplace*** (7855 McCracken Pike; 859–879–1812; www .woodfordreserve.com).

Brown-Forman, an international beverage company based in Louisville, renovated the property as a showplace of the "old ways" of making premium bourbon whiskey. The bulky old stone buildings strung along the creek, the complex aromas from the mash tank, the 25-foot-tall copper stills (unique in modern American distilling), and the lively presentations by the tour guides make this a premium tour, which ends with a taste of bourbon ball candy at the "bar" in the visitor center. By the way, the bourbon distilled on the day you visit won't be available in a bottle for about seven years. The $5 tours are given at 9:30 and 11:30 A.M. from Tuesday through Thursday (must be over 18 years of age). Tuesday through Saturday you can also have a Picnic on the Porch. An a la carte lunch menu includes sandwiches, salads, and desserts priced from $6 to $12. The distillery is about 6 miles from Versailles (so far out that it has its own lake as a source of water in case of a fire). If you're in Versailles, take US 60 toward Frankfort, turn left onto Grassy Spring Road, then right on McCracken Pike. Or take Elm Street out of downtown Versailles.

Continue on Highway 1659 past the distillery, then turn left (west) on Highway 1964 and right onto Germany Road, then follow the signs to the 374-acre **Buckley Wildlife Sanctuary,** which offers an appropriately private and meditative way to explore the wooded Kentucky River Gorge. You can hike on loop trails between ¼ mile and 2 miles long, and there's a bird blind that keeps you concealed while birds come within view (or camera range). You're likely to see everything from warblers to wild turkeys; some people come solely for the hummingbirds. There's an interesting exhibit center, a gift shop, and various events. As a sanctuary should be, it's a peaceful, beautiful place. Admission is $3. Hours are Wednesday through Friday from 9 A.M. to 5 P.M. and on weekends from 9 A.M. to 6 P.M. The nature center is open from 1 to 6 P.M. on weekends. The sanctuary is closed in January and February. Call (859) 873–5711 for event information.

For another worthwhile excuse to take a drive, visit the restored **Jack Jouett House,** circa 1797. This home was built by folks who believed, like Mies van der Rohe, that "God hides in the details." From Versailles go 5 miles west on McCowans Ferry Road, and turn on Craig Creek Pike. Jack Jouett, the original owner, was a legendary Revolutionary War hero who rode all night to save Gov. Thomas Jefferson from the British. His son, Matthew Jouett, became a well-known portrait artist. Tours are free April through October, Wednesday, Saturday, and Sunday between 1 and 5 P.M. The house is closed November through March. Call (859) 873–7902. Check www.jouetthouse.org for special events like the Frontier Day festival or the Matthew Jouett Art Show and Sale.

From Versailles take US 62 north toward **Midway,** named so because it is exactly midway between Frankfort and Lexington. At the Nugent Crossroads, where US 62 intersects Old Frankfort Pike, you will see the old **Offutt-Cole Tavern** building. The building was constructed in the 18th century and has been a tavern, an inn, a stagecoach stop, and a tollhouse. Part of the building contains what may be one of the oldest log structures in the state. One of the old inn's most famous tenants was

trueblue

Frank and Jesse James's mother, Zerelda Cole, once lived in the Offutt-Cole Tavern, located at the intersection of US 62 and Highway 1981 between Versailles and Midway.

Zerelda Cole James, the mother of the infamous Frank and Jesse. Zerelda was born in the building and lived there with her grandfather, who ran a tavern at the site called the Black Horse Inn. Various businesses have occupied the building in recent times, although at press time it sat empty. You can still park and look around the outside of this charming old structure (www.tsgraves .com/blackHorse/LeesTavern.htm).

Midway was the first town in Kentucky built by a railroad company. The tracks are both centerpiece and divider of the tiny downtown. These days it is a quaint college town full of antiques shops, beautiful historic homes, and a few surprises.

One such surprise is an operative, century-old, hydropower grain mill on the South Elkhorn Creek. The **Weisenberger Mill** is the oldest continuously operating mill in Kentucky and one of the few in the nation to remain in the same family. In 1866 a German steamboat and mill specialist named August Weisenberger bought the mill that had been built on the site in 1818. He revamped the entire system and began grinding all manner of grain at the rate of 100 barrels a day. His great-grandson, Philip J. Weisenberger, and Philip's son, Mac, have modernized some of the methods and now grind about 3,000 tons of grain a year. The Weisenbergers introduced the use of the mill's electricity-making capacity by having Kentucky's alternative energy whiz, Dave Kinlock, rebuild the mill's hydropower turbines and add an efficient generator. Now most aspects of the business are water powered, even the computers. Although visitors are not allowed inside the work area, you can walk around the property. Everything at Weisenberger mills is sold by the package in the front office (the 50-pound bags are a very good bargain). As an avid bread maker, I can attest to the excellent quality of the products. Call (859) 254–5282 or go to www.weisenberger.com for more information.

From Railroad Street, turn east on Winter Street (US 62), veer to the right at the Corner Grocery, and go about ¼ mile. You will find yourself at the **Holly Hill Inn,** an 1830 Greek Revival house that has been home to fine dining for more than 20 years. In 2000 the inn also became home to Ouita and Chris Michel, who came well prepared to add their own special touches to the Holly Hill tradition. Both are graduates of the Culinary Institute of America and have cooked at fine restaurants in the Lexington area. Their Holly Hill Inn serves dinner Wednesday through Saturday beginning at 5:30 P.M., as well as Sunday brunch from 11:30 A.M. to 2:30 P.M. The dinner menu changes monthly and the brunch menu changes weekly, but you can be sure of two things: Whatever comes out of Ouita's kitchen is going to be delicious and creative, and whenever possible, it will be made with locally grown produce, Kentucky-raised beef, lamb, and pork, and fresh seafood. A four-course dinner—your choice of appetizer, entree, and dessert—is offered for a fixed price of $35 per person. Brunch is $15, and the Kentucky Heritage Lunch is served Wednesday through Saturday from 11:30 A.M. to 2 P.M. Call (859) 846–4732 or visit www.hollyhillinn .com for reservations.

Ouita's sister Paige and her husband, Jared Richardson, are also extraordinary chefs. They are owners of **Wallace Station,** an unusually excellent deli at 4000 Frankfort Pike, just outside of Midway. From 8 A.M. until 5 P.M., Monday through Saturday and 11 A.M. to 4 P.M. on Sunday, these hard workers make wonderful carry-out food, including innovative sandwiches on bread made from scratch daily. (They also bake bread and cakes for Holly Hill Inn.) You can take food with you or eat at tables on their big patio that is practically in a horse field near a barn. Finish the meal with hand-dipped, locally made ice cream or a cold beer. The Richardsons also do catering. Paige makes gift baskets for sale that feature all Kentucky-made goods. The building itself was an old depot and later a general store. Now it's a real favorite with locals and travelers alike. Call (859) 846–5161 with questions.

In the late 1800s Kentucky was the third-largest grape and wine producer in the United States. Prohibition, however, uprooted not just the vines but also the industry. Cynthia Bohn and Cynthia Hall are among a new generation of vintners working to help grapes make a comeback in the Bluegrass State. At their **Equus Run Vineyards,** 35 acres located on Moores Mill Road, off US 62 between Midway and Georgetown, they've renovated a tobacco barn into a wine-making facility and added a taste of fun to the whole experience. Virtually every month there's some kind of special event—a concert, a barbecue, or an open house. Any day, visitors are invited to go fishing or bring a picnic to enjoy amid the flower gardens or by the old gristmill along the banks of Elkhorn Creek. There's even a life-size art horse, *Vegetariat*, part of Lexington's Horse Mania community art event from summer 2000. And, of course, there are acres of vineyards, a tasting room, and a gift shop, where Equus Run wines sell for $9 to $14 a bottle. Regular operating hours are 11 A.M. to 5 P.M. Tuesday through Saturday; from April through October, the winery stays open until 7 P.M. Call for information or a schedule of special events (859–846–9463 or 877–905–2675; www.equusrunvineyards.com).

trueblue

Because of its many 19th-century houses and old-fashioned charm, Danville was chosen as the location for the 1956 film *Raintree County* starring Elizabeth Taylor and Montgomery Clift.

Danville is a handsome little college town just south of Harrodsburg. From town take US 127; from Shakertown take Highway 33 through Burgin.

Drive or walk around Danville and the Centre College campus to admire the architecture. For arts and cultural events, check the gallery and schedule of performances at the Frank Lloyd Wright–style *Norton Center for the Arts* (859–236–4692; www.centre.edu.nc) on campus.

Right across West Walnut Street, a place of simple beauty awaits to nourish your inner spirit. McDowell Park, the lawn of the Presbyterian church, is the setting for *Pathway of Peace: The Danville Labyrinth Project.* A marker explains: YOU ARE ENTERING SACRED SPACE. A MEDITATIVE TOOL, THE LABYRINTH IS AN ANCIENT PATH OF PRAYER. UNLIKE A MAZE, ITS SINGLE PATH LEADS TO THE CENTER. THIS LABYRINTH IS BASED ON THE ONE IN THE CATHEDRAL AT CHARTRES, FRANCE. PAUSE AND RELAX. WALK AT YOUR OWN PACE. YOU MAY PASS OTHER PEOPLE QUIETLY. ONCE YOU REACH THE CENTER, STAY AS LONG AS YOU LIKE. EXIT BY RETRACING YOUR STEPS. The centuries-old idea of the labyrinth takes on a special Kentucky beauty here. Envisioned and funded by an interdenominational group of local citizens, the Danville labyrinth was created by Robert Ferre, an internationally known mason. The large stone blocks that form the 43-foot circular foundation are made of sandstone quarried in McCreary County, Kentucky, with the pathway etched into the beautiful stone. Shaded by the park's huge trees, this is a pleasant place to find your own contemporary meaning in an ancient idea.

You know an Italian place is good when there's always a customer at the counter reading an Italian newspaper. *Freddie's Restaurant* (140 Stanford Street; 859–236–9884) serves quick, primo cuisine for lunch and dinner Monday through Saturday.

The hospital in Danville was named for a local medical hero, Ephraim McDowell, who performed the first successful removal of an ovarian tumor in 1809. Something should be named for his patient, Jane Todd Crawford, who survived the surgery without the aid of antisepsis or the comfort of anesthetic. The site of the operation, the *Ephraim McDowell House and Apothecary* at 125 South Second Street, has been accurately restored and is open Monday through Saturday from 10 A.M. to noon and 1 to 4 P.M., Sunday from 2 to 4 P.M. From November through February it is closed Monday. Admission is $7. Call (859) 236–2804 or visit www.mcdowellhouse.com.

Across the street is *Constitution Square State Park,* a reproduction of the state's first courthouse square and the site of the first post office in the West, circa 1792. All the buildings are

trueblue

The Kentucky School for the Deaf in Danville was established in 1823 with only three pupils. It was the first state-supported school of its kind in the nation. Today, a large number of its graduates go on to attend college or technical school and join the workforce.

log replicas, and most have recorded interpretations (kids like to push the buttons and run when the voice begins to drone). The lawn is a good place for a downtown picnic, and dessert is right across the street at **Burke's Bakery,** 116 West Main (859–236–5661). Burke's is in its fourth generation of owners and customers and makes good, old, sweet pastries for times when you just don't want whole grains and carob powder.

Since 1950 Danville's **Pioneer Playhouse** has been offering audiences live theatrical performances (and dinner) under the stars. Its claim to fame is being the oldest summer stock theater in the state and having "the most unique outdoor theater history in America." Founded and run by Eben C. Henson (1923–2004) and his wife, Charlotte, the playhouse is now being run by Charlotte and their children: Holly, a comedian; Robby, cinematic director; Eben, businessman; and Heather, novelist. Everything on the complex "campus" is cobbled together creatively and economically from salvaged materials so that the effect is charming full-scale folk art. For example, the amphitheater is paved with brick Henson reclaimed from one of Danville's historic buildings, the Ephraim McDowell apothecary shop. Overhead are two standard-issue streetlights that serve as house lights; the stage lights are C-clamped all along the lights' cross bars. Every structure has a quirky story.

trueblue

John Travolta, Lee Majors, and Jim Varney are among the actors who once performed summer stock at Pioneer Playhouse in Danville.

Every two weeks a new play is produced from mid-June until late August. The plays are primarily romantic comedies, "rib-ticklers," as Charlotte puts it, performed by actors from New York and from the region. Showtime is 8:30 P.M., Tuesday through Saturday. Southern "comfort" dinner food is served at 7:30 P.M. Dinner and show are $27, and show only is $15. A real treat with dinner is hearing Charlotte Henson play guitar and sing folk songs. For information and reservations call (859) 236–2341 or (859) 236–2747; www.pioneerplayhouse.com. The playhouse is at 840 Stanford Road, just on the edge of town. Follow the clearly marked signs from downtown.

It takes a lot of brass to envision being home to a national museum, and for at least one weekend of the year, Danville has more brass than just about any place else. Stop by the stately old Federal Building at Main and Fourth Streets, and you'll see what many Danvillians hope is the future home of a national museum devoted to the rich history of bands in the United States. They figure that since Danville attracts some 40,000 people and dozens of bands from around the world to its **Great American Brass Band Festival** in mid-June, it's the natural place to locate a Great American Band Museum celebrating the role of band music in community life. For information about the festival (a full four-day weekend of everything from Sousa to Civil War songs) or the museum's progress, call (859) 236–4692.

The **Antique Mall of Historic Danville** (158 North Third Street; 859–236–3026) is housed in a large brick Presbyterian church, circa 1867, across the street from the public library. The booths are full of goodies—a great place for poets. Hours are Tuesday through Saturday from 10 A.M. to 5 P.M. and Sunday from 1 to 5 P.M. Check out www.fabric-unlimited.com/antique.html.

A number of acclaimed visual artists call Danville home. At the **Jones Visual Arts Center at Centre College,** you can see the blown-glass creations of Stephen Rolfe Powell. Powell, a Centre College professor (and self-proclaimed pyromaniac), is recognized as a master hot-glass blower. His glass vessels (some weighing up to 30 pounds) are known for their vivid colors, elegant form, and fascinating texture (created by the thousands of beads of color integrated into the surface). The arts center is open by appointment; call (859) 238–5737. A small gallery inside the art center exhibits rotating shows as well as student work.

Exhibits of local and regional art, gifts, and coffee in a clean, well-lighted place are in store for you at Danville's **Community Arts Center** (401 W. Main Street, 859–236–4054). The handsome *beaux arts* building was formerly home to the region's federal government offices. Three galleries offer rotating shows—you may see the stunningly complex still-life paintings of Danville artist and Centre College professor Sheldon Tapley or quirky folk art miniature houses by a local unknown. Classes in dance, drama, and visual arts are offered regularly. The coffee is always good and everyone is welcome, Tuesday through Saturday during regular business hours and evenings during special events.

Just a few more miles east on Highway 300 brings you to the **Isaac Shelby Cemetery State Historic Site.** Shelby became Kentucky's first governor in 1792 after having earned a reputation by fighting in Lord Dunmore's War and in the Revolutionary War. He won the gubernatorial race again 16 years later and victoriously fought the British (again) in the War of 1812. In 1818 he and Andrew Jackson were responsible for the negotiations with the Chickasaw Indians to purchase the land to the west of the Tennessee River for Kentucky, an area now known as the Jackson Purchase. This state-owned site is where his farm, Traveler's Rest, was and where he and his family are buried.

Near Forkland, **Penn's Store** may be the oldest continuously operated one-family-owned store west of the Alleghenies, and it looks like it. Everyone falls in love with the wise, tumbledown appearance of the general store, which was opened in 1852 by Dick Penn. The original building burned, and this replacement is more than 100 years old. In the winter, the little potbellied stove is stoked up hot, and at least three men are playing checkers on a barrel in the middle of the room at all times. (It takes two to play and one to shake his head and chew on his toothpick.) In the summer there's no better place in the world to have a Dr Pepper than on Penn's front porch, where you can hear the creek rumble by. The store is usually open Thursday, Friday, and Saturday spring through fall, but before you go, be sure to call Jeanne Lane to make sure Penn's is open. The store phone number is (859) 332–7706. From Forkland continue on Highway 37 south to Highway 243, turn right, then right again just after crossing a concrete bridge. When you see the store by the creek, cross the new bridge.

Leaving Danville to the west, Main Street becomes U.S. Highway 150 (or 52) and leads to the historic town of **Perryville.**

On Perryville's main street is an area known as **Merchants' Row,** a small row of renovated buildings that house antiques and gift shops, a pizza place, a dry goods store, and an active saddlery. Moving away from creature comforts, proceed in an appropriately somber spirit to the **Perryville Battlefield State Historic Site.** Go north on Highway 1920 for 3 miles and follow the signs. Eighty thousand men fought for one bloody day at this site on October 8, 1862, when Confederate soldiers in search of water accidentally encountered Union troops who were guarding nearby Doctor's Creek. More than 7,500 soldiers were killed, wounded, or missing by sunset. This battle was the largest ever fought on Kentucky soil and, when the Confederate general Braxton Bragg retreated into Tennessee after the battle, there was no real hope left that Kentucky would ever join the Rebel states.

"The Knobs"

If you leave Junction City on Highway 37 south, you will suddenly enter "the knobs," a narrow belt of fairly isolated, wooded hills that encircles the bluegrass region. (Rock lovers: The creeks here are loaded with geodes.) In the heart of this alluring terrain is a little town called Forkland, where there's a good country festival the second weekend of October at the **Forkland Community Center.** Notice the huge, round piece of sandstone in the yard. It measures 51 inches in diameter, is 18 inches thick, and probably weighs more than a ton. What in tarnation is it? No one knows. Sandstone is never used for grinding grain, so a millstone is out. Archaeologists say it's not prehistoric. The best guess is that it was a "hemp brake," a heavy rock rolled by hand or by oxen over hemp stalks to break the fibers apart for making rope.

A Teetotaler with a Mission

Just north of Lincoln County and east of Boyle County is Garrard County, birthplace of a radical antiliquor activist oft neglected by history books. From Lancaster take US 27 north to Highway 34 and go east to its junction with Fisher Ford Road to find **Carry A. Nation's birthplace** at "the jumping-off place," as local folks call it. The house was built about 1840, and Carry was born there in 1846. In 1900, after a short, disastrous, and life-changing marriage to a severe alcoholic, Carry single-handedly wreaked havoc on the saloon at the Hotel Casey in Wichita, Kansas, and, consequently, spent seven days in jail, her first of more than 30 jail sentences on similar charges. I've seen fearsome pictures of Ms. Nation in her prime: hatchet in one hand, Bible in the other, purse to the front, and a glare that would make any bartender's blood run cold.

There's a small museum (859–332–8631) with artifacts and battle displays on the 270-acre grounds. A walking tour introduces visitors to important landmarks. There is also a driving tour of the area; ask for maps. The best time to visit is on the weekend closest to October 8, during the massive annual reenactment of the battle, when people in full period costume, with weapons and horses, stage the long, gory combat. The park is open daily from April through October from 9 A.M. to 5 P.M. and by appointment the remainder of the year. Admission is charged. Call the Perryville Battlefield Preservation Association at (859) 332–1862 for more information about the ongoing development of the site (http://parks.ky.gov/findparks/histparks/pb).

The town of **Stanford** is about 13 miles south of Danville on US 150. There's a charming restored railroad depot used as a community meeting center.

The **William Whitley House State Historic Site** is southeast of Stanford on US 150. Famous "Indian Fighter" William Whitley built the elegant brick house in the mid-1780s, making it one of the oldest brick buildings west of the Alleghenies. It was called "a guardian of the Wilderness Road" because it stood next to the important overland route and served as a place of refuge for white travelers. The high upper windows and barred lower windows, the gun ports, and a hidden staircase were built as precautions against attacks.

Whitley's big contributions to Kentucky (and American) culture were building the first racetrack in the state and running the horses counterclockwise, a practice he encouraged to rebel against the British custom of racing clockwise. Having served as a colonel in the Revolution, Whitley was passionately anti-British. (I'm sure he hated kippers and, if he had been around in the 1960s, would have disliked the Beatles, too.) Whitley died in the 1813

Battle of the Thames River after he supposedly killed the great chief Tecumseh. Tours of the house are given Tuesday through Sunday from mid-March through December 31, 9 A.M. to 4:30 P.M. For further information, check http://parks.ky.gov/findparks/histparks/ww.

Downtown **Lancaster** is a small but bustling central square around which you will find a number of antiques malls. One of several worth checking is the **Lancaster Market** (859–792–4536; www.carrawaycolddesigns.com) at 102 Hamilton Avenue, open 9:30 A.M. to 4:30 P.M., Monday through Saturday. The **Garrard County Jail Museum,** at 208 Danville Street, is an interesting building featuring local historic artifacts. It is free and open to the public from noon to 4 P.M., Monday through Friday. A local historic home that is open for tours is **Pleasant Retreat,** at 656 Stanford Road, the 1804 home of Gov. William Owsley, after whom the 96th county was named. Hours are 9 A.M. to 3 P.M. Tuesday and Thursday through Sunday. Admission is charged. By request, tours can focus on genealogy, architecture, or quilts and wallpaper. Call (859) 792–2500 to make an appointment for a tour, or you can stop by to see if it's open.

Tradition Meets Invention

An old jail, a lot of used furniture, 12,000 locks, and a cemetery—that is what **Nicholasville** has to offer. Go almost due south of Lexington, via US 27, then take the business loop into downtown Nicholasville. Write or make a quick stop at the Chamber of Commerce office at 611 North Main Street, Nicholasville 40356, for a list of the many antiques malls and maps for walking the historic district. The **Old Jail,** 200 South Main Street, is actually interesting, though it would not have been a good place to spend the night after committing a crime. There are no regular tours of the restored 1870 building, but if you go to the county judge's office in the Jessamine County Courthouse, at the corner of Main and Maple, you can pick up the key and take a look around.

Without doubt, the most fascinating site to visit in town is the **Harry C. Miller Lock Collection,** south on Main Street inside Lockmasters Inc. (859–887–9633; www.lockmasters.com). From the time he was a locksmith's apprentice at the age of twelve to the years he traveled the world developing locks for the State Department's classified materials, Harry Miller collected an astounding variety of locks in order to study their designs. The oldest lock in the collection is Arabic and dates to 1303. A lock removed from the Oval Office during Lincoln's presidency and a key to the Capitol's 16-ton doors are in the collection. Many of the locks were invented by Miller himself; he holds some 54 lock patents. Some locks have been donated to the Smithsonian, but the rest are on view in the Lockmasters Security Institute for free on Monday, Wednesday, and Friday from 1 to 4 P.M.

The first commercial wine grape operation in the United States was established in sloping fields along the Kentucky River more than 200 years ago by Jean Jacques Dufour. Prohibition in the 1930s led to the closure of many of the vineyards. In recent years there has been a renewed interest in viticulture in the Bluegrass State and our mild climate and rich soil is promising success for contemporary projects. One example is the ***Chrisman Mill Vineyards and Winery,*** just outside Nicholasville, at 2385 Chrisman Mill Road (859–881–5007). Denise and Chris Nelson planted their first vines in 1997 with the goal of making all their wines from Kentucky-grown fruit. With 1,000 vines producing nine varieties of grapes and fruit from 13 additional growers, Chrisman Mill has won over 24 international wine competition awards. Lunch is served Thursday through Saturday.

Head south of town on US 27 for 5 miles to the ***Camp Nelson Heritage Park,*** a large Union supply depot and recruitment center. Founded in 1863, Camp Nelson was the preeminent recruiting and training ground for African-American soldiers. More than a thousand slaves were "impressed" to construct the camp, its roads, and its railroads, and many of the same men subsequently enlisted. Any Kentucky slaves who enlisted were immediately freed.

campnelson

A group of local citizens has created a foundation to restore and preserve Camp Nelson. You can view the progress of restoration of the Oliver Perry House, an 1855 house that was appropriated for military use during the Civil War. The group also sponsors numerous reenactments and living-history events at Camp Nelson throughout the year. For more information call (859) 881–9126 or (859) 885–4500.

Later, their families were also freed and allowed to live nearby in a refugee camp. Despite the army's attempts to administer the camp, many people died of exposure and disease. The army even joined forces with evangelical abolitionists to provide schools at the camp. One such missionary was Rev. John Gregg Fee, who, shortly after his work at the camp, formed an integrated school in Berea that later became Berea College. When all of Kentucky's slaves were freed in 1865, Camp Nelson served as an issuing station for emancipation papers, and the next year the site was designated the ***Camp Nelson National Cemetery.*** If you drive another 2 miles south of the supply depot site, you can visit the actual cemetery, where some 4,000 Civil War soldiers are buried (www.campnelson.org).

To go any farther east, you have to get across the Kentucky River, and there is no bridge. From Nicholasville take Union Mills Road (Highway 169) down to the river's edge and wait for the ferry. In 1785 the Virginia Assembly granted the **Valley View Ferry** a "perpetual and irrevocable franchise." Let me emphasize the word *perpetual*. More than 200 years later, the little boat is still carrying anyone and anything that needs to cross between Madison and Jessamine Counties at the mouth of Tates Creek. This ferry is Kentucky's oldest recorded business continuously in operation. Originally, workhorses pulled the ferry across; later a motor was connected to the ferry's paddle wheel and the boat was guided between fixed cables. Now a motorized ferryboat can carry three cars at a time. Recently the governments of Jessamine, Madison, and Fayette Counties decided to purchase and jointly operate this sole functioning ferry on the Kentucky River. Operating hours are Monday through Friday from 6 A.M. to 8 P.M., Saturday from 8 A.M. to 8 P.M., and Sunday from 9 A.M. to 8 P.M., except when it is closed due to high or turbulent water. There is no charge to use the ferry, but it's a good idea to check the running status in advance by calling (859) 258–3611 (press "1" after the first traffic message) or check www .lexingtonky.gov/index.aspx.

When you arrive on the east bank, keep driving and you'll soon be in **Richmond,** home of Eastern Kentucky University and very much a university town, full of restaurants, bars, hotels, and shops. For the stargazer, the **Hummel Planetarium** on Kit Carson Drive on campus is totally cosmic. This is the 12th largest planetarium in the nation, and it feels even larger as you crane your neck in the dark dome to catch a view of the galaxy 9.3 billion miles away from Earth. Public shows are offered

trueblue

A sequence of the movie *Flim Flam Man,* starring George C. Scott and Sue Lyon, was filmed in Valley View, near the present-day ferry.

Monday through Saturday at 2 P.M. and 2:30 P.M. and Thursday through Saturday at 6 P.M. and 7:30 P.M. Call (859) 622–1547. To get there from I–75, take exit 87 onto the Eastern Bypass. Follow the signs to Kit Carson Drive and the planetarium (www.planetarium.eku.edu).

Local history comes to life at **Irvinton House Museum,** 345 Lancaster Avenue. This Federal-style house has been restored and filled with furniture, clothing, and other artifacts reflecting local history. There are no rope barriers in the rooms. The idea is to make it feel as if you're visiting the family; they have stepped out for a few moments. The guided tour fills you in on the histories of the wonderful vintage clothing, furniture, and rare artifacts from nearby Fort Boonesborough that are on display, many items donated by local citizens. The house is open 9 A.M. to 5 P.M. Monday through Friday, and the tour is free. From May through September, there are Saturday hours from 10

A.M. to 2 P.M. Call (859) 626–1422 for more information. The Richmond Visitors Bureau is located at the rear of the house, so you can find out about other area attractions before or after your tour of the house.

One of those attractions is **White Hall State Historic Site,** accessible from I–75 (exit 90) or directly from Richmond. Take U.S. Highway 421/25 and follow the signs to the restored home of one of Kentucky's best-loved big mouths and influential abolitionists, Cassius Marcellus Clay, the "Lion of White Hall." The White Hall building is well fortified in part because Clay's ideological and political opponents were not beyond attempts at physically sabotaging the basement press where he produced his radical paper, the *True American.* After a failed political career, Clay served under President Lincoln as minister to the court of Czar Alexander II in St. Petersburg, Russia, then retired and lived bankrupt at White Hall until his death in 1903. The building is open from April through Labor Day daily and from Labor Day through October, Wednesday through Sunday, 9 A.M. to 4:30 P.M. Call (859) 623–9178 or visit http://parks.ky .gov/findparks/histparks/wh. Admission is charged.

Berea is a nationally well-known folk arts-and-crafts center located just south of Richmond in southern Madison County off I–75. Stop by the Welcome Center, 201 North Broadway, for brochures about all the crafts businesses. You'll find more than 30 craftspeople—chair makers, potters, leather makers, blacksmiths, stained-glass artisans, weavers, spoon makers, basket weavers, quilters, and on and on—whose studios and salesrooms are open to the public.

The place to start is the **Kentucky Artisan Center** (859–985–5448; www .kentuckyartisancenter.ky.gov), just off I–75 at exit 77. This center is designed

Native Americans in Kentucky

You've probably heard that Native Americans did not have permanent habitations in Kentucky because it was a commonly owned hunting ground. Not true. Thirty-five hundred acres in southeastern Clark County were occupied, farmed, kept clear, and hunted by Shawnee. Archaeologists are in search of the Shawnee village called Eskippakithiki, meaning "blue lick place" because of salt-sulfur springs in or near the present-day town of Oil Springs. This relatively permanent settlement was established around 1718 and was occupied by as many as 200 families, according to legend and to a 1736 census taken by French Canadians. By 1754 the village was probably abandoned as the Shawnee moved north across the Ohio River, where many other Shawnee lived. Later, the structures burned and the cornfields returned to a wooded state. Some historians believe that the name Kentucky came from an Iroquois name for this particular area, *kenta*, which means level, and *aki*, which indicates location, or "place of level land."

to showcase the diversity of Kentucky craftsmanship in one stop, much as West Virginia's Tamarack Center spotlights that state's handmade heritage. The primary forum of the center is a large gallery that exhibits and sells the work of artists and craftspeople from the state. Also for sale are Kentucky-made food items, music, and books by and about anyone associated with the state. The Artisan Center also contains a cafeteria-style restaurant. Hours are 8 A.M. to 8 P.M., seven days a week, except Thanksgiving, Christmas, and New Year's Day. There are three annual outdoor fairs—in spring, summer, and fall—that feature members of the **Kentucky Guild of Artists and Craftsmen,** a juried organization. In mid-June there is a really fun event called **Bluegrass in the Park** (www.hendersonky.org/bluegrass) that features all-Kentucky bluegrass music bands with a big fish fry on Friday night. The latter festival is held in Memorial Park on Jefferson Street in Old Towne. For festival information call the Berea Visitor Center at (800) 598–5263.

The following are samples of the many crafts studios you can visit in Berea: Warren May is the state's best-known dulcimer maker. Dulcimers are graceful, Appalachian, wooden string instruments played flat on the lap, usually to accompany vocals, often in a minor key. This is an instrument many Americans had probably never heard of before Jean Ritchie. The **Warren A. May's Woodworking Shop** (110 Center Street; 859–986–9293; www.warrenamay.com) is open Monday through Saturday. At **Churchill Weavers** (Lorraine Court at US 25; 859–986–3127; www.churchillweavers.com), you can walk through the loom house and see master weavers hard at work creating shawls, throws, and blankets.

From Chestnut Street (also called KY 21 or Lancaster Road), turn into Old Towne on Lester Street. On the same side of the road as the turn onto Lester, you'll notice the **St. Clare Catholic Church** at 226 Chestnut Street. The architecture of the new church building, completed in 2003, is what I would call "truth-in-materials" style—raw wood, unaltered concrete, brick, all in a spare clean space. If you walk into the church you will immediately see a sculptural baptismal font, designed and built by my husband, Mike Frasca, and me. (Yes, the Catholics are now doing full immersion baptism.) The baptismal pool is octagonal and is lined with deep blue, handmade cross-shaped tile, some of which have a line of gold leafing that reflects in the water. The outer form of the piece is clad with hundreds of chestnut oak leaves made of patinated and textured copper. The upper pool is a massive bowl that Mike made. St. Clare herself belonged to the Franciscan order, nature-oriented sect; the design of the baptistery pays homage to that history by appearing as if it had been sitting in the forest for ages and is completely covered with jewel-like leaves. Many of the other furnishings and ceremonial objects were made by regional artists, like the crucifix made by sculptor Jeanne Dueber, the communion chalice and plate made by a Berea potter, and the altar and other liturgical furniture made by a local woodworker who milled lumber from a giant tree that was felled on the exact site where the new church stands. You can visit the church weekdays between 9 A.M. and 1 P.M. or by special appointment (or during mass!). Call (859) 986–4633.

An elegant place for fine regional foods and downtown lodging is the **Boone Tavern Hotel and Dining Room** (859–985–3770 or 800–366–9358; www.berea.edu/boonetavern), owned and run by Berea College. There's even a dress code for evening meals (if you fellows forget your jacket, they'll loan you one). It's open daily for all meals. Berea College is a highly acclaimed liberal arts college that serves talented, low-income students from southern Appalachia. Students pay no tuition but work ten to 15 hours a week at any of 138 college-owned businesses, which include the Boone Tavern and studios for pottery, weaving, woodworking, broom making, and other crafts. The student-made crafts are sold at the **Log House Sales Room** on Jackson Street. After you've surveyed the student-made crafts on the first floor, head upstairs to the **Wallace Nutting Museum,** where you'll find fine reproductions of 17th- and 18th-century furniture. The Log House Sales Room's phone number is (859) 985–3226.

Five generations of Cornelisons have kept **Bybee Pottery** (859–369–5350; www.bybeepottery.com) thriving since at least 1845, making it the oldest existing pottery west of the Alleghenies. If you're from this region, you've probably seen Bybee's pots. The wheel-thrown, slip-cast (molded), and jiggered stoneware pots are pretty clunky and chip easily, but they are based on traditional designs. The hilarious droop of the studio building itself reflects the age of the pottery. The clays used in all of Bybee's pieces (more than 125,000 annually) come from a small, remarkably pure clay mine less than 2 miles away. Visitors are welcome to mosey around the entire work area. To get there from Richmond, take U.S. Highway 52 east for 9 miles. The Bybee salesroom and workshop are open on weekdays from 8 A.M. to noon and from 12:30 to 3:30 P.M. You'll find the best selection if you go early on the days when the kiln is unloaded—Monday, Friday, and sometimes Wednesday.

trueblue

Of Kentucky's 120 counties, 77 are completely dry (of alcohol sales, that is), and in 16 counties, the largest town is wet and the rest of the county is dry.

Fort Boonesboro State Park is on the beaten path and pretty self explanatory. From I–75 take exit 95 on Highway 627 and follow the signs. The reconstructed fort is at the site of Kentucky's second settlement, established in 1775 by Boone and Richard Henderson when they worked as surveyors for the Transylvania Company. Interpreters at the park dress in period clothing and demonstrate pioneer crafts, such as making lye soap. The park also offers a campground, swimming pool, beach, and more. Hours from April through October are 9 A.M. to 4:30 P.M. daily. Hours from November 1 through March 31 are Wednesday, Thursday, and Sunday from 10 A.M. to 4 P.M. Call (859) 527–3131 or visit http://parks.ky.gov/findparks/recparks/fb.

If you continue north on Highway 627 toward **Winchester,** you may want to veer to the left (west) 3½ miles after crossing the bridge onto Old Stone Church Road and see the lovely little church by the same name. This was supposedly the first church established west of the Appalachian Mountains. It still

Kentucky's Re-Covered Bridges

Almost any time of the year is a good time to take the winding road KY 1262 off U.S. Highway 60 between Georgetown and Frankfort to the small community of Switzer. There, at the center of a small country park, the *Switzer Covered Bridge* spans Elkhorn Creek. It's a picture-postcard scene, this wooden beauty with sawtooth entrances, flanked by trees, and atop stone foundations on each side of the creek.

Switzer looks like a part of the landscape, and it has been since 1855. But if you had made that winding drive, as I did, in March 1997, you would know that Switzer's presence is nothing short of a miracle.

In March of that year, the worst flooding in more than a century hit central Kentucky. The waters of the Elkhorn swelled and pushed downstream with enough force to lift the Switzer Bridge right off its foundation. Had it not been for a modern concrete span just down the creek, Switzer would have been washed away into oblivion. Instead, it hit the concrete bridge and crumpled into the creek like a folded cardboard box. There were more than a few teary-eyed central Kentuckians standing on the banks in the days after the flood.

But Switzer, one of just 13 covered bridges remaining in a state that once boasted 400, was too precious to be lost. Through a community and state effort, the bridge was lifted, removed, and, ultimately, rebuilt, with new materials added to what could be salvaged. The bridge that spans Switzer today is not exactly the same as it was, but it's close enough.

Switzer isn't the only central Kentucky covered bridge to be "re-covered" in recent years. *Colville Covered Bridge,* which crosses Hinkston Creek near Millersburg, was damaged by flooding in 1999. This bridge, too, was removed, repaired, and reinstalled. You can now drive though this "timbered tunnel." To get to Colville, take Highway 1893 west off US 68, go about 3.1 miles, then turn right at an unmarked road lined by stone walls.

has an active congregation, but they don't mind visitors as long as you don't leave trash.

In 1925 the **Leeds Theatre,** at 37 North Main Street, was probably the most popular place in Winchester because it had one of the town's first air conditioning systems. The theater operated as a movie house until 1986, when it closed in a dilapidated condition. A citizens group, the Winchester Council for the Arts, raised enough money to give the place a facelift, and in 1990 it reopened as the **Leeds Center for the Arts.** Along with local productions, this reborn entertainment palace features national arts performances from dance to jazz concerts. Write the center at P.O. Box 836, Winchester 40392, call (859) 744–6437 or (888) 772–6985, or visit www.leedscenter.com for information on upcoming performances.

Though the telephone has radically altered our society and world, it is seldom commemorated. Winchester's **Pioneer Telephone Museum** is one of a kind. The collection of antique phones, phone booths, switchboards, and memorabilia was long housed in a phone company maintenance building. In 2000 the whole collection was moved to Winchester's new **Bluegrass Heritage Museum,** at 217 South Main Street. The museum, created by a combination of citizen activism and city/county support, is located in a stunning Romanesque Revival building that served as the Guerrant Clinic from 1927 to 1971. Dr. Guerrant's offices were located in the building until 1989. The museum focuses on local and regional history, including agriculture, transportation, and Native American and pioneer heritage, according to curator Sandy Stults. Call (859) 745–1358 for hours and more information (www.bgheritage.com).

The clinic building was donated by Wallace and Lana Guerrant, who operate **Mountain Mission Bed and Breakfast** at 21 Valentine Court in what was the nurses' home for the clinic. There are two nicely self-contained units, one with a Jacuzzi and one with a fireplace and balcony with a view of the courtyard fountain. You can have breakfast anywhere, even in bed! Call (859) 745–1284 for more information.

If you are driving near the Mount Sterling Plaza on the bypass, stop at Arby's. Please don't eat. Just get out of the car and look for a rather abrupt grassy knob. That's not a Maya Lin earth sculpture, but the **Gaitskill Mound,** an Adena burial mound dating to between 800 BC and AD 700.

In downtown **Mount Sterling** there is an artifact from the 1950s. **Berryman's Tasty Treat,** open since 1951 on East Main Street, is a full-fledged vintage take-out dairy freeze famous for its chili hot dogs. Berryman's is open from 7 A.M. to 9:30 P.M. daily. It closes for the winter in mid-November. Its annual reopening in early March is a sign to area residents that spring has arrived. For information call (859) 498–6830.

For more area information, stop by—or write—the Mount Sterling Chamber of Commerce, 51 North Maysville Street, Mount Sterling 40353, in the old **Bell House** building, circa 1815, previously a hat shop and county jail. Ask about October Court Days, a big trading festival reminiscent of earlier times when each county held court once a month in a central location so the more remote farmers didn't have to come to town more often. During this three-day extravaganza, approximately 100,000 people crowd into the town of 5,400.

Just uphill from the Bell House at the corner of Broadway and High Street is the **Ascension Episcopal Church,** a beautiful little church with walnut paneling, exquisitely carved wood, exposed beams, and stained-glass windows thought to be the first to cross the mountains (by oxcart!). The doors are open during the day so visitors can drool at the 1877 gem.

If you're a history buff, be sure to drive by **Morgan Station,** the site of the last Indian raid in Kentucky. Daniel Boone's cousin, Ralph Morgan, built the big stone house east of Mount Sterling at 3751 Harpers Ridge Road.

Mount Sterling is sweet-tooth heaven. Make a molasses run (but not as slowly as molasses itself runs) to **Townsend's Sorghum Mill,** at 11620 Main Street (also US 460) in Jeffersonville, south of Mount Sterling. Go any time of year because they always have pure sorghum syrup (and occasionally maple syrup) on hand, but in September and October you can watch them process cane. The Townsend family has been raising cane for 150 years. Although they use tractors to do the real work, at festivals they bring out the mule team to turn the old-fashioned cane break. Call Judy and Danny Townsend at (859) 498–4142, or plan to come by after 4 P.M.

The ultimate dessert is chocolate—real food for real people. If you are a chocoholic, you might be in mortal danger upon entering **Ruth Hunt Candies.** The aroma of liquid chocolate, sweet cream, and roasting nuts will cause lightheadedness in even the strong of heart. Everything is handmade and very fresh. Just like in the old days, you can ask the clerk for a quarter pound of pulled cream candy, a half pound of caramel and bittersweet chocolate balls, and a handful of hot cinnamon suckers, and they'll reach into the big, colorful bins for the goods.

This operation is small and friendly enough that Larry Kezele, the owner, may have time to show you the whole production process. Ruth Tharpe Hunt started the business in 1921 after her bridge buddies encouraged her to go public with her candy making. The Blue Monday Sweet Bar is a dark chocolate with pulled cream in the center and is perhaps the most famous of the company's products. The candy bar was named by a traveling minister who was eating Sunday dinner at the Hunts' and claimed that he needed candy to get through those blue Mondays. Look for Larry and his staff dressed like Blue

Mondays in parades. The company, located at 550 North Maysville Road, is open Monday through Saturday from 9 A.M. to 5:30 P.M. and Sunday from 1 to 5:30 P.M. Call (859) 498–0676 if you need more information or if you are jonesing and need an order FedExed now. Their Web site is www.ruthhuntcandy .com. (If you're in Lexington, Ruth Hunt has a new store at 2313 Woodhill Drive, in the Woodhill Center.)

City Lights

More than 95 percent of the bourbon whiskey made in America is made in Kentucky, and most of it comes from this area. *Wild Turkey Distilleries* (of Boulevard Distillers and Importers Inc.) is a place to get a fascinating bourbon education. From Lawrenceburg take US 62 east of town until it splits with Highway 1510. Bear right, go downhill, and watch for the visitor information center on the right. (Note the high train trestle spanning the Kentucky River. Young's High Bridge is a single-span, deck-over cantilever 281 feet high and 1,659 feet long, the last of its kind.)

The Wild Turkey Distillery has been operating continuously since the mid-1860s, except during Prohibition, when nearly all distilleries were shut down. During World War II this facility made only surgical alcohol. Federal law states that for whiskey to be called straight bourbon, it must be manufactured in the United States, of at least 51 percent corn, and stored at 125 proof or less for at least two years in new, charred, white-oak barrels. Char caramelizes the wood, which gives the bourbon its rich color and flavor. The corn is ground, cooked, and cooled. The distillers add rye for starch, then barley malt, which converts the starch to sugar (unlike moonshiners, who simply dump cane sugar in the corn mash). Yeast is added, and when the fermented mash is steamed from below, whiskey vapor rises to the top where it is condensed into liquid form. The whiskey is distilled again, put in barrels, and aged from four to twelve years. It's tasted at every stage, and meticulous production records are kept for every batch. Free tours are available Monday through Friday between 8 A.M. and 4:30 P.M. The distillery runs 24-hour days every day except Sunday, when liquor is not made anywhere in the United States. Call (502) 839–4544 or visit www.wildturkeybourbon.com.

trueblue

Lawrenceburg, county seat of Anderson County, was named for 19th-century U.S. Navy captain James Lawrence, who is credited with coining the phrase "Don't give up the ship."

From Lawrenceburg take US 127 north into *Frankfort,* the state capital. At the corner of Capital Avenue and Second Street is an ornate Queen Anne–style house with gingerbread trim, the official Frankfort Visitor Center (502–875–TOUR; www.visitfrankfort.com). Because the city's layout is confusing, a map is good headache prevention.

Directly across Capital Avenue from the visitor center is *Rebecca-Ruth Candy Inc.,* at 112 East Second Street. Chocolate and candy addicts will love the tour of one of Kentucky's oldest houses of sweet repute. In 1919 Rebecca Gooch and Ruth (Hanly) Booe quit teaching and went into business making candy. Ruth's grandson, Charles Booe, carries on the tradition today.

Tour the production area to see pipes running full of liquid Dutch chocolate and churning vats of sugar and thick cream. Some candies are made completely by hand on the original 1919 marble slab. Rebecca-Ruth sells hundreds of varieties, including delicate mints, crunchy chocolate turtles, fudge galore, and variations on the theme of the bourbon ball. Hours are Monday through Saturday 8 A.M. to 5:30 P.M. Tours are given Monday through Thursday from January through October between 9 A.M. and 4:30 P.M. (excluding the lunch hour, noon to 1 P.M.). Call (502) 223–7475 or (800) 444–3766 for a tour schedule or a free catalog (www.rebeccaruth.com).

The *Thomas B. Clark Center for Kentucky History* is the definitive high-tech repository of documents, photos, and all manner of important archival material concerning the history of our commonwealth. View such things as Daniel Boone's original survey note, in his handwriting. For years the Kentucky Historical Society had dreamed of having a permanent, state-of-the-art facility for research and education, and this impressive 167,000-square-foot facility was the dream-come-true and then some. The center, at 100 West

In the Grain

"When I start working, I might as well climb into the wood—that's how intimate it gets," says woodworker **Connie Carlton** of Lawrenceburg. Connie looks for the perfect tree in the woods, cuts it before the sap runs, splits long sections of the trunk lengthwise with a sledge and froe, and shapes the wood on a vise-bench of ancient design called a "shaving horse" amid a tiny sea of curled wood shavings. (The place smells like heaven.) The results are long, smooth, shapely pitchforks, rakes, barrel staves, woodworking tools, and the like. He also makes sorghum molasses. If you want to buy fine, functional wooden tools, from US 127 take US 62 west about 2 miles and turn left on Rice Road. His is the first house on the left. Be sure to call ahead (502–839–6478). You might catch Connie demonstrating techniques and selling his work at festivals held at the Shaker Village at Pleasant Hill (see page 24).

Broadway, is in downtown Frankfort, next to the railroad tracks on the corner of Broadway and Ann Street. History Center hours are 10 A.M. to 4 P.M. Tuesday through Saturday. Admission of $4 for adults and $2 for children also includes the Old State Capitol and the Kentucky Military History Museum. Call 502–564–1792 for information about changing exhibits and special events at the center (www.history.ky.gov).

Just across and down a block on Broadway you'll find numerous interesting shops. There are several antiques malls with everything from antique linens to cannonballs. ***Poor Richard's Books,*** at 233 West Broadway, carries a mix of new and used tomes (including some hand-printed at Larkspur Press in Owen County). Call (502) 223–8018. A few doors away is ***Completely Kentucky,*** at 237 West Broadway, which, as its name implies, carries products made in the Bluegrass State. Call (502) 223–5240. Outside of Berea, stores that specialize in regional crafts and other indigenous products are surprisingly few, and Completely Kentucky has variety in both items and price range. From wonderful and affordable cherry kitchen tools and foods to fine raku pottery and handmade jewelry to whimsical metal yard "critters," you're sure to find something of interest.

true*blue*

Kentucky towns bear an international array of names. Kentucky has a Moscow, Athens, Cairo, Dublin, London, Manila, Paris, and Warsaw.

One of Frankfort's newest attractions is actually old—a resurrected bit of Civil War history (and in-town forest) called ***Leslie Morris Park on Fort Hill.*** There were two Civil War earthwork forts on the hill, Fort Boone and New Redoubt. In 1864 Confederate general John Hunt Morgan's raiders attacked Fort Boone, but local citizens successfully defended the city. You can take a self-guided walking tour (begin at the Fort Hill visitor center in the Old Capitol Annex, 100 Broadway). It's a moderately strenuous trek up Old Military Road, but the reward is a chance to see the walls of Fort Boone and earthworks of New Redoubt, as well as a commanding view of downtown Frankfort.

About 8 miles north of Frankfort is ***Canoe Kentucky*** (7323 Peaks Mill Road; 502–227–4492 or 888–CANOEKY; www.canoeky.com), home base for Ed Councill, canoeist and Elkhorn Creek conservation activist extraordinaire. Canoe Kentucky offers a variety of excursions on a dozen Kentucky waterways, but it is the one in his own backyard, Elkhorn Creek, that is most dear to his heart. Take an excursion and you'll soon understand why. This long and winding waterway—which flows for more than 100 miles through parts of six counties—played an important role in the settlement of the bluegrass area.

Poet Walt Whitman, whose soldier brother was encamped in Kentucky in 1863, wrote of "the vale of the Elkhorn." Whether your interest is historic sites, fishing (some sections are great for catching bass), picnicking, or just a quiet-at-your-own-pace getaway, Councill can suggest a good paddle route. Canoe Kentucky even offers moonlight excursions for groups. ("We found that these weren't as much fun when it was a group of people who didn't know each other," Councill explained.) If you want to learn all about the Elkhorn, its history, its wildlife, and the need to protect it in light of rapidly encroaching development, or if you want to try a more unusual aspect of canoeing, such as winter canoeing, Ed Councill's the one to go up (or down) the creek with. Prices vary depending on length and type of excursion. An unguided, 6-mile (2½-hour) excursion costs $45 per person; two people to a canoe. Kayaks are also available, and the 12-mile trip is also popular. A guide on the trip would cost $50 more per group. Office hours are Monday through Friday, 9 A.M. to 5 P.M.

From Frankfort go west on Interstate 64 or US 60 to Shelbyville. In 1825 Julia Tevis founded **Science Hill,** a girls' school at 525 Washington Street in downtown **Shelbyville,** because she believed young women needed an education in math and science, not just needlepoint and etiquette. During its 114-year operation, Science Hill was known as one of the best preparatory schools in the country. Etiquette, however, never lost its essential place. A former student remembers this story about Miss Julia Poynter, the last principal of the school: The mother of a "town boy" had a party in her home. One of the students thanked the hostess by saying, "I enjoyed myself thoroughly." Miss Julia reprimanded the girl, saying, "You do not go to a party to enjoy yourself, you go to enjoy others. Tell your hostess that you enjoyed her party."

Today the fully restored Science Hill complex houses six boutiques, the Wakefield-Scearce Galleries, and a restaurant, the **Georgian Room.** In keeping with the 19th-century atmosphere, the restaurant serves fine American food with a heavy Kentucky accent. Lunch is served daily, except Monday, from 11:30 A.M. to 2:30 P.M.; dinner is served Friday and Saturday from 5:30 to 8:30 P.M. You must call ahead for dinner reservations (502–633–2825). The **Wakefield-Scearce Galleries** (502–633–4382; www.wakefield-scearce.com) are full of elegant English (plus a touch of Oriental, American, and European) furniture, silver, china, rugs, paintings, and other decorative objects. Much of the furniture is antique, and the reproductions are beautifully made. The quality is high, as are the prices. Whether or not you can afford the decor, these museum-like galleries provide room after room of visual and tactile delight. Hours are 9 A.M. to 5 P.M. Monday through Saturday.

There are several other charming shops along Washington Street. Needlepoint enthusiasts won't want to miss **The Needle Nest,** 702 Washington Street

(502–633–4701), which carries an extensive selection of patterns, fabric, thread, and accessories.

There is a cluster of antiques stores downtown, all within walking distance of one another. The Ruby Red Rooster is at 514 Main Street. Antiques for You is at 528 Main Street. Tam's Antiques is nearby at 610 Main Street. And the Country Cottage Collectibles is a block away at 137 Frankfort Road (also US 60). It's a good town for walking and browsing.

Follow US 60 (or, if you're in a hurry, take I–64 West) to **Louisville,** largest city in the state and home of the world-famous **Kentucky Derby.** The greatest two minutes in sports are also part of the greatest 24 hours in fashion. For a week before the Derby, everyone and everything is dressed to the nines—houses are repainted, yards are relandscaped, hair is coiffed, and bodies are clothed in the latest styles, no matter the cost or the weather. For Kentuckians the Derby marks the beginning of early summer and, therefore, the first day that it's acceptable for women to shed their dark winter garb and wear white again. Fashion sometimes follows need and sometimes it leads. Several years ago we had a bitter cold, rainy Derby Day, but the dresses were already purchased, and hats were garnished. Women simply wore thermal underwear under sleeveless gowns, and men, for once, were happy to keep on their coats and ties.

The Kentucky Derby is run the first Saturday in May at Churchill Downs Race Track on Central Avenue (502–636–4400; www.churchilldowns.com). The gates open at 8 A.M., and you can join the party on the infield or wander the paddock area for $50—standing room only or bring your own chair or blanket. Racing begins at 11:30 A.M., but the Run for the Roses isn't until 6:04 P.M. Dress however you want, and keep your eyes peeled for celebrities. Churchill Downs also hosts thoroughbred racing during a Spring Meet, which runs from the end of April to the beginning of July, and a Fall Meet, from late October through late November.

If you're planning to be seen at the Derby and want to be on the cutting edge of fashion, you may want to check out the annual pre-Derby fashion show held in mid-April at the **Kentucky**

Derby Museum on the grounds of Churchill Downs. Celebs and local media personalities model the latest in hats and clothes, setting a precedent for the masses. Any time of year the Kentucky Derby Museum is an interesting stop. Naturally, the exhibits feature the Derby's history, but there are others concerning the whole thoroughbred industry. Hours are 9 A.M. to 5 P.M. Monday through Saturday, noon to 5 P.M. Sunday. Also on-site is the Finish Line Gift Shop and The Derby Cafe. Call (502) 637–1111.

Far from the madding crowd, but not far from Churchill Downs, are several peaceful sites. The most surprising is just inside the Interstate 264 loop between Poplar Level Road and Newburg Road: the *Beargrass Creek State Nature Preserve* (502–458–1328). The best way to get there is to turn onto Illinois Avenue off Trevilian Way (behind the Louisville Tennis Center), then park in the lot next to the *Louisville Nature Center,* where you'll find informative exhibits and a friendly staff. There's a bird blind viewing area behind the building. Trails in the preserve are well defined, though not marked, so pick up a map at the center. No dogs or bicycles are allowed. The preserve encompasses 41 acres and has a remarkably diverse community of flora and fauna. Because it's smack-dab in the middle of the city, it is constantly in use for environmental education. So if you placed all your bets badly at the track, here's a balm. This lovely spot is open

trueblue

Zachary Taylor grew up and is buried in Louisville.

daily from sunrise to sunset, and there's someone at the nature center Tuesday through Saturday, 9 A.M. to 5 P.M. (www.louisvillenaturecenter.org).

The park is named after Beargrass Creek, which empties into the Ohio River just above the famous *Falls of the Ohio,* a rocky series of rapids over a 3-mile descent, which stopped early travelers on their way south. Beargrass Creek proved to be a place to rest and to develop a strategy for getting around the falls. In 1778 George Rogers Clark set up a military and civilian camp nearby, on Corn Island. Floods on the island caused the settlers to move to the mainland (somewhere between what are now Twelfth and Rowan Streets), where they started building the city of Louisville. Since the installation of the Portland Canal and the McAlpine Dam (easily seen from town near the Northwestern Parkway and Twenty-seventh Street), the Falls of the Ohio is an exposed coral reef, a fossil bed over 350 million years in age. Some 600 fossil species can be seen; 400 species have never been seen anywhere else. To get a good look at the fossils, cross the river into Clarksville, Indiana, park at Riverside Park, and walk near where the Fourteenth Street railroad bridge and five dam gates meet the shore. From Interstate 65 take exit 0 and follow the signs. There is an interpretive center (812–280–9970; www.fallsoftheohio.org) open Monday through Saturday from 9 A.M. to 5 P.M. and Sunday from 1 to 5 P.M. Admission is $5 for adults, $2 for students and children.

The **Portland Museum** (502–776–7678; www.goportland.org) features exhibits illustrating 200 years of the city's river history. One of the most enthralling items is an old newsreel of the great 1937 Ohio River Flood. A few exhibits are located in the Beech Grove antebellum home. Admission is $5 for adults, $4 for children and seniors; hours are Tuesday through Friday from 10 A.M. to 4:30 P.M. From I–64 take the Twenty-second Street exit, turn right, and go to 2308 Portland Avenue. It's a good idea to call ahead.

Jefferson County has restored and opened to the public a grand-style Greek Revival brick house, circa 1835, known as the **Farnsley-Moreman House.** With an extremely high front portico that haughtily faces the river, the house represents a showy attitude prevalent in prosperous river cities in the 19th century. In the 1860s this house sat at the center of what was the largest farm in the county at the time. If you visit Riverside (as the property is now known), you'll see period antique furnishings and historically authentic kitchen gardens in addition to exhibits reflecting life on the river as far back as 4,000 years. (It is considered the best view of the Ohio River in Louisville.) Call (502) 935–6809 or check www.riverside-landing.org for information on special events. Normal hours are Tuesday through Saturday from 10 A.M. to 4:30 P.M., Sunday from 1 to 4:30 P.M. Admission is $6 for adults, $5 for seniors and children, or $15 for the whole family. To get there, head west on Gene Snyder Freeway (you can access this from I–64 and I–65), and stay on the "greenbelt," as it's called, until you reach Lower River Road. Then just follow the signs. The house is 7410 Moorman Road, at the intersection of Lower River and Moorman Roads.

Fascinating Facade

One of Louisville's most fascinating house tours isn't really a house; it's just the front of a house. Like a piece of a movie set, the front of the **Charles Heigold House** sits forlornly in Thurston Park, off River Road east of downtown Louisville. If this were a movie, it would be a historical drama, set in the mid-1800s, when Heigold, a German immigrant and stonemason, decided to carve his political feelings in stone—on the front of his house. "The Union Forever, All Hail to This Union, Let It Never Desolve It" is among the sayings and figures elaborately carved into the facade in exuberant fashion. The rest of the house was razed when the street on which it originally stood became part of the city landfill. Luckily, city officials decided to save this face for visitors and future residents to ponder and enjoy.

In 1810 John and Lucy Fry Speed had a Federal-style mansion built based on a design by Thomas Jefferson. ***Farmington*** has octagonal rooms, hidden stairs, and orderly gardens. Abraham Lincoln visited this home of his friend, Joshua Speed, for six weeks in 1841 during a temporary break in his relationship with Mary Todd, his future wife.

Originally the house was in the center of a 552-acre hemp plantation. Now it's on 18 acres, all of which are carefully restored and maintained in keeping with its early-19th-century history. You can visit it Tuesday through Saturday from 10 A.M. to 4:30 P.M., Sunday from 1:30 to 3:30 P.M. The address is 3033 Bardstown Road. Call (502) 452–9920 for more information.

Another spectacular Federal-style structure, which has been exquisitely restored, is the 1900 Ferguson Mansion, 1310 South Third Street, now home to the ***Filson Club Historical Society*** (502–635–5083; www.filsonhistorical.org). The society has a nationally renowned genealogy library (which costs $10 to use) and extensive manuscript, photography, and museum collections (which can be viewed for free). Stop by between 9 A.M. and 5 P.M. Monday through Friday or 9 A.M. to noon Saturday. Tours are every hour on the hour Tuesday through Saturday and at 1:30, 2:30, and 3:30 P.M. on Sunday at a cost of $6 for adults, $5 for seniors, and $3 for children between six and 18.

Next to Beargrass Creek Park is the ***Louisville Zoological Garden,*** at 100 Trevilian Way, home to more than 1,300 animals. The zoo has an exhibit of birds of prey and a Herp Aquarium, which features a simulated rain forest. It is open daily, year-round. Admission is $7.95 for everyone. Call (502) 459–2181 for current hours or check www.louisvillezoo.org.

From the zoo take Newburg Road to Eastern Parkway, and go west to Third Street; turn right and you're on the University of Louisville campus. The ***Speed Art Museum*** at 2035 South Third Street (502–634–2700; www.speedmuseum .org) is a small but outstanding museum not to be missed at any cost. The permanent collection includes works from all periods, including some distinguished medieval, Renaissance, and Dutch masterpieces, and a broad representation of contemporary art. The museum also maintains a stimulating schedule of traveling exhibitions. Hours are 10:30 A.M. to 4 P.M. Tuesday, Wednesday, and Friday; 10:30 A.M. to 8 P.M. Thursday; 10:30 A.M. to 5 P.M. Saturday; and noon to 5 P.M. Sunday. During the summer, more culture is in store at the corner of Fourth and Magnolia Streets in Central Park. The

trueblue

In 1893 a pair of Louisville sisters penned the kindergarten greeting song, "Good Morning to You," which later became the most-sung song in the world rewritten as "Happy Birthday to You."

Kentucky Shakespeare Festival performs free, high-quality, live Shakespeare productions in June and July.

Curtain time is 8 P.M. Tuesday through Sunday. Call (502) 637–4933 for current schedules or check www.kyshakes.org.

Indoor theater is always happening in this town. Consult the *Louisville Courier Journal* for performances by the myriad little theaters, and check the schedule at ***Actors Theatre,*** 316 West Main Street. In addition to producing a surprising variety of plays all year (except during July and August), Actors has become nationally known for the Humana Festival of New American Plays in March and April. Shows in the festival are booked early, so get the schedule and make reservations by calling (502) 584–1265 or (800) 428–5849 or check www.actorstheatre.org.

Main Street is art street in Louisville. The glass structure with the big whimsical sculpture is the ***Kentucky Center for the Arts*** at 609 West Main Street. The center hosts a little of everything, including the Louisville Opera, ballet, orchestra, theater for all ages, and a series of national and regional performers. Call (502) 584–7777 or (800) 775–7777; www.kentuckycenter.com. A block west, at 715 West Main Street, the ***Kentucky Museum of Art and Craft*** (502–589–0102; www.kentuckyarts.org) features the work of some of the state's finest craftspeople. Hours are Monday through Friday, 10 A.M. to 5 P.M. and Saturday, 11 A.M. to 5 P.M. The ***Zephyr Gallery,*** at 610 East Market Street (502–585–5646; www.zephyrgallery.org), is another place worth exploring. This art cooperative never fails to hang imaginative shows.

The ***21C Museum Hotel,*** at 700 West Main, is a renovated luxury hotel as well as a museum of international contemporary art collected by the owners, Laura Lee Brown and her husband Steve Wilson. The 21C Museum collects and exhibits solely contemporary art of the 21st century in a wide range of media (Wilson has joked that, were an artist to die, their work would be removed from the collection!). The artwork is exhibited throughout the hotel, with the main atrium/lobby serving as the primary gallery—it is here that a series of guest curators organize engaging, intelligent, even pioneering exhibitions of contemporary art. The collection includes artists such as Tony Oursler, Yinka Shonibare, Kara Walker, and Red Grooms. The hotel consists of five historic tobacco and bourbon warehouses combined and reconfigured into a clean-lined, minimalist, contemporary structure that occasionally reveals its architec-tural memories—exposed brick walls and massive wooden beams overhead.

The 90 rooms include high quality modern amenities such as an iPod loaded with each guest's music of choice (determined and pre-programmed a week in advance when the hotel has contacted you to ascertain your needs, whether they be theater tickets or rental cars), 42-inch HDTV screens standard in each room, Wi-Fi connections, headboards (made from recycled plastic) that display purchasable poster art of artworks on display in the hotel, and mint julep makings awaiting activation—classic sterling silver julep cups, fresh sprigs of mint, and a bottle of bourbon. It's worth noting at this point that Brown and her family control the Brown-Forman liquor corporation. In addition to their support of contemporary art on the national and international scale, Brown and Wilson have been longtime supporters of regional arts projects and institutions. Rooms are between $165 to $405 a night. For more information, call (502) 217–6300 or (877) 217–6400 and see www.21cmuseumhotel.com. The valet, astride his Segway, will be waiting to whisk you away into this elegant engagement with the present.

The restaurant at 21C, **Proof on Main,** features regional ingredients, like Kentucky striped bass and locally grown produce, in American-style dishes "with Tuscan influences." They're open weekdays for lunch and daily for dinner and late-night offerings (until midnight and 1 A.M.). Closed Sunday. Of course, you'll dine with art. For reservations call (502) 217–6360; www.proof onmain.com.

Another not-to-be-missed arts attraction is **Glassworks,** located in a renovated commercial building at 815 West Market Street. Here you can see the art of glassmaking in numerous forms, from glassblowing to the creation of stained glass and architectural glass. Guided studio tours are given Monday through Saturday for $6.50 and last about an hour. Self-guided tours are $3.50 and $4.50. There's no charge to see the changing glass exhibits in the main floor gallery. Call (502) 584–4510 for more information or visit www.louisville glassworks.com.

With the 2004 opening of **Flame Run Gallery and Studio,** Louisville is on its way to becoming a hot spot for hot glass. At 828 East Market, the studio is just blocks away from Glassworks (above). The 12,500-square-foot space is primarily a functional hot shop, but there is also a gallery that showcases changing exhibitions of studio glass art. The gallery is open Tuesday through Saturday from 10 A.M. to 4 P.M., by appointment, and by chance at other times. When the glassblowers are working in the shop, you're welcome to observe the activity.

trueblue

Louisville is second only to Boston in number of registered historic sites.

Special tours can be arranged for groups. They offer classes in all aspects of hot glass, from blowing to kiln casting or sand casting to making paperweights; they also rent shop time. For more information, call (502) 584–5353 or visit www.flamerun.com.

The next stop is for kids. The *Louisville Science Center,* 727 West Main Street, is a big, colorful, hands-on place orchestrated for discovery. The selling point for adults is the IMAX theater, a four-story screen surrounded by speakers; the experience blows your confidence in logic to pieces. "It's just a movie," you tell yourself as you clutch the nearest person's arm to keep from falling. Call the museum at (502) 561–6100 or (800) 591–2203 for show times and admission charges (www.louisvillescience.org).

In case you didn't notice, there's a 120-foot baseball bat at Main and Eighth Streets. The erect bat is a beacon for the *Louisville Slugger Museum* (502–588–7228 or 877–775–8443; www.sluggermuseum.org). Baseball fans of all ages will love the museum and tour of the world's largest manufacturing plant of baseball bats. (Over one million are made there annually.) There's a full-size dugout, a replica of Orioles Park, a replica of a northern white ash forest, and exhibits tracing the history of the game and its most famous brand of bat. Despite being called the Louisville Slugger, for 22 years the bats were actually made across the Ohio River in southern Indiana. In 1996 the manufacturing plant returned to Louisville. Tour hours are Monday through Saturday, 9 A.M. to 5 P.M. Tours are also given Sunday afternoon April through November, but production does not occur on Sunday, so you'll get a video tour instead. Admission is $9 for adults, $8 for seniors, and $4 for children.

Directly across from the Louisville Slugger Museum, is the *Frazier International History Museum* (829 West Main Street; 502–753–5663; www .fraziermuseum.org). The city's new three-story museum is primarily devoted to American military history and related artifacts and weaponry. Some notable items in the permanent collection include Daniel Boone's family Bible, Geronimo's bow, and President Theodore Roosevelt's "big stick." In addition to traditional displays, history is presented in lively reenactment performances by elaborately costumed actors in several parts of the museum. There are also interactive multimedia presentations and frequently screened films in the internal theater. Not a fan of arms? Pacifism is given its due, too. There is, for example, a fascinating display of World War I photos by a pacifist soldier named Andre Jeunet. Carrying a simple folding camera, Jeunet captured more than 200 images of the war depicting everyday life as a foot soldier and documenting his travels to the Balkans and Greece as a participant of the Salonica campaign. The museum is open Monday through Saturday from 9 A.M. to 5 P.M. and on Sunday from noon to 5 P.M. Admission is $9 for adults and $6 for students and children.

Since there are so many restaurants of every kind in town, let's just consider breakfast and dessert. If having breakfast at *Lynn's Paradise Cafe* (984 Barret Avenue; 502–583–3447; www.lynnsparadisecafe.com) doesn't get your day off to a smiling start, you might as well just give it up and head back to bed. Owner Lynn Winter's taste in decor is certainly eye-opening— there's an 8-foot red coffeepot out front and all manner of knickknacks inside—but there's nothing silly about her efforts in the kitchen. This place serves great breakfast burritos, chunky French toast topped with fruit and whipped cream, fabulous cheese home fries, and all sorts of other inventive approaches to "home cooking." Lynn's is open Monday through Friday 7 A.M. to 10 P.M., and 8 A.M. to 10 P.M. Saturday and Sunday, so if you like to sleep in, you can also get lunch or dinner. Lynn has added an attached store, the World of Swirl, (502–583–4434) where you can buy zany knickknacks like those in the cafe as well as some pants of her own design called "Magic Pants."

Kizito Cookies (502–456–2891; www.kizito.com) wins a prize for the most unusual method of dessert distribution. Elizabeth Kizito started her business by carrying baskets of scrumptious chocolate cookies through the downtown streets on her head during lunch hours. (She still sells from her head basket at ball games, parades, and special occasions.) She is from Uganda, where it's commonplace for folks to keep their hands free by means of this balancing act, but in Louisville, she's become famous for it. These days she has a retail store at 1398 Bardstown Road, where you can buy coffee, cookies, and muffins while looking over a colorful selection of African earrings or small

Tattoos—While You Wait (Is There Any Other Way?)

A little-known cultural reference library of sorts is found in the halls of *Tattoo Charlie's,* a dermagraphic extravaganza. Tattoo art has come a long way since bones and charcoal or needles in a cork. For the uninitiated, you can watch consenting clients being decorated by a certified tattoo technician wielding an electric needle that looks and sounds like a dentist's drill. Prices range from $25 for a single music note, for example, to more than $3,000 for a series of full-color illustrations. Even if you aren't personally interested in a tattoo, check out the tattoo design gallery and museum featuring photos, tattoo machines, and other memorabilia. Then there are hundreds of photographs and slides of customers displaying actual tattoos, no matter where they are. Although there are now four locations, the original Tattoo Charlie's is located at 1845 Berry Boulevard, on the south side of town; the easiest way to get there is to take U.S. Highway 31 south and turn east on Seventh Street Road, then veer onto Berry Boulevard. No appointment necessary. Call (502) 366–9635. Hours are Monday through Thursday noon to 8 P.M., Friday noon to 10 P.M., and Saturday noon to 6 P.M. (www.tattoocharlies.com).

carvings from Kenya and wonderful baskets from Uganda. Hours are 7 A.M. to 5 P.M. Tuesday through Friday, 8 A.M. to 5 P.M. Saturday.

If you're looking for fragments of almost anything imaginable, pay a visit to *Joe Ley Antiques* at 615 East Market Street. Joe Ley's place is two acres under one roof full—and I mean full—of antique treasures. For architects and home-restoration folks, this is an endless toy shop. Stained glass, chandeliers, mantels, carousel horses, stuffed moose, fine silver—you name it, it's here. Hours are Tuesday through Saturday from 8:30 A.M. to 5 P.M. Call (502) 583–4014. Also check www.joeley.com. Want more? Head down to *Architectural Salvage* at 618 East Broadway for more of the same. This place is crammed full of mantels, hardware, stained glass, doors, wrought iron, and on and on. Call (502) 589–0670 if you care to ask specifics. I recommend the browsing method myself. Or for the whole gamut, stop by the *Louisville Antique Mall* (502–333–6195 or www.louisvilleantiquemall.com) in a 19th-century cotton mill at 900 Goss Avenue.

On the mezzanine level of the Seelbach Hilton Louisville, at 500 Fourth Avenue, is the *Oakroom,* Kentucky's first and only AAA Diamond restaurant. Awards (of which there are many) aside, the truth is that the chefs use fresh local ingredients (Amish free-range chickens, wild morel mushrooms, pungent Trappist monk–made cheese, still-dripping-with-dew fruits and vegetables, etc.) to very creatively conjure palate-tingling, eye-popping-gorgeous dishes. The restaurant is in the hotel's 1907-era gentlemen's billiard hall—the aesthetic is still powerfully present in the carved lion's head columns, ornate molding, dark wood beam ceiling, brass chandeliers. They offer 1,200 wines and a huge collection of Kentucky's many bourbons (also used in many of the dishes). Call (502) 807–3463 to make reservations (recommended). They are open daily from 5:30 to 10 P.M., and on Friday for lunch between 11 A.M. and 1 P.M. and on Sunday for an elegant Champagne Piano Brunch between 10 A.M. and 2 P.M. (www.seelbachhilton.com/hoteldining_theoakroom.html).

Bardstown Road has long been home to countless artists, musicians, playwrights, and people of diverse backgrounds. Over the years that cultural richness has grown, and now includes many of Louisville's most popular and successful small businesses. For international cuisine and an usually wide selection of vegetarian dishes, try *Ramsi's Café on the World* (1293 Bardstown Road; 502–451–0700). While you wait for your table, be sure to walk next door to a pair of favorite and very complementary local businesses, *Carmichael's Bookstore* (1295 Bardstown Road; 502–456–6950; www.carmichaelsbookstore.com) and *Heine Brothers' Coffee.* (There are seven locations in town—this one is at 1295 Bardstown Road; 502–456–5108; www.heinebroscoffee.com). Don't worry about missing your reservation at Ramsi's because the host is happy to retrieve you when your table is ready. Across the street from Ramsi's are the ***Baxter Avenue Theatres*** (1250 Bardstown Road; 502–459–2288), a small set of movie theaters tucked into the middle of town, that show the usual blockbusters as well as a variety of foreign films, documentaries, and indie art films.

For music lovers, Mecca is near! Louisville's home-grown business ***Ear X-tacy*** (1534 Bardstown Road; 502–452–1799) is the place to get music—any kind of music, and in almost any format. The shelves are stocked with music from around the world and from a range of time periods. If you prefer the crisp sound of vinyl, then Ear X-tacy is a real resource; they have many of your old favorites in stock, along with a lot of new music you may not expect to find for a turntable. If you don't see exactly what you have been searching for, ask someone, because they special order music for customers. Ask, too, about buying tickets for local live shows. You may not have to leave the store to hear live music—there are in-store performances by the likes of the Del McCoury Band or Sam Bush. Hours are Monday through Thursday from 10 A.M. to 10 P.M. and Friday and Saturday from 10 A.M. until midnight. You can find daily sales, performance schedules and other information at www.earx-tacy.com.

If you want to stay in town but escape briefly, escape to ***Cherokee Park,*** off Eastern Parkway east of downtown, for bicycling, jogging, and picnicking. Or take Third Street south to ***Iroquois Park*** and admire a nearly 200-year-old forest. Louisville has some of the most beautiful public parks found anywhere, thanks to foresight on the part of city leaders. In 1891 Louisville hired Frederick Law Olmsted to design and construct the city's park system. Olmsted is known as the father of landscape architecture; his other credits include New York's Central Park, Biltmore Gardens, and the 1893 Chicago World's Fair. When Olmsted retired in 1895, his stepson, John C. Olmsted, completed the Louisville plan. In all, the Olmsteds created 16 Louisville parks between 1891 and 1935. Although a 1974 tornado took its toll, citizens rallied in the late 1980s to conserve and, where necessary, restore the parks' beauty.

To explore the world in all its infinite detail is a lifelong process demanding your every sense. But not every sense is challenged equally by those of us who have the use of all human senses. The blind can access nearly any information that seeing people can if they have the tools; and some of their senses, like touch and hearing, are sharpened by intensive use. The ***American Printing House for the Blind,*** established in 1858, is the world's largest and oldest publisher and manufacturer of education aids for visually impaired people. The printing house has recently opened a museum of rare artifacts relating to the history of technology developed for the blind—from the tactile language of Braille to the audio recording of almost any text that exists in the world. This museum is one of the most important and unique sites in Louisville. Tours are given Monday through Thursday at 10 A.M. and 2 P.M., and you can browse the museum before or after. For more information call (800) 223–1839. The printing house and museum is located at 1839 Frankfort Avenue (www.aph.org).

Abbeys and Art

What was once an abused tract of tired farmland is now **Bernheim Forest Arboretum and Nature Center,** a 10,000-acre native forest protected since 1928. Available in this legacy of "the knobs" are hiking, picnicking, limited fishing, unlimited daydreaming, and a self-education in the nature center's museum or in the arboretum, where an enormous variety of ornamental plants are grown in meticulously labeled, manicured beds. I used to skip high school in the spring to make an annual pilgrimage here, armed with my bicycle and a sketch pad. The forest is open from 7 A.M. to sunset daily. The visitor center, art gallery, and nature shop are open from 9 A.M. to 5 P.M. daily. Call (502) 955–8512 for information. Bernheim Forest is right next to the intersection of I–65 (exit 112) and Highway 245. Admission is free weekdays, $5 per vehicle on weekends (www.bernheim.org).

While traveling, Mark Twain was asked by the luggage inspector if he had anything besides clothing in his suitcase. Twain said no, but I guess he looked suspicious because the man opened his case anyhow and found a fifth of bourbon whiskey. "I thought you had only clothes!" the man roared. "Ahh," Twain answered, "but that's my nightcap." Twain's drink of choice had to be bourbon, and it had to be from the limestone hills of Kentucky, which provide the water that gives Jim Beam and other regional bourbons a distinctive flavor that makes them the best in the world. For a crash course in whiskey mash, take a free tour of the **Jim Beam American Outpost and Museum** (502–543–9877; www.jimbeam.com) on Highway 245, a mile east of Bernheim Forest. Hours are 9 A.M. to 4:30 P.M. Monday through Saturday, 1 to 4 P.M. Sunday.

Bardstown is dense with well-advertised, historically significant treasures, such as **My Old Kentucky Home State Park** and house of John Rowan. Rowan invited his cousin from Pittsburgh, Stephen Foster, to visit in 1852, and shortly afterward, Foster wrote the tune that is now our official state song. The mansion and gardens are open from 9 A.M. to 5 P.M. daily year-round. Admission is $5.50 for adults and $3.50 for children. From early June through Labor Day, the famous musical, *The Stephen Foster Story,* is performed outdoors. You can't miss the signs. Call (800) 323–7803 for more information or check http://parks.ky.gov/findparks/recparks/mo.

Run, Rooster, Run!

If you're going toward Bardstown from the west on Highway 245, not stopping at **Rooster Run General Store** (502–348–8753) is like being in Memphis and skipping Graceland. The store, formerly called Evans Beverage Depot, was the only place in Nelson County in the late 1960s that sold alcohol. One day a man had too many drinks, and his wife showed up with fire in her eyes, stood in the Depot door, and snarled his name. When the drunk man sped obediently to her side, someone remarked, "Well, would you look at that old rooster run." Such is the history of town names in our state. I still wonder whether the name had anything to do with the fact that the next town over is called Hen Peck. Whatever the truth may be, Joe Evans put the place on the map by selling over a million Rooster Run caps to truck drivers and celebrities alike.

Near the park on Highway 49 is **Heaven Hill Distilleries,** touted as the largest family-owned distillery in the country. The free tour includes a lesson in bourbon making and a visit to the bottling operation. This distillery makes Heaven Hill, Elijah Craig, and Evan Williams. Open 10 A.M. to 5 P.M. Tuesday through Saturday and, from March through October, also on Sunday from noon to 4 P.M. Call (502) 348–3921 or visit www.heaven-hill.com.

Two on-the-beaten-path restaurants in town are **Old Talbott Tavern,** the oldest western stagecoach stop in America, circa 1779, which also has bed-and-breakfast lodging in the old inn (502–348–3494; www.talbotts.com), and **My Old Kentucky Dinner Train** (502–348–7500; www.kydinnertrain.com), where you dine in vintage 1940s dining cars pulled by old diesel-electric engines on a two-hour ride to Limestone Springs and back.

At the corner of US 62 West, also called Stephen Foster Avenue, and Fifth Street is the **Saint Joseph Proto-Cathedral.** The cathedral, circa 1823, is the oldest west of the Alleghenies and contains a collection of paintings given by the French King Louis Philippe, Francis I, King of the Two Sicilies, and Pope Leo XII. Here's what impresses me: Six solid tree trunks, lathed and plastered, were transformed into the building's huge Corinthian columns. St. Joseph's is open every day. Guided tours are given April through October from 9 A.M. to 5 P.M. Monday through Friday, Saturday from 9 A.M. to 3 P.M., and Sunday from 1 to 5 P.M. You can tour on your own November through March. Admission is free, but donations are encouraged. Call (502) 348–3126 or visit (www.bardstown.com/~stjoe).

Behind the cathedral is **Spalding Hall,** circa 1826, a large brick building that was originally part of Saint Joseph College, and later Saint Joseph Prep School. Two adjoining museums housed here are the **Bardstown Historical**

Who Really Invented the Steamboat?

Pay your respects to John Fitch, the unhappy inventor of the steamboat in 1791. Then listen to the earth rumble when Robert Fulton turns over in his grave—wherever he's buried, may he rest in some peace. John Fitch was not born in Bardstown, but he died here after a lifetime of work on steam navigation and a lifetime of struggle with inventor James Rumsey, who, like Fulton, claimed to have been the first to apply it successfully. After failing to get sponsors, comparable to today's lusted-after research grants, Fitch came to Nelson County, built steamboat models, and tested them in local streams. *John Fitch's grave* in the square is marked by a small steamboat replica.

Museum and the ***Oscar Getz Museum of Whiskey History,*** both free. Displays range from items like Jenny Lind's cape and Jesse James's hat to an original 1854 E. G. Booz bottle, which inspired the word booze, and a Carry Nation exhibit. Hours from May through October are 10 A.M. to 5 P.M. Monday to Saturday and noon to 5 P.M. Sunday. From November through April the museums open at 10 A.M. and close at 4 P.M., except on Sunday, when they are open from 1 to 4 P.M., and Monday when they're closed. Call (502) 348–2999 for information.

Think about the basis of homesteading—self-sufficiency. Now apply the concept to the visual arts and you will begin to appreciate Jim and Jeannette Cantrell. The ***Bardstown Art Gallery,*** at 214 West Stephen Foster Avenue, is a fine-art gallery, a framing shop, pottery and painting studios, a hand-set printing press operation, an office, a home, and a small book-sales business, which boasts one of the country's most comprehensive collections of Thomas Merton's writings. That both Cantrells have a love of high quality is apparent in everything from Jim's treatment of light and reflections in his oils to Jeannette's hand-set letterpress gallery announcements. Jeannette curates group and solo shows in addition to displaying Jim's originals in oil, watercolor, pen and ink, and anything else that catches his eclectic eye.

It was by accident that Jeannette became a Merton expert. One of the monks at the nearby abbey asked if she wouldn't mind selling a few of Merton's books to tourists. She started with a few copies of *Seven Storey Mountain,* and now she carries a respectable line of Merton's out-of-print writings, valuable limited editions, related scholarly works, and cassettes of Merton himself reading from his works or just talking about such subjects as Rilke's poetry, silence, art, and beauty. Hours at the Bardstown Art Gallery are officially By Chance or By Appointment, but someone is usually there from 10 A.M. to 5 P.M.

Monday through Saturday and from 1 to 5 P.M. Sunday. Contact the Cantrells by writing to P.O. Box 417, Bardstown 40004 or calling (502) 348–6488. They have two Web addresses: www.bardstownartgallery.com and www.thomas mertonbooks.com.

To visit Thomas Merton's residence, the ***Abbey of Gethsemani,*** oldest Cistercian monastery in the United States, follow US 31E south from Bardstown, veer left at Culvertown onto Highway 247, and watch for TRAPPISTS signs. From the heart of Italy around AD 500, Saint Benedict developed a set of rules to help monks in a spiritually based community follow the example of Christ as closely as possible. These Trappist monks take vows to renounce the capacity to acquire and possess goods, to obey the house rules and the abbot's advice, and to remain celibate. Silence is encouraged but not required. "Enclosure," I've been told, "is enforced not so much to keep laypeople out as to keep the monks in." But these monks do indulge in some wandering. Thomas Merton, quintessential ascetic, aesthete monk from this abbey, was known to go "out"

Merton the Monk

Perhaps no one in Kentucky has done more to translate the personal journey of the spirit into a universal dialogue of understanding than Trappist monk, author, and poet, Thomas Merton. Born in Paris (France, not Kentucky), Merton traveled throughout Europe as a child with his parents, both of whom were artists. After graduating from Cambridge and later from Columbia, Thomas joined the Trappist order of monks, the most ascetic of the Roman Catholic monastic orders, at the Abbey of Gethsemani in the hills outside Bardstown. At his quiet retreat Merton immersed himself in prayer, mediation, and writing. His many books, essays, and articles address a breadth of issues with intensity and grace, including pacifism, race relations, world peace, and meditation. In his later work, Merton used his insight and wisdom to encourage an interfaith dialogue between the East and West, even traveling to meet with the Dalai Lama and to learn from Buddhist monastic orders. It was on one of these journeys in December of 1968 that Merton was tragically electrocuted by a faulty fan while in his bathtub. There is lingering suspicion that his death was not accidental. Merton's unflinching insistence on the universality of spiritual experience caused him to be both loved and despised during his lifetime—many Christians believed his work with other faiths to be blasphemy. Although the voices of discontent have quieted over the years, Merton's insights have continued to shape discussions of faith into the present day.

To learn more about Thomas Merton's life and works, visit the **Merton Center** at Bellarmine University, 2001 Newburg Road, Louisville, where his many photographs, drawings, and writings, are preserved. The center is open from 8 A.M. to 5 P.M. Monday through Friday. The center is closed on all major holidays, including the university's spring break, so call ahead (502–452–8100).

to lecture, to meet with other spiritual people, and occasionally to hear jazz. While visiting the abbey, I met a monk who travels to Owensboro for the barbecue festival. No matter what else you think, their life choice is radical.

Economic survival is perhaps the greatest difference between early and modern cloisters. The 76 resident monks make and sell fruitcakes, bourbon fudge, and three kinds of Port Salut Trappist cheese, a pungent, creamy, French-style aged cheese. Everyone takes part in all aspects of the work, from making cheese to doing dishes to answering the phone or laying sewer pipes. The slogan *Ora et Labora* means "prayer and work," but they don't have "all necessary things" on their 2,000-acre farm. They use hired help to raise the beef cattle and to do some construction and maintenance. Health care, for example, is sought in the secular world, including modern services such as weight-loss centers. To learn more about the abbey's farm products or to place an order, call (800) 549–0912 or use the Web site, www.gethsemanifarms.org.

Laypeople are welcome to join in parts of life at the abbey. Mass is always open to the public, if you can make it at 5:30 A.M. on weekdays (the monks will have been awake for hours by then), and there are a variety of other prayer services and vespers throughout the day. Sunday Mass is at 10:30 A.M. in the main chapel, a long, narrow, modern building where the choir's chant reverberates as if produced in outer space. Hospitality is historically part of the living monastic tradition. Saint Benedict instructed that the guest represents Christ and is to be welcomed and cared for by the community. Anyone is welcome to make a retreat at the Abbey, in the words of Merton, "to entertain silence in the heart and listen for the voice of God—to pray for your own discovery." Abbey retreats are silent, unstructured, and undirected (speaking is permitted in designated areas). Gethsemani has a retreat house with 30 rooms (with private bathrooms and air-conditioning) that can be reserved for personal or group retreats. Women are welcome during the first and third full weeks of each month (that's Monday to Monday), and men can make retreats during the second and fourth weeks. Call far in advance at (502) 549–3117. For a group day visit, call (502) 549–4129. For more information, write Abbey of Gethsemani, 3642 Monks Road, Trappist 40051 or visit www.monks.org.

trueblue

Marion County is located at the geographic center of Kentucky.

If you drive south from Bardstown on US 31E, you will arrive in the tiny town of *New Haven.* Downtown on Main Street the old train depot now houses the *Kentucky Railway Museum,* where you can hop a train to Boston—that's Bawston, Kentucky—11 miles away on the old Louisville & Nashville Railroad's former Lebanon Branch.

Members of the museum completely restored an L&N steam locomotive (No. 152) and the streamlined No. 32 of the former Monon, made in the late 1940s. When these babies pump by, you feel your heart making reply. From March through December trips run between 10 A.M. and 4 P.M. on weekends, when the museum and gift shop are also open. In the summer there are excursions daily, except Monday. For exact fares, times, and dates, contact the Kentucky Railway Museum, P.O. Box 240, New Haven 40051-0240, or call (502) 549–5470 or (800) 272–0152 or check www.kyrail.org.

To visit one of the state's most famous and picturesque whiskey distilleries, take US 52 east from New Haven, or Highway 49 south from Bardstown, to Loretto; then take US 52 east until you see the sign on the left for **Maker's Mark Distillery.** Like the process, the facility is old. In 1953 Bill Samuels Sr. bought the shabby country distillery where folks were accustomed to filling their own jugs straight from casks of whiskey in the Quart House. Now Maker's Mark is known around the world for its super-smooth bourbon (nicknamed "Kentucky champagne"). The distillery is open year-round every hour on the half hour from 10:30 A.M. TO 3:30 P.M. and at 1:30, 2:30, and 3:30 P.M. Sunday. For more information, call (270) 865–2099 or visit www.makersmark.com.

In Loretto take Highway 49 north, then veer right at a fork in the road onto Highway 152. You'll soon see the sign for **Loretto Motherhouse.** The Sisters of Loretto, founded in central Kentucky in 1812, was one of the first American religious communities of women. The sisters moved here in 1824 from Little Loretto at nearby St. Charles. Near the entrance of the grounds is the restored cabin, circa 1808, of Father Charles Nerinckx, founder of the order. Going toward the cemetery you'll see one of the country's first outdoor Stations of the Seven Dolors, installed in 1911. On the east side of the drive, you'll see **Knobs Haven Retreat,** a center at which folks can reserve space for taking a serious, personal retreat. For rates and further information, write Director, Knobs Haven, Nerinx 40049, or call (270) 865–2621; www.nerinxhsorg/LKYhist.html.

Next to the main church and convent, circa 1860–63, you'll notice a group of abstract sculptures in various media. This is the work of Jeanne Dueber, nun and artist in residence at Loretto. Her studio is in **Rhodes Hall Art Gallery,** at the north end of the driveway. Her work is amazing in its variety and feeling, and her exploration of form is almost religious. Large, refined abstract sculptures in wood, resin, metal, and paper fill the big rooms. A large willow, struck by lightning, has been transformed into a powerful piece called *Tempest*, in which Dueber strategically added heads and arms of a man and a woman in such a way that they seem to be sliding away from each other while reaching toward each other. Many pieces are playful, like a series on Pelé, the soccer star, or an academic charcoal drawing of a heavy, drooping nude woman entitled *Homage to Gravity*. Pieces about Prometheus, ecstasy, companionship, and yoga positions accompany overtly religious work such as crucifixes for churches. If she's working in the first-floor studio and isn't too busy, tell her what you think. You can visit the gallery daily from 9 A.M. to 5 P.M. To buy a piece, just put your money in the slotted box by the stairs—a self-service fine-art gallery! Write Jeanne Dueber, Rhodes Hall, Nerinx 40040, or call the Loretto Motherhouse, (270) 865–5811, ext. 2068.

Another retreat center located near New Haven and the Abbey of Gethsemani is **Bethany Spring** (115 Dee Head Road; 502–549–8277; www.bethany spring.org), sponsored by the Sisters of Charity of Nazareth. Private or directed spiritual retreats are offered to adults of all faiths and cultures. There are three housing options available. The Main House can accommodate up to eight people and includes a home-cooked dinner nightly and simple fare made available for other meals. The cottage for couples, called Emmaus, is a simple and lovely retreat spot for two with a kitchen where guests cook their own meals. And Wellspring is a hermitage for one person, a self-contained cabin designed by architect Ted Johanson with a bath, kitchen, fireplace, and porch overlooking a lake. The retreat is open year-round and rates are $55 per person on weeknights and $65 per person on weekends (Friday and Saturday).

For more local lodging head south on Highway 49 into **Lebanon** and check into the **Myrtledene Bed and Breakfast** at 370 North Spalding Avenue. The house is an 1833 formal brick affair with a colonial columned portico. Famous Confederate raider Gen. John Hunt Morgan used Myrtledene for headquarters in 1862, and a year later, when he returned with the intention of destroying Lebanon, it was from here that he waved the white flag of truce. During his stay, Morgan rode his horse into the front door of Myrtledene and up the front steps; the hoof prints survived well into the 20th century. A room with full breakfast costs $85 a night. Call (270) 692–2223 or (800) 391–1721 for reservations. Also check the Web site, www.myrtledene.com. By the way, Union soldiers from the 1862 Battle of Perryville are buried in **Lebanon's National Cemetery.**

Since Lebanon is out of the way, you might be happy to know that the little town boasts a classy eating establishment at 157 West Main Street called **Henning's Restaurant** (270–692–6843; www.henningsrestaurant.com). In addition to occupying a handsomely restored building in the historic district, the restaurant offers homemade soups, entrees, breads, and desserts, recommended by the locals. Dinner only is served Tuesday and Thursday from 4:30 to 9 P.M. and on Friday and Saturday from 4:30 to 10 P.M. Reservations are recommended.

New in Lebanon is the **Blues on Tap Restaurant and Bar,** at 110 North Proctor Knott Avenue, just a half block off Main Street. Not new is the handsome 1870s-era building. Nor is the owner, James Spragens, new to creating great food in a comfortable environment; he also owns the Myrtledene B&B (above). The blues music is live on Thursday through Saturday night. The food features locally grown produce made into New Orleans–style dishes, like gumbo and red beans and rice, and Southern classics like peach-grilled pork chops and marmalade-grilled chicken breast. They serve lunch on weekdays and dinner Monday through Saturday. Call (270) 699–BLUE (2583).

Although there were once more than 400 covered bridges in Kentucky, there are now only 13. The **Mount Zion Bridge** (referred to in some quarters as the Beech Fork or Mooresville Bridge), in the northwest corner of Washington County, is the only remaining example of two-span Burr Arch construction and, at 102 feet, is the longest in the state. It was almost lost recently before the county restabilized the piers, and it may yet be moved to a more accessible location. For now, the easiest way to see it is to get off the Blue Grass Parkway at exit 34 and go south on Highway 55; at Mooresville take Highway 458 north and watch for the bridge on the left spanning the Beech Fork Creek. The bridge is closed to traffic, but you can walk through it.

Like nearby **Hodgenville** (covered in the South-Central Kentucky chapter), central Washington County is a repository of sites and stories connected to Abraham Lincoln. Abe's parents, Thomas Lincoln and Nancy Hanks, were from this area, and several of their family buildings are restored or replicated. For details go by the **Lincoln Homestead State Park** at the intersection of Highways 438 and 528, just 5 miles north of Springfield off US 150. An 18-hole golf course has been built on old Mordecai Lincoln's land, and I'll bet he's rolling over violently in his grave. The park also has several log structures, such as the original Berry Home, where Nancy Hanks lived when she and Thomas were courting. While the golf course is open year-round, the museum is seasonal; it's open May to September from 8 A.M. to 6 P.M. and on weekends in October. Ask at the park for a map of the Lincoln Heritage Trail. For more information call (859) 336–7461 or visit http://parks.ky.gov/findparks/recparks/lh.

In downtown **Springfield** notice the **Washington County Courthouse** on Main Street (859–336–5425; www.kycourts.net/counties/washington). Built in 1816, it is the oldest courthouse still in use in Kentucky. Records in the files, including the marriage certificate of Abraham Lincoln's parents, date back to 1792. If court isn't in session, look at copies of this and other documents hanging on the walls. It's open from 8:30 A.M. to 4:30 P.M. Monday through Friday and from 9 A.M. to noon Saturday.

In 1822 Father Samuel Wilson, a Dominican priest in Springfield, asked young women of the parish to dedicate their lives to Christian education. One of those who answered the call was Maria Sansbury. A year later she and eight other women opened St. Magdalen Academy in a converted building on the banks of Cartwright Creek. As Mother Angela, Maria is considered the founder of the first order of Dominican Sisters in the United States. In 1891 their school became Saint Catharine Academy, and in 1920 the sisters established a teachers college. The academy has long been closed, but the college survives today as Saint Catharine College, a two-year liberal arts institution (859–336–5082; www.sccky.edu). The *Saint Catharine Motherhouse* (859–336–9303; www .opkentucky.org), 2 miles west of town on US 150, is under renovation, but visitors are welcome. Not too far away on US 52, about ½ mile off US 150, is the *Saint Rose Proto-Priory.* Founded in 1806, this was the first Catholic educational institution west of the Alleghenies. Students included Jefferson Davis, who would become the president of the Confederacy. Tours of the priory are by appointment; call (859) 336–3121.

More Good Lodging in Central Kentucky

Ask about lower-priced weekend specials and other special rates.

BARDSTOWN

Beautiful Dreamer Bed & Breakfast
440 East Stephen Foster Avenue
(502) 348–4004 or
(800) 811–8312
www.geocities.com/ bdreamerbb
A new home built in classic Federal style, across from My Old Kentucky Home. $119 to $199 per night.

Hampton Inn Bardstown
985 Chambers Boulevard
(502) 349–0100 or
(800) HAMPTON
Newer motel with pool. About $99 per night.

Jailer's Inn
111 West Stephen Foster Avenue
(502) 348–5551 or
(800) 948–5551
www.jailersinn.com
Renovated 1819 historic limestone jailhouse, with Jacuzzi suites and one humorously decorated "cell room." $115 to $145 per night.

BEREA

The Doctor's Inn
617 Chestnut Street
(859) 986–3042
www.berea.com/ accommodations
Luxurious B&B accommodations in an elegant colonial style mansion. About $135 per night.

DANVILLE

Old Crow Inn
471 Stanford Avenue
(859) 236–1808
www.oldcrowinn.com

Bed-and-breakfast in "Kentucky's oldest stone manor house." On the premises are a working arts studio and walking trails. $75 to $100.

FRANKFORT

Meek House
119 East Third Street
(502) 227–2566 or
(866) 646–7650
www.bbonline.com/ky/ meek
This 1869 Gothic Revival home takes its name from Benjamin F. Meek, a silversmith who helped develop the Meek and Milam fishing reel. Downtown. Rooms start at $115.

The Meeting House
519 Ann Street
(502) 226–3226
www.themeetinghouse bandb.com
1849 Civil War–era home located in the historic district.

GEORGETOWN

Jordan Farm
4091 Newtown Pike
(502) 863–1944 (evening)
or (502) 868–9002 (day)
www.jordanfarmbandb.com
Bed-and-breakfast in a carriage house on thoroughbred horse farm. It has a fishing lake! $100 to $125.

Pineapple Inn
in town at
645 North Broadway
(502) 868–5453
www.travelassist.com/reg/
ky001.html
Bed-and-breakfast in an 1876 historic house with period antiques. $75 to $95.

HARRODSBURG

Bauer Haus
downtown at
362 North College Street
(859) 734–6289
www.bbonline.com/ky/
bauer
Bed-and-breakfast in an 1880 Victorian home. Full breakfast is included. $100 to $145.

Baxter House B&B
1677 Lexington Road
2 miles east of town at the road's junction with Highway 1343
(859) 734–4877 or
(888) 809–4457
www.baxterhousebb.com
Theme rooms in a large country home with unusual pets. Kids are allowed (the owners have some), and bonfires and wagon rides will be offered. Rates are between $109 and $149.

LEXINGTON

Gratz Park Inn
120 West Second Street
(800) 752–4166
www.gratzparkinn.com
A historic downtown hotel complete with a ghost or two. Rates are about $179 to $429.

Swann's Nest at Cygnet Farm
3463 Rosalie Lane
(859) 226–0095
www.swannsnest.com
Distinctively appointed suites and rooms on a thoroughbred farm near Keeneland Race Course.

LOUISVILLE

Camberley Brown Hotel
Fourth Street and Broadway
(502) 583–1234 or
(800) 555–8000
www.brownhotel.com
A 1920s landmark with an excellent restaurant. $159 and up.

DuPont Mansion
1317 South Fourth Street
(502) 638–0045
www.dupontmansion.com
Elegant 1884 Italianate house with marble mantels and period furniture. $129 to $209.

Galt House
Fourth Avenue at River Road
(502) 589–5200
www.galthouse.com
Overlooking the Ohio River. Rooms are about $115.

Seelbach Hilton
500 South Fourth Avenue
(502) 585–3200 or
(800) 333–3399
www.seelbachhilton.com
A luxurious Beaux Arts showplace in the heart of downtown. Rooms $99 and up.

NEW HAVEN

Sherwood Inn
138 South Main Street
(502) 549–3386
Bed-and-breakfast in a restored railroad hotel next to the Kentucky Railway Museum. About $70 per night.

PARIS

Country Charm Historic Farmhouse Bed and Breakfast
505 Hutchinson Road
(859) 988–1006 or
(866) 988–1006
www.countrycharm.net
Bed-and-breakfast with one room or suite in the main house and a three-bedroom stand-alone cottage. $80 to $125.

The Treehouse at Stoner Creek Bed and Breakfast
131 Taylor Avenue
(859) 987–6251 or cell
(859) 707–0369
www.treehouseatstoner
creek.com
Bed-and-breakfast right downtown in an unusual creekside house. Canoes and pontoon rides are available to guests. $90 to $110.

RICHMOND

The Bennett House
419 West Main Street
(859) 623–7876 or
(877) 204–3426
www.bennetthousebb.com
Romanesque-style house,
on the National Register of
Historic Places.

SPRINGFIELD

Maple Hill Manor Bed and Breakfast
2½ miles east out of
Springfield on U.S. Highway 150
(Perryville Road)
(859) 336–3075 or
(800) 886–7546
www.maplehillmanor.com
An antebellum Greek
Revival mansion, circa
1851, restored with
Jacuzzis and porch grills
with every room.

VERSAILLES

Bluegrass Bed and Breakfast Reservation Service
(859) 873–3208
Information about private
bed-and-breakfasts and
cottages in the Versailles
and Lexington area that do
not advertise.

Montgomery Inn
270 Montgomery Avenue
(859) 251–4103
www.montgomeryinnbnb
.com
Large restored Victorian
home with numerous
Jacuzzis and electric fireplaces. Gourmet breakfast
is featured. 10 guest suites
$109 to $179.

Rose Hill Inn
233 Rose Hill Avenue
(800) 307–0460
www.rosehillinn.com
An 1820s official landmark
home within walking distance of town. Seven guest
rooms are available. $129
to $184.

WINCHESTER

Day's Inn Winchester
Mount Sterling Road at
Interstate 64, exit 96A
(800) DAYSINN
About $79 per night.

House on Belmont B&B
331 Belmont Avenue
(859) 745–0177
www.houseonbelmont.com
Renovated, elegant 1872
home in the downtown.
Fireplace, Jacuzzi. $20 high
tea. $120 to $150.

Mountain Mission Bed and Breakfast
21 Valentine Court
(859) 745–1284
www.bbonline.com/ky/
mountmiss
$110 and up.

More Fun Places to Eat in Central Kentucky

BEREA

Hometown Cafeteria
Interstate 75, exit 76
(606) 986–7086
Popular for its home cooking—enjoy real mashed
potatoes and straight-from-the-oven pie.

Ground Effects Specialty Coffee House
440 Chestnut Street
(859) 986–8597
www.groundeffectscoffee
house.com
Open all day every day but
Sunday for specialty coffees and espresso drinks,
tea, smoothies, pastries,
free wireless Internet, and
live music—local musicians
Friday and Saturday, open
mic on Thursday.

BURGIN

The Village Inn
501 East Main Street
(at intersection with Highway 33 by the only traffic
signal in town)
(859) 748–5943
If you like country cooking and also like to smoke
while eating, this is your
place. Locals who have
moved away are drawn
back like moths to flame.

CYNTHIANA

Biancke's Restaurant
102 South Main Street
(859) 234–3443
Open for three meals
daily, except Sunday. It's
the spot where everyone
goes—teenagers on prom
night, local grandmas and
tile setters, and visitors
alike. Great homemade
pies.

Gibby's
212 West Broadway
(502) 223–4429
Lunch only. Monday
through Saturday, 11 A.M.
to 3 P.M. Hot Italian entrees,
pasta, fresh gourmet salads, sandwiches, soups,
and ice cream.

Jim's Seafood
950 Wilkinson Boulevard
(502) 223–7448
Seafood while you watch
the Kentucky River out the
window.

Serafini Broadway at the Saint Clair
pedestrian mall
(502) 875–5599
Monday through Friday
11 A.M. to 2 P.M. and 5 to
10 P.M.

HARRODSBURG

Aunt Gravy's
419 East Office Street
(859) 734–2151
Home cooking, located
downtown.

Kentucky Fudge Company and Cafe
225 South Main Street
(859) 733–0088
www.kentuckyfudge
company.com
An 1865 pharmacy serving floats, fudge, and ice
cream.

LEXINGTON

a la lucie
159 North Limestone
(downtown)
(859) 252–5277
www.alalucie.net

Possibly the best restaurant in Lexington. Excellent,
creative nouvelle cuisine
in a glamorous and tightly
packed space. Reservations are recommended.

Natasha's Cafe
112 Esplanade
(859) 259–2754
www.natashascafe.com
Eclectic international
cuisine with an attached
boutique selling items from
Slavic cultures and live
entertainment on weekend
nights.

Parkette Drive-In
1216 New Circle Road
Northeast
(859) 254–8723
Drive-through? No, a real
drive-in, with sign, service,
and menu much the same
as when it opened in 1952.
A new 50s retro dining
room has been added.
Slide into a seat and relive
those happy days.

Planet Thai
2417 Nicholasville Road,
#2
(859) 373–8269
www.planetthaiinc.com
Linen napkins, moderate
prices, plentiful vegetarian
options, fabulous flavors,
enough said.

Ramsey's Diner
Woodland and High Streets
in downtown Lexington
(859) 259–2708
4371 Harrodsburg Road
(859) 219–1626
and 3090 Helmsdale Place
(859) 264–9396

Down-to-earth menu of
"classy comfort food"—
even Brussels sprouts and
crawfish.

LOUISVILLE

Lilly's
1147 Bardstown Road
(502) 451–0447
www.lillyslapeche.com
Upscale bistro and
gourmet-to-go with award-winning chef.

Queen of Sheba
2804 Taylorsville Road
502–459–6301
www.queenofsheba
louisville.com
Authentic Ethiopian cuisine. Traditionally served
by tearing off a piece of
Ethiopian flat bread, scooping the food with it and
placing it in your mouth.
However, the restaurant is
happy to serve entrees with
silverware.

Vincenzo's
150 South Fifth Street
(502) 580–1350
www.vincenzositalian
restaurant.com
Fine Italian cuisine by
Agostino Gabriele. Winner
of more than 20 awards.
Check out the Web site for
photos and names of some
of its diverse clientele,
including Hillary Clinton,
Usher, Muhammad Ali, and
Al Pacino.

MIDWAY

Bistro La Belle
117 East Main Street
(859) 846–4233
Lunch weekdays, dinner
Wednesday through Satur-
day, and Sunday brunch.

MOUNT STERLING

**Melini Cucina Italian
Ristorante**
908 Indian Mountain Drive
(859) 497–7066
www.melinicucina.net
Owned by a fabulous cook
born and raised in Italy.
Ham calzone, spinach and
veggie calzones, Melini
stromboli, and baked lasagna. Select Italian wines.
Open daily for lunch and
dinner.

NEW HAVEN

Sherwood Inn
138 South Main Street
(502) 549–3386
Dinner served Wednesday
through Saturday.

PARIS

Paradise Cafe
Corner of Eighth and Main
Streets
(859) 987–8383
Reasonably priced lunch
and dinner in the world's
tallest three-story building
(yes, it's in the *Guinness
Book*!).

WINCHESTER

Hall's on the River
1225 Athens-Boonesboro
Road
(859) 527–6620
www.hallsontheriver.com
Hall's is also famous for
seafood entrees and
take-home foods like beer
cheese.

EASTERN KENTUCKY

Most of North America is inhabited by a wild soup of dissenters' descendants, but what makes eastern Kentucky different is the mountains.

The Appalachian Mountains are a long, beautiful line of steep, nearly impregnable rock that has always tended to keep outsiders out and insiders in. Although the Appalachian culture initially strikes outsiders as foreign, visiting can have the strong allure of a homecoming, in part because your roots may be in European cultures that are better preserved here than anywhere else in the big melting pot. The isolation also has caused eastern Kentuckians to live close to the land, close to one another, and to survive self-sufficiently. As you meet people, listen to the language of this region, the beautiful phrases loaded with humor, knowledge of quirky human nature, and sensitivity to the cycles of the natural world.

There are opportunities in this region to expose yourself to very fine traditional craftsmanship by meeting individual artists or craftspeople and by visiting craft cooperatives where knowledge and tools are being shared with those who want to take the baton. Music and dance, for which mountaineers have always been admired, have developed in fascinating

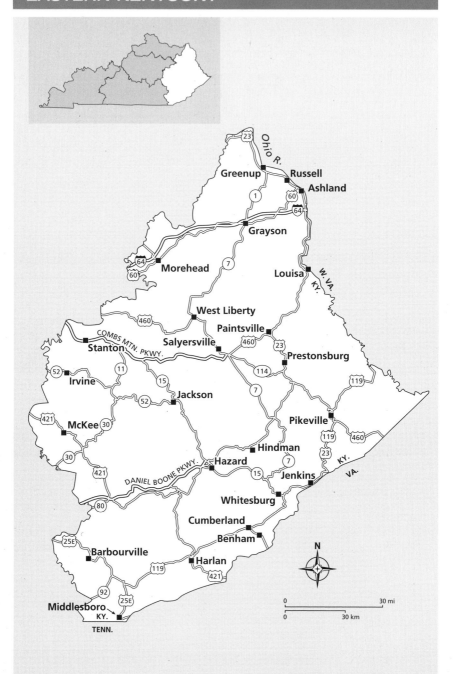

ways and play an important role in the life of this region. Festivals and community dances, which are always open to visitors, are good events to attend if you want to get an authentic taste of the music here. In addition to music, the mountains themselves can soothe the soul.

I have a wonderful recent memory of traveling through the mountains at the end of a long, hot day and stopping on a bridge where a "passel" of people had gathered. Below, by the side of a wide brook, a small revival was in progress. Babies were being passed from lap to lap, and people of all ages were sitting in folding chairs by the little stage, clapping and singing. A sweet hymn in an irresistible minor key rising just above the constant tumble of the water calmed me and opened my eyes to the changing mountains, rosy in the last light of the setting sun. Even in the heat of summer, a mist gathers in the folds and hollows of the land and baptizes everyone equally, even passersby.

AUTHOR'S FAVORITE PLACES IN EASTERN KENTUCKY

Bad Branch State Nature Preserve
near Whitesburg
(502) 573–2886

Carter Caves State Resort
Park Olive Hill
(606) 286–4411 or (800) 325–0059
www.parks.ky.gov

Furnace Mountain
Write for information to the Abbess Box 545
Clay City 40312
www.furnacemountain.org

Lilley Cornett Woods Skyline
(606) 633–5828
www.naturalareas.eku.edu

Little Shepherd Trail
(in the Kingdom Come State Park)
Cumberland
(606) 589–2479
www.kingdomcome.org

Lost Squadron Museum
Bell County Airport
Middlesboro
(606) 248–1149

Mine Portal Number 31
Lynch
(606) 589–5812

Mountain Homeplace
Paintsville
(606) 297–1850
www.mountainhomeplace.com

Red River Gorge
(contact Natural Bridge State Resort Park) Slade
(606) 663–2214

Seedtime on the Cumberland
music festival in early June at Appalshop
Whitesburg
(606) 633–0108
www.appalshop.org

Through the Gap

Dr. Thomas Walker was hired by Virginia's Loyal Land Company to go west in search of fertile settling land. In 1750, when Walker found the only natural route west, a divide he named Cumberland Gap, he built a small cabin to claim the territory, mapped the route, and went home. You can visit a replica of Walker's crude cabin at the **Dr. Thomas Walker State Historic Site** on Highway 459 off U.S. Highway 25E just southeast of Barbourville (606–546–4400; http://parks.ky.gov/findparks/histparks/tw. Though Walker and his group missed reaching the bluegrass region by just a few days of traveling, they did succeed in blazing a trail through the mountains for more than 300,000 pioneers to roll toward a new life in the West. The house and grounds are open year-round.

The 20,000 acres of **Cumberland Gap National Historic Park,** off U.S. Highway 25E south of Middlesboro (www.nps.gov/cuga), include the 800-foot natural break in the Cumberland Mountains through which Native Americans and, later, Daniel Boone and other settlers entered Kentucky. Go to Pinnacle Overlook and you can see three states, as well as the twin tunnels that go 4,600 feet through the mountain to connect Kentucky and Tennessee. Seventeen years in the making, the tunnels finally opened in 1996, replacing a stretch of US 25E so treacherous that it was known as Massacre Mountain. Near the overlook is **Fort McCook,** which was built by Confederate troops to guard the passage.

trueblue

Between 1750 and 1783, some 12,000 settlers had entered Kentucky through the Cumberland Gap.

More than 55 miles of hiking trails wind through the park, but one of the most interesting is the **Ridge Trail** on Brush Mountain, which runs the entire length of the park from the Pinnacle Overlook to a site on the far eastern side of the park called White Rocks, where, on a clear day, you can actually see the Great Smoky Mountains. Early pioneer records note that the 600-foot-high white limestone rock face was an important landmark. Other great hiking destinations include an area called **Indian Rocks,** where Native people used to fashion flint tools (there are still remnants of their work), and the **Goose Nest Sink,** a massive sinkhole created when part of a cave ceiling collapsed. Civil War sentries viewed the valley from this spot, where now you can look down into the canopies of 100-foot-high trees. The Sand Cave is an extraordinarily beautiful and humbling space, a wide cave with a one-and-a-half-acre sand floor next to a 100-foot-high waterfall. One popular stop on the trail is the **Hensley**

Settlement, a restored cluster of farms and houses inhabited from 1903 until 1951. To drive, take the Brownies Creek Road from Cubbage, or take a shuttle from the visitor center in Middlesboro, which is open daily from 8 A.M. to 5 P.M. For all park information, stop by the center during business hours, or call (606) 248–2817. Write to the Cumberland Gap National Historic Park for campsite reservations and so forth at P.O. Box 1848, Middlesboro 40965.

On the second floor of the visitor center at the national park is the Southern Highland Craft Guild's retail gallery, *Cumberland Crafts* (606–242–3699; www.southernhighlandguild.org/shop.php). The guild is a highly competitive juried craft organization that showcases about 250 artists from southern Appalachia. All the work is handmade and includes pottery, glass, fiber, paper, quilting, wood, metals, jewelry, and more. Artist demonstrations go on from Memorial Day until Labor Day and during October. Gallery hours are seven days a week from 9 A.M. to 6 P.M. The gallery closes at 5 P.M. from Labor Day until Memorial Day.

Much of the Wilderness Trail that early settlers used was paved to become US 25E. But the rerouting of motorized traffic between Middlesboro and Tennessee through the modern Cumberland Gap Tunnel, which opened in 1996, is enabling the original trail to be restored so visitors can have a better sense of what the area looked like in the 1700s. Pursuing the same goal in his own way is Tom Shattuck, a former mining engineer who worked on the early phases of the Cumberland Gap Tunnel and founder of *The Wilderness Road Company.* While doing research for the tunnel project, Shattuck became interested in the trails and tales of early Gap area history. His company now offers a variety of guided tours that focus on facets of local heritage from mining to hiking. The three-hour Cumberland Gap Area Tour is an overview that includes sites in Middlesboro as well as the Gap area. These air-conditioned van tours run from $12 to $42 depending upon length and subject matter. Shattuck has distilled the area's dramatic history down into memorable narratives, while the countryside speaks eloquently for itself as you watch it flow by your window. Call (606) 248–2626 or write The Wilderness Road Company at 408 Arlin Hills, Middlesboro 40965, for reservations or information. The Web site offers detailed information and images, www.wilderness-road.com.

Middlesboro is just north of the Gap, outside the national park, in a circular basin that was probably formed between 30 million and 300 million years ago by a large meteor that disintegrated or was blown back into space upon impact. Another possibility is that the depression was formed by the collapse of an underground cavern, since no meteor fragments have been found.

Coal fragments, chunks, and seams, on the other hand, are everywhere and at the heart of the recent history of the area. The *Bell County Chamber of Commerce* (www.bellcountychamber.com) on North Twentieth Street is housed in a building faced with 40 tons of bituminous coal. Next door is *The Coal House Museum,* a little open-air collection of mining artifacts—old mine train cars, headlamps, drill bits, and photos. Ask about the *Cumberland Mountain Fall Festival,* which is held annually in Middlesboro during late October as a celebration of the area's English heritage. Call the Tourism Office at (606) 248–2482, or visit www.mountaingateway.com for information about any of these topics.

Follow North Twentieth Street to the top of the hill, turn left on Edgewood, right onto Arthur Heights, and left when the road comes to the edge of the cliff. The second house on the left at 208 Arthur Heights is *Cumberland Manor,* a 20-room grand Victorian home built in the early 1890s especially for John B. Cary, the secretary-treasurer of Middlesboro Town Company, the English company that developed the Cumberland Gap area. (In the early 1900s the U.S. Post Office Americanized the official spelling of the town's name from the English *-ough* to *-oro,* but you still see both spellings in use.) The street is named after Alexander Arthur, Middlesboro's founder. Cumberland Manor has four rooms available for between $89 and $109 per night. A tornado that narrowly missed the house in the late 1980s managed to clear the trees from the front hillside, leaving an open view of the town below. Call (606) 248–4299 for reservations.

A favorite autumn spot is the *Mason Farm* in Frakes, west of Middlesboro, where pumpkins, gourds, and Indian corn are grown for sale during the month of October. They also host a big *Pumpkin Patch Festival* every harvest season. For more information call the farm at (606) 337–9915 or the county extension agent at (606) 337–2376.

With genius and fine craftsmanship in mind, stop by the Bell County Airport, located just 2 blocks off Cumberland Avenue on the west side of Middlesboro at the *Lost Squadron Museum. Glacier Girl,* a World War II fighter plane, was the fourth in a formation of six Lightnings that made forced landings on a remote glacier in Greenland on July 15, 1942, because they ran out of fuel. For 50 years the planes were buried deeper and deeper under glacial snow and ice until Pat Epps, the owner of Epps Aviation at Atlanta's DeKalb-Peachtree Airport; Richard Taylor, an Atlanta architect; and a group of technical specialists formed the Greenland Expedition Society in order to find and retrieve a plane. The story of the expedition is amazing. Over a three-year period, the crew located the planes, then dug through 268 feet of glacier with a huge hole-melting device designed just for this project, then carefully removed the plane, part by part, and flew it to a hangar in Middlesboro. Supported by a Middlesboro businessman, corporate sponsors, aviation groups, and numerous volunteers and interested individuals around the country, the restoration began in October 1992. As the work progressed, this remarkable saga spread and soon *Glacier Girl* had legions of devoted fans and supporters around the world, from serious aviators and war veterans to the merely curious who would stop by the Middlesboro hangar with cameras and camcorders in hand. On October 26, 2002, about 25,000 people showed up in Middlesboro to watch the reborn *Glacier Girl* make her first flight. Now the restoration group is building a museum to house the aircraft and to tell this remarkable story. Visitors are welcome from 8 A.M. to 5 P.M. daily. Call (606) 248–1149 or check the Web site, www.thelostsquadron.com, for more information about the project as well as upcoming flights.

Between Middlesboro and Pineville is the **Kentucky Ridge State Forest,** which includes **Pine Mountain State Resort Park.** Both have entrances off US 25E. Follow signs to the Herndon J. Evans Lodge at the top of the mountain, where you can get trail maps and park information. Call (606) 337–3066 or (800) 325–1712 or visit http://parks.ky.gov/findparks/resortparks/pm. At the park's nature center, notice what looks like a petrified tree trunk by the entrance. The trunk was found at a strip mine in northwest Bell County. The tree, which may be 300 million years old, grew in a swampy area and was buried in flood sediments, which caused it to rot. Over the course of a few million years, sand percolated through the cavity and hardened, making a fossilized sandstone cast of the tree.

trueblue

Middlesboro is home of the oldest municipal golf course in the nation.

One of the most special trails in the whole state park system is the **Hemlock Garden Trail,** which goes through a 782-acre area protected by the Nature Preserves system. The Hemlock Garden is a ravine featuring massive hemlocks, tulip poplars, beech trees, and a beautiful mountain brook. On the southwestern boundary of the park, it can be reached on the **Laurel Cove Trail** or the **Rock Hotel Trail.** Linger as long as you are able. After all, how often are you in the presence of living beings more than 200 years old?

During the last weekend in May, the **Mountain Laurel Festival** is held to celebrate the blooming of the much-loved mountain flower. The whole event is held in the Laurel Cove Amphitheater, a beautiful natural stage that seats more than 3,000 people, and culminates in the crowning of a Mountain Laurel Queen. The **Great American Dulcimer Festival** is also held outdoors during the third or fourth weekend of September. This is a wonderful, small festival during which dulcimer makers sell, demonstrate, and teach in booths during the day. At night spectators wrap up in quilts under the stars and watch some of the best performers play on a stage behind a reflective pond. Styles range from traditional to classical, pop, big band, and country rock, all played on lap or hammered dulcimers.

There is a special place to eat any meal of the day or to get an afternoon pick-me-up in the form of an old-fashioned hot-fudge sundae in downtown Pineville. You just have to stop by the **Flocoe Restaurant** (606–337–2034) at 122 Kentucky Avenue at Walnut Street directly across from the Bell County Courthouse. The building was formerly an apothecary and soda fountain. The daughter of the pharmacist restored it to its glory and opened this comfortable restaurant. The Flocoe—named for a woman named Flo (daughter of the man who built the building) and her friend Coe—dates back to the 1920s. It's been a gathering place for generations. The fare is hearty "homestyle"—barbecue, potato salad, soup, beans, and lots of fruit cobbler. The Thursday special is the best seller—chicken and dumplings with mixed greens. Friday features soup beans and cornbread. Meals are accompanied, of course, by strong black coffee.

Eighteen miles southwest of Pineville via Highway 190 in Frakes is the **Henderson Settlement,** a United Methodist ministry started in 1925 as a school and community outreach center. Now Henderson Settlement is a multipurpose community service facility and the only Methodist mission in the country with an agricultural development program—1,300 acres of land, livestock, orchards, gardens, and a big community greenhouse. The old high school houses a library, offices, and a weaving room where people can learn and pursue the craft. Visitors are welcome to tour the place or to come for an extended stay for a retreat or work camp. Call ahead for reservations at (606) 337–3613; www.hendersonsettlement.com.

The Red Bird Mission in Beverly is another similar United Methodist mission complex with a school, health clinic, community outreach program, work camps, and a craft shop. From Pineville follow Highway 66 north for 26 miles. From the Daniel Boone Parkway, take exit 34 and go south on Highway 66 into the mission. Directly across the street from the mission hospital is **Red Bird Mission Crafts,** in operation since 1921. The area craftspeople represented there are especially skilled at making hickory bark furniture, exquisite willow baskets, and handwoven rugs. Hours are 9 a.m. to 4 p.m. Monday through Friday. You can reach the craft shop at (606) 598–2709, (800) 898–2709, or www.rbmission.org.

trueblue

Among the country music stars from eastern Kentucky are Billy Ray Cyrus from Greenup County, the Judds from Ashland, Tom T. Hall from Carter County, Keith Whitley from Elliot County, Loretta Lynn and Crystal Gayle from Johnson County, and Dwight Yoakam from Floyd County.

Head northeast on U.S. Highway 119 to *Harlan,* a little mountain town populated primarily by people of Welsh descent. Natives say that because the Welsh have always been fantastic vocalists, it's no surprise that Harlan's fame is musical. The *Harlan Boys' Choir,* an all-male, award winning choir, received national acclaim after performing at the inauguration of President George H. W. Bush in 1989. What most people don't know is that the choir was an offshoot of a 1945 girls' group called *The Harlan Musettes,* now under the direction of Marilyn Schraeder. David Davies directs the boys, who range from third grade through high school. The repertoire is classical and the sound exquisite. Visit the Web site at www.harlanboyschoir.com for a performance schedule.

Another Harlan original is the *Poke Sallet Festival,* held during the first full weekend in June. The festival affords you plenty of opportunities to eat poke sallet, barbecued chicken, corn pone, and buttermilk—a mountain meal if ever there was one. Poke sallet is a cold salad of very young poke plant leaves (which are bitter and mildly poisonous when the plant is several months older); the leaves are cooked way down, like turnip greens, and have a flavor similar to asparagus. They're said to have healing powers. Call the Harlan Chamber of Commerce at (606) 573–4717 or visit www.harlancountychamber .com for more information on the festival.

Some people perpetually have fishing on the brain. If that describes you, call the Army Corps of Engineers at (800) 261–5038 to get fishing reports and other information about the two wildlife management areas, *Cranks Creek Lake* and *Martins Fork Lake,* that are just south of Harlan. Both are beautiful spots for just relaxing, too.

If you like to explore on foot, another gorgeous place to spend time in any season is *Stone Mountain,* a 200-acre gorge that is part wilderness and part history lesson. From Harlan take U.S. Highway 421 south to Highway 1138 and park in the Herb Smith lot. The long, twisty hike up the hollow of Stone Mountain follows a historic, hundred-year-old wagon road that leads to an amazing tunnel, which was built for wagon-carried freight to be connected with a Virginia railroad. The tunnel was built by punching through the sandstone caprock with hand-operated drills, hammers, and not a little black powder. At the Virginia end of the tunnel, you can see the vast Powell Valley.

Head north of Harlan on US 421, straight up the mountain. At the summit of Pine Mountain, you'll see a sign for *The Little Shepherd Trail,* a 38-mile gravel trail that runs along the ridge of the 2,800-foot Black Mountain all the way to Whitesburg.

On the other side of Pine Mountain, make a hard right onto Highway 221, go east "a fur piece" (in this case, about 10 miles) and turn onto Highway 510, then immediately into the driveway of the ***Pine Mountain Settlement School*** (606–558–3571; www.pinemountainsettlementschool.com). Here you will find 800 acres of forest and farmland, native woods, and stone buildings. The history of the place begins with an early settler named William Creech, who recognized the need for a school based on what he knew of a settlement school in Hindman. That school was founded by Katherine Pettit, who, in turn, based her ideas on Jane Addams's work in urban settings. From 1913 until 1972 the Pine Mountain Settlement School was a remarkably wholesome and successful school, community center, and medical facility.

After the regular school closed in 1972, the folks at Pine Mountain decided to flow with the real needs of the community, and it became an environmental education center. Good timing—eastern Kentucky was and is suffering massive environmental exploitation in a nation tending toward over consumption, waste of resources, overpopulation, and a general lack of concern for and understanding of the fragile, crucial cycles of the natural world. The school definitely takes an activist approach. In 2000 the school led a successful effort petitioning the state of Kentucky to declare 5,226 acres unsuitable for surface mining. The acreage includes the school, its view shed, and a water source area on the south face of Pine Mountain. To introduce the petition, school representatives used the words of founder William Creech Sr., just as he wrote them in 1915: "I don't look after wealth for them. I look after the prosperity of our nation. I want all young-uns taught to serve the livin' God. Of course, they won't do that, but they can have good and evil laid before them and they can choose which they will. I have heart and cravin' that our people may grow better. I have deeded my land to the Pine Mountain Settlement School to be used for school purposes as long as the Constitution of the United States

Harry M. Caudill

Be sure to stop at one of the high lookout points along U.S. Highway 119, where you can get a more abstract sense of the texture and shape of the land. You'll also get a very nonabstract sense of the meaning of "mountaintop removal," a method of strip mining coal by taking off whatever is above it, usually the entire top of a mountain. With this panorama before you, pay mental tribute to one of Letcher County's great native sons, the late Harry M. Caudill: writer, teacher, lawyer, politician, and outspoken activist in Appalachian social and economic issues. His historical writings, including *Night Comes to the Cumberlands* and *Theirs Be the Power*, are disturbing and powerful books about the troubled power relations in these mountains. In his storyteller (preserver) mode, Caudill has written a number of honest, intimate portraits of his people in books such as *The Mountain, the Miner and the Lord*.

stands. Hopin' it may make a bright and intelligent people after I'm dead and gone." For more information, write Pine Mountain Settlement School, 36 Highway 510, Bledsoe 40810. Visitors are welcome to tour the fascinating campus daily from 8 A.M. to 8 P.M.

The next major town to the east is **Cumberland.** It's small (population 2,780) but busy. In the beginning, though, it was really small; in 1870 six families settled this spot, and by 1911 Cumberland was incorporated with a population of 185 souls.

In town follow the signs to the campus of Cumberland's Southeast Community College, then to its **Appalachian Cultural and Fine Arts Center,** at 700 College Road, for more mountain history. Tours of the entire facility, including the three-story atrium space with rotating art exhibits and traditional crafts on display, are free. Most interesting for scholars or casual travelers is the center's amazing photo and oral history archives. Call (606) 589–2145, ext. 1313, for general information or to find out about special events.

Downtown on West Main Street, next to the Rebecca Caudill Public Library (named for the famous children's book author, who was born nearby), is the **Poor Fork Arts and Craft Guild,** a shop that features the craft items made by the guild's 75 members. Hours are 10 A.M. to 5 P.M. Monday through Saturday, but the shop may be closed in January and February. Call (606) 589–2545.

Directly up the mountain from Cumberland off US 119 is the **Kingdom Come State Park** (606–589–2479; www.kingdomcome.org). Here is another access point to the Little Shepherd Trail. The trail and the park are named after John Fox Jr.'s famous novel about Appalachian life, *The Little Shepherd of Kingdom Come.* In 1903 Fox's book became the first American novel to sell over one million copies. This park is known for its incredible vistas and rich mountain woodlands. Two of the most spectacular sites are the Log Rock, a natural rock arch that looks like a log, and Raven Rock, a huge hunk of stone that thrusts some 290 feet into the air and has at its base a capacious sand cave, which is used as an amphitheater for concerts and other performances. Stop by the visitor center for trail maps.

Follow the valley (and the railroad) just 2 miles southeast from Cumberland along Highway 160 to a tiny little town called **Benham,** a place that instead of evolving was made, every bit constructed intentionally, in 1911 by International Harvester as a company town right "on" the seam of coal that the company was mining. In the preceding decade, company towns had gotten terrible reputations for the sordid conditions of such isolated, temporary communities. Benham, however, was among the company towns built after national attention had been drawn to the situation, and large, profitable companies chose to show off their benevolence by building exceptionally pleasant and civilized "encampments" for their workers. The rows of identical houses were often pre-made kittype structures ordered from Sears or Montgomery Ward.

All this social history and more about the mining process is illustrated by excellent displays in the *Kentucky Coal Mining Museum,* at 221 South Main Street, in the original commissary building. The scale-model coal tipple is wonderful! Admission is $5, and hours are Monday through Saturday from 10 A.M. to 5 P.M. and Sunday from 1 to 4 P.M. Call (606) 848–1530 or visit www .kingdomcome.org/museum. Next door is the *Coal Miner's Park,* which features a walking track, picnic and shelter area, an old L&N caboose, and the Coal Miner's Wall. You can't miss it. Just watch for the two-ton lump of coal and the 1940s electric locomotive engine that moved the miners inside the mine. Across the street and up the hill in the old community school building at 100 Central Avenue, is *The Benham School House Inn* (606–848–3000 or 800–231–0627; www.kingdomcome.org/inn), a restaurant and an active inn with 30 rooms.

Continue on Highway 160 for 2 more miles to another company town, *Lynch,* built in 1917 by U.S. Steel, Coal, and Coke Company. It's worth the trip to see the *Kentucky Coal Museum and Portal 31 Exhibition Mine Tour* of what was at one time the largest coal camp in the world, where 10,000 people of 38 nationalities lived and worked in more than 1,000 structures. Today you can see the original lamp house, rail depot, firehouse, bath facility, powerhouse, water supply plant, conveyor, coal tipple, and mine portal. For 40 years more than one million tons of coal per year came out of that very portal. Visitors don protective gear and view animated exhibits as they ride several hundred feet underground through a portion of the mine. Museum hours are 10 A.M. to 5 P.M. Monday through Saturday and 1 to 5 P.M. on Sunday. Call the museum at (606) 848–1530.

trueblue

Kentucky's highest point is Black Mountain, off Highway 160 near Benham: 4,145 feet.

Go down another 4 miles to the south and up to 4,145 feet on *Big Black Mountain,* the highest point in Kentucky. There's an old fire tower at the peak. This is one of the few places in the state where it would not be unusual to find a rattlesnake or even a black bear. Bird-watchers should keep their binoculars handy—this mountain supports breeding populations of species that are not usually seen anywhere else in the state, including the solitary vireo, the Canada warbler, and the rose-breasted grosbeak.

If you go back to Cumberland, head east along the gap line and US 119 will take you northeast into Letcher County.

As you continue to wind along the Cumberland River bottom on US 119 for 15 miles, watch for Highway 806. Check out *J. D. Maggard's Cash Store,* an authentic kind of place that was run by the same family since it was built in 1914. Maggard's provided the location for scenes in the movie *Coal Miner's Daughter,* the story of Loretta Lynn. They're closed now, but the building is still interesting to see.

In just 2 miles, Highway 806 leads to a little community called Eolia. Nestled between Pine and Black Mountains, the two highest in Kentucky, Eolia is said to get its name from the Native American word meaning "valley of the winds." So you'll know what it means when you see the sign for the *Valley of the Winds Art Gallery* (606–633–8652; www.valleyofthewindsart.com), the studio and sales gallery of a family of artists, Jeff and Sharman Chapman-Crane and their son, Evan. For sale are original works by all three family members, as well as prints of Jeff's simple, expressive line drawings, which make great note cards. Visitors are welcome but should call first; the gallery is open by chance on most weekdays and many weekends.

Get back on US 119 and head east 1 mile to Highway 932 on the right (east) side of the road. Turn and go 1.7 miles to the entrance of the *Bad Branch Nature Preserve* (606–633–0362; www.naturepreserves.ky.gov/ stewardship/badbranch.htm) on the left. This place is so special that I barely have the nerve to include it here, but if you visit, you must promise to treat it with great care, to soak it into your soul, and to support nature preserves here and everywhere in any way that you are able. This gorge, which is rimmed by 100-foot cliffs, is home to a unique ecosystem of rare plant species and breathtaking wildflowers. The trail leads you through a hemlock and rhododendron kingdom along some of the only clean, pure water you're going to see. At the end is a spectacular 60-foot waterfall arching over the edge of a sandstone cliff. Open sunrise to sunset daily.

Get back on US 119 again and head over Pine Mountain into *Whitesburg.* Downtown, next to the north fork of the Kentucky River, is the *Appalshop* building, which is open to visitors. Appalshop is a community-oriented, not-for-profit arts and education center working to preserve traditional culture and history and to encourage conscientious involvement in contemporary arts and social issues. Appalshop is best known for making powerful documentaries about folk-culture figures and about social activism in Appalachia. While visiting, you can ask to watch almost any of Appalshop's videos—for example, *On Our Own Land,* about the history and demise of the broad form deed in Kentucky, or *Chairmaker,* about the life and work of Dewey Thompson, a furniture maker from Sugarloaf Hollow. The Headwaters Television series is a weekly broadcast of these documentaries on public television.

June Appal Recordings, Appalshop's own record label, also has made a massive cultural contribution by recording Appalachian musicians and storytellers, famous and obscure, ranging from contemporary folk dulcimer artists, such as John McCutcheon, and traditional mountain banjo players, such as Morgan Sexton (who won a National Heritage Award from the National Endowment for the Arts in 1990), to mountain storytellers, including Ray Hicks. Appalshop's Roadside Theatre is a small theater and storytelling troupe that delights and instructs folks all over the region. Appalshop also runs a community radio station, WMMT 88.7 FM, to which you are hereby commanded to tune in while in the area. Like the river, Appalshop's efforts flow out into the whole Kentucky-Virginia area, giving us all an education and a renewed sense of pride and hope. For literature and catalogs write Appalshop, 91 Madison Street, Whitesburg 41858, or call (606) 633–0108. Also, ask about the schedule of live performances held in the theater year-round. The Web site is interesting: www.appalshop.org.

Have a meal downtown at the ***Courthouse Cafe*** (606–633–5859; www .kaht.com/multiple/courthousecafe.htm), a charming little restaurant that serves healthy, delicious lunches and dinners made from scratch—baked turkey breast sandwiches, large salads, and ever-changing special meals. Hours are 10 A.M. to 8:30 P.M. Monday through Friday (the daily specials are ready at 11:30 A.M.). Read through a copy of the local paper, *The Mountain Eagle*. There's a very democratic section called "Speak Your Piece," for which you anonymously call an answering machine, mail a letter or e-mail a comment and the editor prints, verbatim, what you say. The "pieces" range from heated discussions about international issues to layoffs at the coal mines to "I hate my boyfriend's guts, and I hope he knows it."

One of the owners of the Courthouse Cafe (above), Josephine Richards, used to sell the work of regional artists and craftspeople right off the walls of the cafe where it was displayed. Now she has opened a space just for the artwork, ***Cozy Corner Crafts*** at 104 North Webb Avenue (606–633–9637). The store includes all sorts of folk art and woodcarving, but you'll immediately sense that Josephine's passion is for quilts. All the quilts in the store are pieced and quilted by hand. And the prices are reasonable enough that you will feel comfortable actually using them on your bed; as any quilter would tell you, the bed is the best place for a quilt. Hours are Monday through Friday from 10 A.M. until 8:30 P.M.

Other works by area craftspeople are featured in the ***Pine Mountain/ Letcher County Crafts Co-op*** in town on US 119. Stop by to see demonstrations of work. Admission is free. Hours are Monday through Saturday from 10 A.M. to 5 P.M. Closed Tuesday and Sunday. In the winter they close at 4 P.M. daily. Call (606) 633–0185.

On the west side of the county in a community called Blackey is an area museum disguised as a general store, the *C. B. Caudill Store and History Center;* www.appalshop.org/cbcaudill. From Whitesburg take Highway 15 north, then turn on Highway 7 south toward Isom. The store is just past Blackey on the right. There are usually a few fellows chatting on the big front porch. The store, which opened in 1933, was for man years owned by Joe Begley, an upbeat, dedicated activist who used his store to unite diverse groups over issues such as the 77th Strip Mining Bill and the area health clinic. "Everyone should be a politician," he said. "Even Christ was a protester, and a strong one at that." But the walls of the store tell some of their own stories, Joe intentionally collected mining artifacts, everything from hats, boots, lights, and tools to scrip, old mine company currency useful only within the mining camps. His unintentional collections are amusing—scan the shelves for things like 50-year-old tubes of hair restoration cream. Begley, who died in March 2000, was honored as a man of rare courage who never failed to take a stand on issues facing the people of the mountains. With assistance from Appalshop, the store has remained open as a museum.

Also ask at Appalshop about the *Carcassonne Dance* at the Carcassonne community center. Beginning at 7 P.M. on the second Saturday of each month, people get together for a big square dance, the traditional kind with a caller and usually a live "house" band including the well-known Lee Sexton Band and the Trough Sloppers. You don't need experience or even a partner—just comfortable shoes and lots of spirit. All ages are welcome. From C. B. Caudill Store, stay on Highway 7 for a few hundred yards and turn right on the first road on the right, Elk Creek Road. Follow the pavement to the very top of the mountain.

Back on Highway 7, go west past Blackey and the Caudill Store, turn south on Highway 1103, and follow the signs to the *Lilley Cornett Woods.* Because this is one of the only old growth forests in the state, it is of great value to ecological researchers and to beauty addicts alike. The wise and eccentric Lilley Cornett purchased this land just after World War I and did not allow any live timber, except for blighted chestnuts, to be cut. His chil-

true blue

Some of the trees in Lilley Cornett Woods predate the arrival of the Pilgrims in America in 1620.

dren continued the tradition, and finally in 1969 the state purchased the land and continues to preserve it. Time is the key. Old-growth forests are characterized by a large number of trees that are more than 200 years old, many of which are of great commercial value.

In order to protect the forest, visitors are not allowed to hike without a guide. The guides, however, are real treats, and they will take you out whenever you arrive. You'll learn more in an hour hiking with these folks than you could in a year reading dendrology books. Come between 9 A.M. and 5 P.M. From May 15 to August 15 the woods are open daily, and in April, May, September, and October, they are open only on weekends. For more information, contact Superintendent, Lilley Cornett Woods, 91 Lilley Cornett Branch, Hallie 41821, or call (606) 633–5828.

On the east end of Letcher County, very near the Virginia border on Highway 805, is a town called *Jenkins,* originally a mining camp built by Consolidation Coal Company—note the rows of identical houses.

During the third week of August you are welcome to join the local folks for a real hometown festival, *Jenkins Days.* It's just what you'd hope for—kids' carnival, craft booths, lots of silly festival food, music, and some pretty zany contests. For festival information, call the people at the railroad museum.

Jenkins, like Lynch and Benham, was built as a company town. You'll notice the telltale signs: rows of nearly identical frame houses clustered in a tight grid. This town was once part of the Rockefeller family holdings. To get a real sense of this history, stop by the former train depot that now houses the *David A. Zeeger Coal-Railroad Museum.* Myriad little objects pertaining to the everyday life and work of the miners (non-Rockefellers) in this town are on display, including *scrip,* the only legal, non-money form of currency you're likely to see in America outside of video arcades and subways. Open Tuesday through Saturday from 11 A.M. to 5 P.M. and Sunday from 1 to 5 P.M. Call (606) 832–4676 for information.

Leaving Jenkins to the east on US 119, you'll soon be entering Pike County, the largest county in the state. South of Pikeville, in the center of the county on Highway 1789, is *Fishtrap Lake,* a large lake known for its largemouth bass, bluegill, and crappie. Directly south of Fishtrap Lake on the state border with Virginia is the *Breaks Interstate Park,* where the Russell Fork River, a tributary of the Big Sandy, has done its darndest to imitate the Grand Canyon. For more than 5 miles, the river canyon has high jagged walls, some exceeding 1,600 feet in height. It is the largest canyon east of the Mississippi River. It is believed to have been formed primarily during the late Paleozoic era, some 250 million years ago. Unlike the Grand Canyon, this gorge is lush and tree covered. There are more than 12 miles of hiking trails, and the park has four fantastic overlooks, one of which is at the Rhododendron Lodge and Restaurant. Contact Breaks Interstate Park, P.O. Box 100, Breaks, Virginia 24607, or call (276) 865–4413, www.breaks park.com.

Windows into Geologic History

The ostensible reasons for engineering the massive road cut-through near Pikeville, which straightened the course of the Levisa Fork of the Big Sandy River, were to provide more direct road and rail transportation in the area; to reduce the frequency and severity of flooding in the town; and, after the former river channel was filled with rubble, to create over 400 acres of new flat land adjacent to town. An unintentional but spectacular fringe benefit of the road cut was an opportunity for geologists to see a whole series of "exposures," or windows into geologic history, as opposed to the usual fragmentary view gained from smaller cut-throughs or from core samples. In the series of cuts near Pikeville, someone with a trained eye can see a frontal section view of an ancient river delta, the Pocahontas delta system, which ran off the Appalachians about 300 million years ago, during the Mississippian-Pennsylvanian era. A geologist would see a river with channels, levees, and splay deposits flowing into overbank deposits of shale and coal. She would see vertical layers of former channels of the ancient river as they migrated back and forth across the valley, like rococo layers of marzipan in an Italian wedding cake that has been cut into vertically stepping tiers.

In October white-water rafting is possible on the mighty Russell Fork River. Since it drops in elevation 350 feet in a long series of minor waterfalls and rapids, with a few calm pools in between, it is rated among the best rafting rivers in the country. Some of the rapids are Class VI and require both skill and raw nerve to get through. Guided trips are available through *Sheltowee Trace Outfitters* only in October for between $50 and $125 per person. Call (800) 541–RAFT or visit www.ky-rafting.com.

For better or for worse, Pike County is known nationally as the locale of the infamous Hatfield-McCoy feud, a violent interfamily vendetta that began during the Civil War and was sustained almost until the 20th century. Buried in *Pikeville* in the *Dils Cemetery* are several major figures in the feud from the McCoy side. This cemetery also was the first in eastern Kentucky to be racially integrated. In 1996 a Pikeville College professor began an inventory of the African-American graves; since then, markers have been placed on many that had no headstones. The city of Pikeville has leased the cemetery from Dils family descendants, and it is open year-round during daylight hours. Take Bypass Road to the east side of town; the cemetery is just north of Bypass's split with Highway 1460 on the east side of the road. For more information visit the Pikeville Visitors Center at 101 Huffman Avenue, between 8:30 A.M. and 4:30 P.M., Monday through Friday, or call (800) 844–7453.

The feud is over, but the families aren't quite finished with the whole business. Every year in mid-June Pikeville hosts the Annual *Hatfield and*

McCoy Reunion. It has become a festival of sorts, unifying the two families and celebrating their heritage and genealogy. Visitors are welcome to come learn the history and enjoy regional food, craft booths, dance troops, and all kinds of live entertainment and kids' events. For annual locations and more about it all, call (606) 432–5063.

Authentic Italian cuisine in Pikeville? Yes, indeed. At *Chirico's Ristorante,* in the old Pinson Hotel Building at 136 Pike Street, owner and chef Frank R. Chirico serves classic Italian dishes using recipes from his grandmother Gracia Chirico. The menu includes an extensive collection of calzones as well as pizza and heavier dishes such as spaghetti, lasagna, and Manicotti Chirico. Hours are 10 A.M. to 10 P.M. Monday through Thursday, 10 A.M. to 11 P.M. Friday, and 3 to 11 P.M. on Saturday. Call (606) 432–7070. You can walk off the calories by heading a couple of blocks over to Sycamore Street and climbing the 99 steep steps up to the Administration Building of *Pikeville College,* appropriately known as the "college on the hill." The college was established in 1889 as an outreach of the Presbyterian Church and now offers liberal arts education (plus a great physical workout getting up the hill) to about 1,200 students.

At the visitor center you can also find out about the *Pikeville Cut-Thru,* a massive rerouting of highways, railroads, and rivers on the west side of town. After 14 years of labor, millions of dollars, and a whole lot of blasted and hauled rock and dirt, the cut-through was completed in 1987. You have to see it to believe it. The overlook is at the top of Bob Amos Park. To get there take the Pikeville exit off U.S. Highway 23. You are on Highway 384 West (Cedar Creek Road). Very quickly turn left onto Bob Amos Drive and follow the road to the top. The park is a good place for a picnic but closes at dusk.

Asphalt roads may seem to dominate eastern Kentucky now, but there was a time when railroads were king. Head southeast from Pikeville on U.S. Highway 460, which becomes Highway 80, and you'll end up in Elkhorn City. The *Elkhorn City Railroad Museum* on Pine Street offers exhibits of memorabilia from that time, including a caboose, everybody's favorite extinct railcar; switchstands; meters; and so forth. Know what a velocipede is? Find out. Admission is free, but tours are given by appointment. For details, call (606) 754–8300 or the Elkhorn City Historic Society at (606) 754–5080 or visit www.elkhorncityrrm.tripod.com.

Big Sandy Country

A few miles west of *Paintsville* off Highway 40, you can visit *Mountain HomePlace* (606–297–1850; www.mountainhomeplace.com) and get a sense of what farm life in the mountains was like in the mid-1800s. Set up as a living history farm, the complex includes a home, crib barns, horse-powered grist-mill, chicken house, blacksmith shop, and small school, as well as costumed interpreters going about the activities of daily life—tending gardens, feeding stock, hewing logs, making shingles, processing sugar cane, and even preparing and eating their daily supper. Mountain HomePlace is open April through October. In April, May, September, and October, hours are 8:30 A.M. to 5 P.M. Tuesday through Saturday year-round. If there's a Monday holiday, the Home-Place is also open Sunday and Monday. Admission is $6 for adults, $4 for children. There's a wonderful gift shop with items made by local craftspeople.

In downtown Paintsville you can tour one result of coal mining, the ***John C. C. Mayo Museum,*** a large, ornate house built by the local baron between 1905 and 1912 for a "mere" $250,000. The house is currently home to Our Lady of the Mountains, a Catholic elementary school, so hours are by appointment only. Call (606) 789–3661. Next door to the museum/school is the ***Mayo Methodist Church,*** also built by Mayo. (Local legend has it that there was once an underground tunnel connecting the two buildings.) The church's prized Pilcher organ was a gift from Mayo's friend Andrew Carnegie.

Johnson County's history involves some outstanding women. Country music stars Crystal Gayle and Loretta Lynn are both Johnson County natives. Loretta Lynn was born and raised in a beautiful setting in ***Butcher Hollow,*** near Van Lear. From Paintsville take Highway 302 south and follow the signs to the board-and-batten cabin where she lived. The place was rebuilt for the filming of the 1980 movie *Coal Miner's Daughter*, a biography of the singer's difficult but triumphant life. Remnants of an orchard make the place feel authentic. Stop by Webb's Stop and Shop (606–789–3397), owned by Loretta Lynn's brother Herman Webb, if you want to take a tour. They're given April through October as long as the weather is good for $5. Larger groups should call ahead.

trueblue

A Johnson County native, country and pop singer Crystal Gayle's "real" name is Brenda Gail Webb. Her sister, country music star Loretta Lynn, gave Crystal her stage moniker after the name of a hamburger chain.

Just west of Butcher Hollow on Highway 302, in Van Lear's tiny downtown in the former Consolidated Coal Company office building, is the ***Van Lear Historical Society Coal Miners' Museum.*** If you haven't yet seen a real-life mining camp, check out the model of a typical company town in the museum. Hours are 10 A.M. to 4 P.M. Monday through Saturday from March through November, 11 A.M. to 4 P.M. in the winter. Call (606) 789–8540; www.geocities.com/coalcamp. Admission is $4. To get there, take US 23 south to

The Best-Kept Dirty Little Secret in America

The lush temperate forests of the ancient Appalachian mountains are some of the most biologically diverse on Earth. In the heart of this verdant region, Inez, Kentucky, in Martin County, was the site of one of the southeastern United States' worst environmental disasters in October, 2000. A coal slurry impoundment located over an abandoned coal mine shaft with an illegally thin base (under 15 feet, although Federal regulations require at least 150 feet) failed and released a viscous black sludge of more than 300 million gallons of water and toxic coal waste into the underground shaft and into local streams. About 75 miles of rivers and streams turned an iridescent black, causing a fish kill along the Tug Fork of the Big Sandy River and some of its tributaries. As the spill contained heavy metals, including arsenic, mercury, lead, copper, and chromium, towns along the waterways were forced to turn off their drinking water intakes. The pollution was evident as far away as Cincinnati along the Ohio River.

This tragedy is the result of a relatively new method of extracting coal in Appalachia, called mountaintop removal (MTR)—or "strip mining on steroids."

Recipe for Disaster

1. Purchase mountain

2. Clear-cut forest and scrape away topsoil

3. Set off explosives to blast apart rock

4. Bulldoze millions of tons of overburden (former top 800 feet of mountain) into valley

5. Remove thin vein of coal

6. "Wash" coal with toxic chemicals

7. Store toxic waste liquid in sludge lagoon on hillside

8. Sell coal to power plant

9. Repeat

Repeat the process long enough, and the entire Appalachian mountain range would be annihilated and transformed into a barren, toxic moonscape. There is a swelling movement to rein in and ultimately ban the heinous excesses of MTR. To see heart-stopping photos of the practice, check Ohio Valley Environmental Coalition's Web site at www.ohvec.org. As you travel this region, you will not be likely to see evidence of this or any other style of surface mining from the road—mining companies have made a concerted effort to avoid being visible.

Highway 302, then go east on Highway 78 or Miller's Creek Road. Inside there is a fully restored 1950s-era soda bar called Icky's where these days you can buy snacks and gifts.

During the first full weekend in August, the Coal Miners' Museum comes to life for the ***Van Lear Town Celebration.*** Soup bean and fried catfish dinners are served in the museum. All day Saturday there are sports tournaments in the park.

Another legendary area woman is Jenny Wiley, an early settler of the Big Sandy area who survived a remarkably tragic capture by Shawnee Indians and, after nine months of captivity, during which time she gave birth, subsequently escaped. She died at 71 and is buried in a cemetery 5 miles south of Paintsville on Highway 321 near the site of ***Harmon Station,*** the first white settlement in eastern Kentucky. Mathias Harmon was one of the hunter–Indian fighters now known as Long Hunters because of the length of their sojourns in the wilderness. In 1750 he and his companions built a fortlike log hunting lodge on this site; in the late 1780s they built a more permanent blockhouse.

Jenny Wiley's captors took her north along the Big Sandy River to its confluence with the Ohio River. They went downstream, looking for a place to cross the river. Unable to cross into Ohio, they instead journeyed up the Little Sandy River Valley to Dry Fork and across a ridge to Cherokee and Hood Creeks. Though the landscape has obviously changed greatly since 1789, you can roughly follow their Kentucky route along the ***Jenny Wiley Train Heritage Byway,*** a 154-mile loop drive. You start at ***Jenny Wiley State Resort Park*** near Prestonsburg, travel north to Paintsville, and along US 23 through Ashland to Greenup. From Greenup take Highway 1 to Grayson and Highway 773 from Grayson to Hitchins. Then get back onto Highway 1 Blaine, where you pick up US 23 to return to Paintsville to complete the loop.

Before or after this excursion, Jenny Wiley State Resort Park (606–886–2711 or 800–325–0142; http://parks.ky.gov/findparks/resortparks/jw) is a good place to relax. The park is located between Paintsville and Prestonsburg on Highway 3, just east of US 23/460. At the heart of the park is Dewey Lake, a clear lake famous for its white bass run in April. In the park you can tour one of the last one-room schoolhouses to close in Kentucky. January through March and September through December, the park offers Elk Sighting Tours to nearby areas in which elk have been introduced since 1997. A variety of tours are offered, costing from $5 to $10. If you want to go, make reservations well in advance because the tours have become quite popular. Call the park naturalist at (606) 886–2711, ext. 2269, for information.

The park has the usual array of overnight lodging in the park lodge, at cabins, or at campsites. It may sound a little cheesy, but it's also breathtaking to take the seasonal sky lift out over the wooded hollows.

The ***Jenny Wiley Summer Music Theatre*** presents one very colorful, musical version of the legendary Jenny Wiley story in addition to three

Broadway musicals, which have included *Hello, Dolly!* and *The Sound of Music*. You can take in a different performance every night for four nights in a row. The outdoor performances are at the Jenny Wiley State Resort Park in an amphitheater open from late May through late August, Wednesday through Sunday; the house opens at 7:30 P.M., with curtain at 8:15 P.M. Call (606) 886–9274 or (800) CALLJWT, or visit www.jwtheatre.com for more information.

Prestonsburg is also home to the **Mountain Arts Center,** a beautiful 47,000-square-foot entertainment complex that opened in late 1996. This center, with recording studio, classrooms, and a 1,000-seat performance hall, began as the dream of a retired music teacher, Billie Jean Osborne. Osborne, who is from Betsy Layne (country singer Dwight Yoakam grew up a few houses away), envisioned a theater where eastern Kentucky audiences could enjoy top entertainment. Refusing to take no for an answer, she spurred a coalition of state and local officials to make her theater a reality. The center features top entertainers in all genres—from country and gospel to classical music—along with regular performances by the Kentucky Opry, Osborne's own country music showcase. Performance times vary; call (888) 622–2787 for ticket information. The Web site is www.macarts.com.

The Mountain Arts Center is on a section of US 23 that has been designated **Kentucky's Country Music Highway.** Along a stretch running from Ashland to Letcher County, through seven counties, signs honor a dozen country and bluegrass music stars who came from the region, from Billy Ray Cyrus (Greenup County) and the Judds (Boyd County) to Patty Loveless (Pike County).

The new **East Kentucky Science Center** is drawing crowds from great distances in large part due to its state-of-the-art, 80-seat planetarium. The universe is yours when the star machine creates the night sky for any date, from

The Civil War in Prestonsburg

In addition to being the site of Daniel Boone's winter camp in 1767–68, Prestonsburg was also the site of two wintertime Civil War engagements. Each May a reenactment is held at the **National Historic Landmark.** (For more information call 606–886–1341.) The Battle of Ivy Mountain, which lasted less than an hour and a half, resulted in the Union's capture of Piketown (now Pikeville), where the Confederates had been stationed. The Battle of Middle Creek, in January 1862, occurred along the creek between Paintsville and Prestonsburg. The battle marked the beginning of Union domination of Kentucky and was a major accomplishment for the Union commander, James Abram Garfield, who became the 20th president of the United States and died months later from injuries sustained from an assassin's bullet.

any point on the planet. Show times are Friday between 7 and 10 P.M., and Saturday afternoon at 1, 2:30, and 4 P.M. The exhibit hall hosts changing science shows throughout the year and is open to the public on Saturday from noon to 5 P.M. Special science educational events, with an emphasis on hands-on activities, are scheduled throughout the year. And for pure unadulterated entertainment, the planetarium space is used for rock 'n' roll laser shows on Saturday night at 7:30 and 8:30 P.M. The skies have rocked to the sounds of Pink Floyd and Led Zepplin, so far. There's also a snappy Emporium (gift shop). The science center is located at 7 Bert Combs Drive, on the Prestonsburg Campus of the Big Sandy Community and Technical College. There are plentiful signs in town. Call (606) 889–0303 or (606) 889–8260, or visit www.wedoscience.org for more information.

Built in 1817 as the main residence on a 300-acre farm, **Samuel May House** in North Prestonsburg is now the oldest standing brick house in the whole Big Sandy Valley. The house was built in the classic Federal style. The address is 1035 North Lake Drive. Tours are available weekends between 2 and 5 P.M. for $3. Call the Prestonsburg Convention and Tourism Bureau at (606) 886–1341 or visit www.prestonsburgky.com.

The David community, which is about 6 miles southwest of Prestonsburg on Highway 404, has two surprises in store for you. One is a small crafts shop called **David Appalachian Crafts,** which features quality traditional mountain crafts like split oak baskets, wood carvings, and quilts. Hours are 9 A.M. to 6 P.M. Monday through Friday and from 9 A.M. to 4 P.M. on Saturday. Tuesday through Friday there are usually craftspeople at work at the shop. Write them at P.O. Box 2, Highway 404, David 41616, or call (606) 886–2377; www.david appalachiancrafts.com.

Also in town is the **David School,** a nonsectarian, not-for-profit, wonderful school committed to educating local high school dropouts from low-income families. In 1972 Dan Greene founded the school in an old mining camp with hopes of helping kids who were functionally illiterate. Now, more than 95 percent of the David School students have finished their high school education, and there's always a waiting list. Other schools around the state and nation are looking to Greene's program as a model. If you are inspired, stop by.

Due south of the David School is a longer-lived educational institution built upon similar hopes, **Alice Lloyd College** (606–368–2101; www.alc.edu). Take Highway 7 south, then Highway 899 southwest into Pippa Passes, in Knott County. The school's founder, Alice Lloyd, was a Radcliffe graduate who contracted spinal meningitis at the age of 40 and moved with her mother to the mountains of Kentucky to die in an abandoned missionary house. Despite her illness, she typed letters with her left hand to businesspeople and friends in Boston, asking for help in establishing a school. It was opened in 1917 on the hillsides of Caney Creek Valley, where it stands today.

Alice Lloyd, who lived until 1962, gave her students a free education, but there was one string attached—she requested that after graduation the students return to eastern Kentucky to work and live. Almost 4,000 graduates have become teachers in the region, and more than 1,000 have become mountain doctors and other professionals. Visitors are welcome to tour the beautiful campus all year.

Just a few miles away on Highway 550, slightly south of Highway 80, is Hindman and, strung along Troublesome Creek, the *Hindman Settlement School* (606–785–5475; www.hindmansettlement.org), yet another educational facility that long has been a social and cultural gold mine. The school was founded in 1902 on the folk school plan and operated successfully for many years, but like other settlement schools, it has changed functions and now serves as a special school for area children with dyslexic characteristics. Today it hosts some of the best workshops in the state on traditional dance and mountain crafts and culture, the most famous of which is the Writers' Workshop held at the end of July. Visitors can tour the campus free, Monday through Friday between 8 A.M. and 5 P.M. You'll see a film about Jean Ritchie, the nationally acclaimed folk musician and composer from the nearby town of Viper.

If it's a Wednesday or a Friday when you happen to be in Hindman, stop by the school's *Marie Stewart Crafts Shop* for fresh-baked goods. Actually, you can stop by the restored hundred-year-old cabin on Highway 160 anytime between 9 A.M. and 4:30 P.M. to see a wide range of traditional regional crafts. The shop is a co-op, and all of its members are juried. You may be lucky and be there on a day when the craftspeople are giving demonstrations. For more information call (606) 785–5475 or check the Web site at www.hindman settlement.org.

You're in store for an architectural museum of sorts at the *Pioneer Village,* due south of Hindman. Take Highway 160 south to Carr Fork Lake, then take Highway 15 south just a little farther into Red Fox and watch the east side of the road for the long driveway to the village. This group of cabins was moved to this location in Rainbow Hollow when the Carr Fork Dam was built. Some of the log structures date as far back as the 1780s. Presently the cabins are standing, but the logs are not chinked (filled in between with mud, rock, straw, etc.).

Water-based relaxation, camping, picnicking, swimming, and all sorts of fishing are available April through December at *Carr Creek State Park* and the 750-acre lake, *Carr Folk Lake,* created by the dam that caused the cabins at Pioneer Village to be moved. The lake has been well stocked with crappie and largemouth bass. Water from this lake eventually ends up in the Kentucky River. Call (606) 642–4050 or visit http://parks.ky.gov/findparks/recparks/cc.

Nearby *Hazard* is a booming little riverside town at the end of the Daniel Boone Parkway. Because it sits on and near some of the widest, richest seams of coal in the area, coal is at the heart of almost everything here, a fact made loud and clear during the third weekend of September when Hazard hosts the *Black Gold Festival.* In town, spend a little time at the *Bobby Davis Museum* (234 Walnut Street; 606–439–4325) next door to the visitor information center (606–439–2659). This free museum is a visual history book of the area from the 19th century through World War II. Hours are 8:30 A.M. to 4:30 P.M. Monday through Friday. The town has an interesting Web site with lots of historic images and fascinating stories; www.hazardkentucky.com.

The *Mother Goose House* (downtown Hazard on Route 476) is a local landmark in Perry County and a piece of wacky architecture that has been noted nationally by folk art enthusiasts (including *The New York Times*, PBS, and Oprah Winfrey). The goose house took six years to build and was finished in 1940 by George Stacy, an L&N railroad employee who modeled the building after a goose he had shot. He actually had his wife cook the goose and carefully clean the skeleton so that he could use it as a kind of blueprint for establishing proportions. The exterior walls are built from area sandstone. The space inside has three bedrooms, a living room, kitchen, bath, dining room, and large family room. Later, Stacy added a grocery store and gas station below the house. The windows are egg-shaped and the roof forms the goose head and upper body—obviously a mother because she is sitting on her oval-shaped nest. Her eyes are automobile lights that used to blink in the night. Stacy lived in his house until his death. The building is now a private residence, so you may enjoy it as a drive-by attraction only.

trueblue

Kentucky has 15,000 square miles of water surface and has more miles of running water than any state, except Alaska.

An architectural treat is in store just north of Hazard in Buckhorn on Highway 28, which is off Highway 15 North. The Log Cathedral, now functioning as the *Buckhorn Lake Area Church,* is an unusually large and beautiful log structure built in 1907 as part of the Witherspoon College campus. Harvey S. Murdoch of the Society of Soul Winners helped found a Christian elementary and high school and called it a college in order to give the students extra status. The massive logs are white oak, cut from the surrounding woods. Inside, the space is lovely and impressive. The gem in the crown of the cathedral is a Hook and Hasting pipe organ, which has been restored and sounds great. Sun streaming through the old amber-glass windows bathes the oak sanctuary (and you) in a warm and beautiful golden glow. To experience it, stop by the parsonage next door. If the pastor's not home, try Sparks General Store (open Monday through Friday, 7 A.M. to 5 P.M.) across the road, where caretakers also have a key. You're also invited to come for services, held on Sunday at 11 A.M. Summer (June through September) services are at 10 A.M. If you'd like to make an appointment to tour the church, call (606) 398–7382. For more history, check the Web site, www .buckhorn.org.

To see the region on foot, try some hiking trails in the **Buckhorn Lake State Resort Park** (606–398–7510 or 800–325–0058; http://parks.ky.gov/find parks/resortparks/bk) 20 miles northwest of Hazard. Take Highway 15 North, then Highway 28 to the west and watch for signs. There's a lodge with a dining room overlooking the lake, campgrounds, and a marina where you can slip your canoe into the 1,250-acre **Buckhorn Lake**.

Like the mountain schools in the area, **Frontier Nursing Service,** in Hyden off US 421 (southwest of Hazard in Leslie County), is an institution committed to promoting health and growth, but in this case its main concern is with the physical body. Mary Breckinridge started Frontier Nursing as a school in 1925. Her original students and the generations of nurses to follow have made strong impressions on the minds of everyone who has encountered them riding on horseback to remote hollows and mountain towns to deliver babies and administer health care. Folks at Frontier Nursing have revised their charter and are also involved in child care, general education, and regional economics. The grounds are lovely, and the history of the service is inspirational. Make sure to go in the tiny chapel, which has a 15th-century Flemish stained-glass window, and to see the Wendover Big House, a log home built in 1925 for the founder. Eight rooms for rent in the house and barn are the only lodging in the county. The rate of $85 per night includes breakfast. Add dinner for $10. For information call (606) 672–2317.

The Gorgeous Gorge

The **Red River Gorge** in the Daniel Boone National Forest is one of the most beautiful and best-loved wilderness areas in Kentucky. Actually, the area was quite obscure until its existence was threatened in the late 1960s by a proposed 5,000-acre impoundment on the Red River's north fork. Intense controversy raged until 1975, when the plan was nixed. All the publicity caused the park to be badly overused by visitors who weren't ecologically sensitive. Today the park has been reorganized; large areas are strictly protected, and visitor education is an important part of forest management.

The gorge was formed by erosion and weathering, in much the same way that the Grand Canyon was carved out by the Colorado River. The north fork of the Red River cut through the area more than 340 million years ago and left behind some fantastic geologic phenomena in limestone, conglomerate sandstone, and siltstone, all of which are tucked under a layer of shale. The most outstanding of these phenomena are the 80 natural rock arches, a number surpassed in the United States only by Arches National Park in Utah.

The Daniel Boone National Forest is 60 miles east of Lexington on the Bert T. Combs Mountain Parkway. A good place to begin exploring the Red River Gorge, at the northern end of the forest, is **Natural Bridge State Resort Park** (800–325–1710 or 606–663–2214; http://parks.ky.gov/findparks/resortparks/nb), a full-fledged state park with a big lodge, cottages, camping, a pool, recreation areas, and a variety of hiking trails leading to a spectacular natural stone bridge. This park is not very isolated, but it can serve as a point of reference for outings to more remote places. From Interstate 64 take the Bert T. Combs Mountain Parkway southeast, get off at the Slade Interchange onto Highway 11, and follow signs to the park.

There's a Morel to This Story

Eastern Kentucky communities have festivals celebrating all kinds of foods, from Gingerbread Days in Hindman in September to the Kentucky Apple Festival in Paintsville in early October. There's even a Poke Sallet Festival, honoring a local green, in Harlan in June. But the most exotic eastern Kentucky food festival has to be the **Mountain Mushroom Festival** in Irvine in late April. Up to 20,000 people show up in this town of 2,800 with mushrooms on the mind—grilled, fried, baked, and en casserole mushrooms, that is. For many years folks in Estill County have gone to the woods to hunt for the morels, or wild mushrooms, that pop up in poplar thickets and apple orchards in the spring. Locally, these delicacies are called landfish for their somewhat fishy taste. The annual festival includes a hunt to see who can find the biggest morel, a mushroom cook-off, and even a Fungus Run. Call the Estill County Chamber of Commerce at (606) 723–2558 for the current year's festival dates. If you're planning to do any mushroom gathering on your own, make sure you know what the edible variety looks like. (Check out the poster hanging in the Irvine City Council chambers.) You don't want to take home a poisonous variety.

On the way in or out, you should have a meal at **Miguel's Pizza** (606–663–1975; www.miguelspizza.com), a little building with a beautifully carved wooden front door on the left near the park entrance. Miguel Ventura's parents, who live next door, grow an enormous and wonderful garden. Order a veggie pizza, and you'll be likely to find it laced with whatever's in season—heavenly. Their expanded menu offerings include salads, pasta, sandwiches, fancy ice cream, and a new smoothie bar. If you're a climber, take note that this is the only store in the area that sells a good variety of climbing supplies. Miguel's is open seven days a week, from 8 A.M. to 10 P.M. from March 1 through Thanksgiving.

The **Kentucky Reptile Zoo** (606–663–9160; www.kyreptilezoo.org) is a very well-run and educational reptile center. And its founder, Jim Harrison, is well respected in venom research circles. He is a leading supplier of snake venom for medical research and also is helping a university in Brazil breed rattlesnakes whose venom may be used to help hold human skin together after surgery. In addition to seeing more than 100 species of snakes (including pythons and black mambas) and three alligators, your visit can include an informational demonstration by Harrison or a staff member (1 P.M., 3 P.M., and 5 P.M. Monday through Friday) and possibly a demonstration of venom extraction. From March through Labor Day, the zoo is open daily from 11 A.M. to 6 P.M. September through November, it's open only on weekends. Closed December through February. Admission is $6, $4 for kids. To get there take exit 33 off the Mountain Parkway, turn into the rest area, then turn left at L&E Railroad Place. You'll see the sign.

There is a designated driving loop through the area beginning in Nada, 1½ miles west of the Slade Interchange on Highway 15. Take Highway 77 north through the **Nada Tunnel,** a 10-foot-wide, 13-foot-tall, 800-foot-long tunnel cut by hand in 1877 to give small-gauge trains access to the big timber in the area. Stay on Highway 77 and it will run into Highway 715, which runs parallel to the river. At Pine Ridge, Highway 715 connects with Highway 15 again, which leads back to Natural Bridge. Ask for a map in the lodge at Natural Bridge.

Big timber is the subject of a small museum in the recently restored **Gladie Creek Cabin,** which you'll pass on this loop drive. This was the 1884 cabin of John Ledford, who bought and logged more than 4,000 acres here. The USDA Forest Service recently rebuilt the cabin and filled it with historic objects that refer to the early years of the logging industry in eastern Kentucky, including log branding irons, tools, models of old equipment, and photographs.

Gladie Creek Historical Site/Environmental Learning Center also serves as the visitor center for the north end of the Daniel Boone National Forest.

This is another good place to get trail maps, weather reports, and general advice about hiking or anything else concerning the National Forest. Hours are 8 A.M. to 4:30 P.M. Monday through Friday and vary on weekends. Call the Stanton Ranger District (606–663–8100; www.fs.fed.us/r8/boone/districts/cumberland/index.shtml) for information. Station hours are from 9 A.M. to 5:30 P.M. seven days a week. Aside from the driving loop, another way to reach Gladie Creek is from the north. Take Highway 77 south to Highway 715; go east for about 11 miles and watch the right side of the road.

The absolute best way to be in the Red River Gorge is to be hiking, crawling, if you must, for driving does not do the woods justice. You must sweat, propel yourself by your own energy, drink when you're thirsty, eat when you're hungry (or can't wait any longer for the granola bar), feel the leaves brush against your legs, feel the sunshine on your shoulders when you come to an opening in the forest canopy, hear and see the animals, and so taste the life of the mountains. More than 165 miles of foot trails in the Daniel Boone Forest offer ample opportunity to be here the right way. Get maps from the Hemlock Lodge at Natural Bridge, at Gladie, or anywhere you see a ranger. Hike as many trails as you're able.

Ask at the lodge, or anywhere you see a ranger, about the **Clifty Wilderness** area, a 13,300-acre area that adjoins the Red River Gorge. Hiking, camping, canoeing, horseback riding, and fishing—these are all great ways to spend time here, where there are some 170 species of trees and more than 750 flowering plants, several of which are rare or endangered. Call (606) 663–2852 for maps and information (www.fs.fed.us/r8/boone/districts/cumberland/clifty).

trueblue

There are about 175 species of native and introduced tree varieties that grow wild in Kentucky, including 17 species of oak.

I will concede that canoeing is as good as hiking for seeing the woods. Nothing beats gliding silently through the forest, unless maybe it's crashing dramatically through some wild white water. Either way, if you want to canoe the Red River and didn't bring a boat, contact **Canoe Kentucky** at (800) CANOE–KY or www.canoeky.com for information about trips. From October through May you can hire a guide or self-guide in its boats through Class I, II, or III rapids. Rates are between $45 to $55.

The **Sheltowee Trace** (Trail #100) is the only backpacking trail that traverses the entire length of the Daniel Boone National Forest. It goes 257 miles through nine counties, beginning in Rowan County in the north and ending in Tennessee, where it connects with the John Muir Trail (named for the father of the Sierra Club), which connects to the great Appalachian Trail. If you're planning a backpacking trip, check with a ranger. The Sheltowee Trace is marked with a white diamond or turtle-shaped blaze. The word *sheltowee* is Shawnee for "big turtle," Daniel Boone's Native American name when he was captured and adopted by Shawnee chief Blackfish.

For a taste of the area's social and cultural history, stop by the **Wolfe County Historical Museum** on Main Street in downtown Campton. From the Mountain Parkway take exit 43, go downtown, and watch for the signs. It's only open on Sunday from 2 to 4 P.M.

The **Pioneer Weapons Hunting Area** is a 7,480-acre area in the National Forest, north of the gorge, which is designated for hunting deer, turkey, grouse, and squirrel, but you must use only primitive weapons—black-powder muzzle loaders, bows and arrows, blow guns, spears, rubber bands, whatever. Before you hunt, be sure to call the forest supervisor (606–784–6428) so that you understand the regulations.

If you turn toward the north from the Corner Restaurant on Highway 36, take the first street to the right, follow it to the end, and you'll see a trail going up the hillside. This trail leads to **Donathan Rock,** a great huge rock teetering near the edge of a cliff from which you get a perfect aerial view of Frenchburg below. Park in town and walk over. Traveling a mile farther north on Highway 36 brings you to the **Roe Wells School.** Watch carefully for it on the left—the sign is small. The schoolhouse is a typical, quaint, one-room country school. Look in the windows; the old desks and books, chalkboard, and even a few messages from the teacher remain. It would make a perfect movie set. Visitors are welcome to walk around and look in the windows. Right now there is no one available to give tours.

Strange as It Sounds

Eastern Kentuckians have their own way of saying things, and as you travel this part of the state you'll not only notice a distinctive accent, but you'll also encounter some fascinating local expressions. For example, man or woman, don't be surprised if you're called "honey" by total strangers of both sexes. A ghost is a "haint"; "loaded for bear" means angry or looking for a fight; and a "passel" is one way to indicate a large quantity. If someone tells you to "quit lollygaggin' around," it means to stop delaying or taking so long; and there are a passel of other local expressions. One day a friend from Hazard and I were having lunch at a local restaurant when an acquaintance of hers came in. In the course of conversation, I mentioned that I wasn't from the area. "Oh, honey, I knew that," he said. "You talk way too plain to be from around here."

Leaving Frenchburg in the southeasterly direction, there are several surprises in store for you. Watch for the old ***Botts School.*** Although it's now a community building, you can still feel its age; it was a one-room schoolhouse since before the time Menifee County was a county. If it catches your fancy and you want to see inside, stop by the Botts General Store that's directly across the street. Either way, you'll get some stories.

One of the most special surprises in this immediate area is ***Furnace Mountain Inc.,*** a spiritual community founded in 1986 by Zen master Seung Sahn. The community owns 500 acres of beautiful woodland near Clay City in Powell County, where visitors are welcome to hike or join in daily meditation practices. The main function of Furnace Mountain is to host a variety of retreats, primarily traditional three- to ninety-day Zen Buddhist retreats. Retreats are also conducted in other disciplines such as 12-step programs, Christian meditation, and clinical pastoral education.

Kwan Se Um San Ji Sah, which means "Perceive World Sound High Ground Temple," is indeed a place that sits beautifully on high ground and affects the way one perceives the world, due to its exquisite blend of eastern Kentucky craftsmanship with Far Eastern aesthetics. This timber-frame temple has the classic tapering vertical lines and uplifting roofline of Oriental architecture and the materials of the mountains—recycled Douglas fir siding, a cherry wood floor, and deep sky-blue ceramic roof tiles. For more information, write c/o the Abbess, P.O. Box 545, Clay City 40312, leave a message at (606) 723–4329, e-mail the center at furnacemt@aol.com, or visit www.furnacemountain.org.

what'sinaname?

If I were giving an award for the best town name in the state, the prize would have to go to Leslie County's Hell Fer Certain, a little, not-even-on-the-map community north of Hyden just off Highway 257. Runners-up in the area would include Devil's Jump Branch, Confluence, Cutshin, Thousandsticks, Yeaddis, Smilax, Yerkes, and Krypton (watch out, Superman!).

A nice area for hiking and birdwatching is ***Pilot Knob State Nature Preserve,*** located off Highway 15 near Cave City. The preserve includes one of the tallest "knobs," or large hills, in the area—a 730-footer from which Daniel Boone supposedly looked out over the bluegrass region for the first time. There are so many Daniel Boone exaggerations made in Kentucky that one is always a little suspect of such claims, but it is nonetheless a good spot for modern explorers to gaze upon a lovely vista. Open most days. Also see www .naturepreserves.ky.gov/stewardship/pilotknob.

In downtown Clay City on Main Street, there is a free museum devoted to the area's work history. Artifacts at the ***Red River Historical Museum*** include lots of tools from the railroad and the area's iron and logging industries. Also, there's a huge rock with supposedly ancient carvings. Hours May through October are Saturday and Sunday from 1 to 5 P.M. Call (606) 663–4000.

You can get your bluegrass music inside and out at **Meadowgreen Park Bluegrass Music Hall.** This hundred-acre park with music hall is home base for the Kentucky Friends of Bluegrass Mountain Club, an organization whose goal is to preserve the musical heritage of the Appalachian Mountains. There are indoor shows October through April and large outdoor festivals in spring and fall. For more information write Meadowgreen Park Bluegrass Music Hall, 465 Forge Mill Road, Clay City 40312, or call (606) 663–9008.

You are still in beautiful country when you travel to the south side of the Red River Gorge. From Natural Bridge head south on Highway 11 through Zachariah and Zoe (my name town and the site of my worst bicycle wreck) to **Beattyville,** a friendly little mountain town with the best named restaurant in the world, **The Purple Cow,** on Main Street. Eat any meal there any day of the week, just for the fun of it. The weekend after the third Monday in October, Beattyville is host to the world's only **Woolly Worm Festival,** devoted to the humblest of all meteorologists. Call (606) 464–2888 for festival information.

From Beattyville take Highway 11 south and turn east on Highway 30 to Booneville, home of **Morris Fork Crafts** at 930 Morris Fork Road. The shop offers traditional mountain items including quilts, baskets, toys, and wooden items. Run by volunteers, the shop is usually open during the summer on Tuesday, Thursday and Friday from 10 A.M. to 2 P.M. In the winter and on other days, hours are by appointment. Please call ahead at (606) 398–2194.

Continue on Highway 30 east and you'll come to **Jackson.** This town was originally known as Breathitt, but in 1845 it was renamed to honor President Andrew Jackson, who died that year. The **Breathitt County Museum** (329 Broadway; 606–666–4159; www.breathittmuseum.com) has exhibits on logging and coal mining along with Civil War artifacts. The photo collection of life in the area during the 1940s is especially impressive. Hours are Monday, Wednesday, and Friday, 9 A.M. to 3:30 P.M. From Highway 15 south veer off to the southeast on Highway 476 to Robinson Forest, a large research and educational forest owned and managed by the University of Kentucky. Visitors can take a self-guided hike along a nature trail and see a wide variety of flora and fauna typical of this area. The forest is a unique example of an old-growth forest ecosystem on the Cumberland Plateau. A climb up the Camp Robinson Lookout Tower is worth the effort. To get to the tower, take Highway 426 way into the forest and turn left on Clemons Road to the tower trail. The forest is open daily, year-round. Call (606) 666–5034 for more information or check www.uky.edu/Ag/Forestry/robfor.htm.

The Wild-Bird Charmer

Beattyville's two most important claims to fame are, first, that it is the place where all three forks—north, middle, and south—converge to form the Kentucky River, and second, that Beattyville has been the lifelong home of Nevyle Shackelford, Kentucky's (and my) most loved syndicated nature and mountain culture columnist, and his wife, Gladys, gardener and cook extraordinaire. Some of my earliest childhood memories were of "Uncle" Nevyle's amazing feats, like growing apples and pears on the same tree and charming wild birds. Since his fame was as a writer, let me quote him from a 1972 excerpt from his column, *Outdoor Lore*:

> One of the easiest of all wild songbirds to tame, the chickadee, comes readily to winter bird feeders and, with a little patience and a handful of sunflower seeds or walnut kernels, can be coaxed to feed from the hand. And once its confidence is gained, it will remember from year to year and keep coming back to provide delightful companionship for its benefactor.

> One winter, often to the consternation of visitors dropping by, I had a small flock of chickadees that would fly in at my call and eat from my hand. When I was wayfaring outside these birds would accompany me on my little journeys, buzzing my head, and often alighting on my head and shoulders. Actually, they became so tame that I could reach up and lift them from their perches like picking apples from a twig. Observing this, some of my visitors considered me some sort of a wizard with hidden powers extraordinary. While a bit flattering, this was far from true. The trick was, the chickadees associated me with food and nothing more.

Iron Country

If these United States can be called a body, Kentucky can be called its heart.

These words are from the first stanza of "Kentucky Is My Land," a poem by the late poet laureate of Kentucky, Jesse Stuart, a wholesome, hopeful writer whose work was deeply rooted in his eastern Kentucky homeland. Because W-Hollow was Stuart's home and source of inspiration, more than 700 acres have been made into a pastoral museum and maintained as Stuart knew it—cattle graze in some pastures and young forests are being allowed to grow to maturity. The ***Jesse Stuart State Nature Preserve*** lies between Highways 1 and 2 just west of Greenup, off US 23. Visitors can walk the hills and fields Stuart walked and visit Op's Cabin, the old white clapboard house where he did some of his writing. For those who know his work, the fictional Laurel Ridge is Seaton Ridge. His home borders the preserve but is private property. The Kentucky State Nature Preserves Commission (502–573–2886; www.naturepreserves.ky.gov/stewardship/jessestuart.htm) maintains the nature

Poetry in Motion—Relocated to Eastern Kentucky

It has been 150 years since large numbers of elk ranged freely in these mountains. In fact, every elk was entirely extirpated from Kentucky until now. Every year for the next decade, 200 elk will be released into the wild with the hope that in two decades their population will increase to more than 8,300. This program may be the largest relocation of game animals in modern times. Initially the elk will be released in Perry, Knott, and Breathitt Counties in wildlife refuge lands inside the Robinson Forest and in the Cyprus Amax Wildlife Management Area. It all makes perfect sense. You just have to know the code.

preserve and the Jesse Stuart Foundation, a nonprofit organization devoted to preserving and sharing Stuart's work. To order books, write the foundation at 1645 Winchester Avenue. P.O. Box 669, Ashland 41105, or call (606) 236–1667 or (800) 504–0209.

Continue south on Highway 1 to *Greenbo Lake State Resort Park,* where the lodge is named after Jesse Stuart and even includes a reading room where you can enjoy his novels, short stories, and poems. The last weekend in September the park hosts a Jesse Stuart Weekend, during which speakers lecture on the life and works of Stuart, a guided tour of W-Hollow is given by family members, films are shown, and exhibits are open. Otherwise, the lake is marvelous for fishing, the dining room is popular, and camping is available. The 24-mile-long Michael Tygart Trail connects the park with the Jenny Wiley National Recreation Trail. Call or (800) 325–0083, or check http://parks.ky.gov/findparks/resortparks/go for more information about the park or the festival.

Nine miles south of the park, at the intersection of Highways 1 and 3111, is the *Oldtown Covered Bridge,* spanning the Little Sandy River near the site of a Shawnee village. The 194-foot-long, two-span, Burr-type bridge was built in 1880 and has not been restored. Bennett's Mill Bridge is 1 foot longer, 25 years older, and has one less span than the Oldtown Bridge, and it's functional. It was built in 1855 for access to *Bennett's Grist Mill* on Tygart Creek. What is amazing is that the original frame and footings are intact. This bridge is on Highway 7, just west of the Greenup County Locks and Dam. (Warning: Grays Branch Road, the direct route from the dam, is a rough dirt logging road.)

The county seat, *Greenup,* is a very interesting little river town at the confluence of the Little Sandy and Ohio Rivers. Though it's suffered through some terrible floods (the 1937 flood destroyed its hundred-year-old court-house), there are still some old places worth seeing. Stop by the Greenup

Library at 614 Main Street (606–473–6514) and get a free map of *Greenup's walking tour.*

Follow the Ohio River south on US 23 into *Ashland,* the largest city in Kentucky east of Lexington and headquarters for Ashland Oil and A–K Steel (not to mention that it's the hometown of country music stars Naomi and Wynonna Judd and Wynonna's movie-star sis, Ashley). Downtown you'll notice a surprising number of large, ornate houses built by early industrialists during the last half of the 19th century. My favorite is at 1600 Central Avenue. The highest peaks of the roof sport two cast-iron dragons, reminiscent of French *faitages* or the figures on ancient Macedonian tombs, meant to ward off evil spirits. It was originally built at the corner of Winchester Avenue and Seventeenth Street but was hauled intact to the present site some 20 years later by a team of mules. The dragons did their job.

Downtown in Ashland, at 1620 Winchester Avenue, is the *Kentucky Highlands Museum and Discovery Center.* The museum is organized by subject and period, and exhibits range from Adena, Fort Ancient, and Hopewell Indian cultures to rail, steam, and industrial histories, the evolution of radio, a World War II room, and an impressive antique clothing collection Hours are 10 A.M. to 5 P.M. Tuesday through Saturday. Admission is $5.50 for adults, $4.50 for children ages 3 to 16 and free for children under 2. Call (606) 329–8888 or check www.highlandsmuseum.com for special programs and more information.

Not far from the museum in downtown Ashland is *Central Park,* a 47-acre area set aside when Ashland was laid out in the 1850s. It contains a number of ancient Native American mounds that have been restored to their original proportions. They were found to contain human bones and pottery and other artifacts that correspond with the Adena period (800 BC to AD 800). The mounds and historic houses are part of a 2-mile walking tour of downtown Ashland. Stop by the visitor center at 1509 Winchester Avenue, for a free

Lower Shawneetown

Though no one knows the exact spot, somewhere in Greenup County is the site of Kentucky's very first white settlement before Fort Harrod. (And I do hate to admit this, since Harrodsburg is my hometown and the generally recognized title holder.) Sometime prior to 1753 French fur traders and Shawnee Indians settled across the Scioto River at a place referred to in records as Lower Shawneetown. However, all traces of the settlement disappeared before 1800. So, there's some work here for archaeologists in need of a project.

map between 9 A.M. and 5 P.M. Monday through Friday. Call (800) 377–6249 or (606) 324–1007, or check www.visitashlandky.com.

Architecture buffs, brace yourselves. The *Paramount Arts Center* (1300 Winchester Avenue; 606–324–3175; www.paramountartscenter.com) is out of this world. Art deco has never been better, and the people of Ashland cared enough to give this place an enormous face-lift (but what a face!). If you're in town on a night when a cultural event is scheduled, go, no matter what's playing. It has booked acts from Marcel Marceau to the Sistine Chapel Choir to Ray Charles and continues the excellence. Or you can just tour the building between 9 A.M. and 4 P.M. Monday through Friday. Whether you've ever been to Ashland before or not, you may have already seen the Paramount Center in Billy Ray Cyrus's "Achy Breaky Heart" video. Billy Ray was born in nearby Flatwoods, Kentucky.

In the early 1920s Paramount Famous Lasky Corporation planned to build a chain of "talking picture" theaters like the Paramount across the nation to showcase Paramount Studios films. After a few theaters were built, the Depression hit and truncated the plan. In 1931 this joint was built for $400,000. The ceiling is painted with the famous art deco pseudo-Moravian sunburst surrounded by leaping gazelles. On the red walls are murals of 16th-century theatrical figures. The seats are done in plush red velvet. Ornamental pewter and brass are everywhere, even in the bathrooms. Opulent is the word.

About 10 miles from Ashland on US 23N is *Russell,* home to numerous antiques shops and restaurants. Not to be missed, however, is *Rail City Hardware* (606–836–3121)—part general hardware store, part railroad museum. Owner Scott Darling collects miniature trains as a hobby and has two tracks set up right in the store. Over the years, other people in the area have brought in items from the C&O railroad, which ran through the town. So in addition to the usual hardware goods for sale, at Rail City you also can see a fascinating collection of (not-for-sale) railroad lanterns, oil cans, even potbellied stoves. The store is right in the center of town on Highway 244, and it is open Monday through Friday from 8:30 A.M. to 5 P.M. and until 4 P.M. on Saturday.

Downtown Russell has an antiques district with a number of stores. The largest is the *White Eagle Collector's Mall* (509-511 Bellefonte Street; 606–836–2830), open 10 A.M. to 5 P.M. Thursday through Sunday. There's a plethora of things, new and old, from primitive furniture to glassware, and an unusual assortment of railroad- and boating-related items. In the midst of garden statuary and fountains is a courtyard where you can catch your breath. Also try the *Antique Junction* (440 Bellefonte Street; 606–836–3238 or 606–836–1289).

Just north of Russell on US 23 you will pass *A–K Steel Mill* (formerly Armco; 606–329–7111), an enormous operation perched on the banks of the

Ohio. It was the world's first continuous sheet-rolling mill when it was opened in 1923. By the 1950s a process called hot strip milling replaced the old system. Now many of the trains rolling in and out of Russell's train yard are hauling materials to and from the steel mill and its massive coke ovens on the other side of Ashland, near Catlettsburg.

In this area, US 23 runs right alongside the Big Sandy River, which forms the boundary with West Virginia. It is a route that allows travelers access to the rich culture and history of the entire region. Where the Big Sandy meets the Ohio River sits the town of Catlettsburg, a former timber center where loggers rode rafts of logs down the Big Sandy only to blow their money in the town's saloons. These days more than half a million tons of freight traverse the river annually. Many boats transport petroleum products to and from the massive Catlettsburg Refinery where more than 2 percent of the gasoline made in the United States is produced. The town's Kentucky Harbor is the largest inland port in the United States.

Because Catlettsburg's economy is half nautical, it's no surprise that one of the area grocery and supply stores operates half on land and half on water. **The Boat Store** (1907 Center Street; 606–739–5166) primarily serves tugboats and tows. The boats can stop by for fuel and almost any imaginable supply or they can fax in their order ahead of time and the Boat Store crew can meet them midstream—the boats are lashed together with the trip in progress and supplies are unloaded. Those of us not traveling by boat can't shop from the grocery supply store, but they do welcome us to their gift shop called Towboat Treasures (same phone; www.towboattreasures.com), open from 9 A.M. to 5 P.M., Monday through Friday. A landlubber can buy nautical clocks, brass compasses, clothing, jewelry, model tugboats, license plates that say TUGBOAT POWER, and the like.

The river is the lifeblood of this town, but it has also wrought repeated devastation with each flood. Although any floodwall is a monument to hard times, the one in Catlettsburg also serves as a monument to achievement and pride. One portrait painted on the wall is of native son **Billy C. Clark,** a nationally acclaimed author whose fiction makes use of his hometown's history. As early as his teen years, Clark wrote stories of life on the river and its colorful characters. One of his best-known novels, *A Long Row to Hoe,* is often used in university courses as a study in Appalachian culture. The book's beginning tells an auspicious story of the author's birth in 1928. Although she was going into labor, Clark's mother took a streetcar across the Big Sandy Bridge from Huntington, West Virginia, as terrible floodwaters were rising and lapping at the bridge. She was determined to give birth in Kentucky so that Billy would not be "a foreigner." When that very bridge was replaced in 1999, the town named it for Clark. Billy C. Clark Tours of Catlettsburg, especially elements that relate to Clark and his books, are available through the Boyd County Extension Office (2420 Center Street; 606–739–5184).

The town of **Louisa,** south of Ashland on US 23, is at the confluence of the Big Sandy and its two main forks, the Levisa and the Tug. These rivers are characterized by narrow crooked channels and radically variable depths caused by floods and draughts, and they can be blamed (or praised) for keeping the region relatively isolated, since navigation was so difficult until the mid-20th century. Human beings tend to try to tame rivers and usually lose, either immediately or eventually. An interesting example is the **Louisa Needle Dam,** a unique moveable dam and lock built in 1897 just downstream from the town. You can visit the site. To cross between Louisa and Fort Gay, West Virginia, you'll drive on a bridge that made the pages of *Ripley's Believe It or Not* as the only bridge to cross two rivers (the Tug and Levisa), to connect two cities and two states, and to have a right-hand turn in the middle—a ponderous combination.

Downtown is the newly opened **Kentucky Artisan Center** at Louisa (606–638–9669). Coming toward Louisa on US 23, turn onto Highway 3 south into town. Turn left onto Lock Avenue and look for the sign. The Center is a business incubator for regional artists and craftspeople whose work is exhibited. Items available for sale include wood furniture, folk art, quilts, quilt stands and ladders, ceramic bird feeders, handmade soaps and potpourri, primitive woven baskets, and so forth. Hours are Tuesday to Friday 10 A.M. to 5 P.M. and Saturday 10 A.M. to 3 P.M. Closed Sunday and Monday.

Want a brief respite from culture but not from water? One good antidote is going fishing. The **Yatesville Lake State Park,** southwest of Louisa on Highway 3, is regionally famous for its largemouth bass. There's a full marina. For landlubbers there's an interpretive center with a comprehensive exhibit of all sorts of engineering battles with the Big Sandy River. There's also an interesting reconstructed wetlands area on a high bluff near the entrance to the Yatesville Lake Wildlife Management Area. Camping is available in the park. Call (606) 673–1492 or visit http://parks.ky.gov/findparks/recparks/yl.

In late May there is an annual **Eagle Watch Weekend.** Attendees take a thrilling houseboat tour along the shores of the lake in search of nesting sites of the American bald eagle. The tour, complete with snacks and drinks, offers a brief but comprehensive education about the American bald eagle. Bring binoculars and prepare for your heart to skip a beat, because odds are very good that you'll spot nesting couples. For more information, call (606) 673–1492. Also ask about dates for guided interpretative hikes on the parks trails with special topics like birding and wildflowers.

Must be something in the water, as they say. The very small town of **Blaine,** located on Highway 32 on the western end of Yatesville Lake (about 20 miles from Louisa) is the hometown of two shining stars in country music, Ricky Skaggs and Larry Cordell. Skaggs is known worldwide as a chart-topping ambassador for bluegrass and roots music. His childhood musical roots are in Blaine-area church music. He became famous at the age of six when he performed on stage with the father of bluegrass music, Bill Monroe. Some of Ricky Skaggs' No. 1 hits were written by his boyhood friend and Blaine son, Larry Cordell. A singer/songwriter in his own right, Cordell is well known in country music as the songwriting genius behind hits for the likes of Alison Krauss, Garth Brooks, Kathy Mattea, and Diamond Rio. His own band is called Lonesome Standard Time.

Downtown Blaine, there's a luxurious bed-and-breakfast (the only one in all of Lawrence County) called the **Gambill Mansion,** located at Highway 32 at Highway 21 (606–652–3120 or 800–485–3362; www.gambillmansion.com). Rooms and suites are available for between $100 and $150 per night in a restored 1923 brick mansion, complete with wisteria-covered porch.

Two pig-iron furnace ruins near Ashland are accessible to the public. One is the **Clinton Furnace,** built by the Poage brothers in 1833. Take U.S.

A Pig-Iron Primer

The furnace ruins in the Ashland area were all once part of a much larger community of pig-iron operations. Because the sites are usually in bad condition and none of them are part of guided tours, let me explain how they worked. It was a clumsy process, but these furnaces produced tons and tons of rough pig iron that were refined into steel, wrought iron, and ingot iron. The Civil War was fought with bullets and cannonballs from these humble industries. The earliest furnaces of the late 18th century produced approximately three tons of iron from nine tons of ore—today's steel furnaces need only about half an hour to produce the same amount of steel the old furnaces could produce in a year.

Enormous stones were quarried from the nearby mountains and used to build the furnaces by the sides of hills. A bridge was built to the top of the chimney, where they dumped the "charge," which consisted of iron ore, also mined locally; limestone, which acts as a fluxing agent; and charcoal, for heat. The charcoal, in turn, was made by burning prime hardwood down to lumps of black, porous carbon. When all this was dumped into the top of the furnace, pig iron and slag came out the bottom and cooled in ditches. When you visit these old furnaces, climb inside, if possible, and look up the stacks; often they taper beautifully to a small round opening at the top. In my opinion, the art of stonemasonry of this quality is dead. It's important to know what's possible.

Highway 60 south, turn left (east) on Highway 538, and left again on Shopes Creek Road to the furnace ruins. The other, ***Princess Furnace,*** was put into operation in 1864. From town take US 60 south, then Highway 5 north; watch for a rough stone structure near the road.

The furnace tour continues west of Ashland in Carter County. Just 2 miles north of Grayson is a little community called ***Pactolus,*** which also has a run-down furnace right by the road. This one was a blast furnace that used hydro-power from the Little Sandy River. If your interest is piqued, continue north on Highway 7 to the ruins of the ***Iron Hill Furnace,*** once the largest charcoal-powered blast furnace in the region. Stay on Highway 7 until it merges with Highway 2, then continue to Highway 1773, turn left (west), and go 4 miles to Boone Furnace on Grassy Creek. The blast furnace, built by Sebastian Eifort, started producing iron in 1857.

South of Grayson is the ***Mount Savage Furnace,*** one of the best pre-served and most beautifully made furnaces in the state. If you only want to see one furnace, this is the judge's choice. Take Highway 7 south of Grayson and turn east on Highway 773. The furnace is on the left, about 1½ miles east of Hitchins. The gorgeous stonework was done in 1848 by a Prussian mason named John Fauson.

Carter County is home to ***Carter Caves State Resort Park,*** one of the most magnificent small parks in this region of the United States. From Grayson take Interstate 64 or US 60 west, then go north on Highway 182. In addition to a lodge, camping facilities, a pool, canoe trips, and hiking trails, there are 20 navigated caves, three of which are lighted for tours. Many of the caves are wild and can be seen only if you're excited by the idea of real spelunking. One of the best times to try your hand (and elbows and knees) at caving is during the park's annual Crawlathon in early February, when the best guided tours are given (http://parks.ky.gov/findparks/resortparks/cc).

Two of the park's most significant parts are ***Bat Cave*** and ***Cascade Caverns,*** both of which are state nature preserves. Bat Cave is part-time home to one of the nation's largest wintering populations of the Indiana bat, a federally endangered species. The bats hang in tight clusters in cracks and on the ceiling. There are no winter tours of this cave because it is impor-tant not to disturb these creatures during the winter; they have stored just enough fat to keep them alive during hibernation, and flying would use up their reserves. Cascade Caverns is not contiguous with the rest of the park. Take Highway 182 south, turn west onto Highway 209, and follow signs. Aboveground, on the north slopes by the caverns, are some rare plants that are usually found much farther north, and there are a number of mountain maple trees, shrublike trees found here along the stream that flows out of the cave toward Tygarts Creek, where the hemlock forest and old yews will take your breath away. During the summer the park offers guided canoe trips. Better yet, when the water is high enough—from late winter through early spring—you can take your own trip beginning anywhere upstream and ending in the park. East of Olive Hill, where Highway 1025 goes under I–64, you can launch a canoe and take a gorgeous 12-mile paddle to the park. Though generally innocuous, there may be Class II rapids and dangerous deadfalls along this part of Tygarts Creek, so be careful. For information about any facet of Carter Caves State Resort Park, call (606) 286–4411 or, for lodge reservations (800) 325–0059.

While driving from Carter Caves to Cascade Caverns, watch for the ***Northeastern Kentucky Museum*** and gift shop, a decidedly quirky little joint. From late April through October, 9 A.M. to 5 P.M., seven days a week, you can take a visual crash course in regional history beginning with ancient Native American artifacts through pioneer times, the Civil War, World War II, and into the present. If you're visiting in the winter and want to tour this informative amateur museum, make an appointment with Jim Plummer at (606) 286–6012 (www.kymuseum.org). Admission is free.

Another look at the Civil War and its effect on Carter County is offered in the form of a summertime outdoor musical called *Someday*. It's a love story with Class II rapids and deadfalls, just like the creek. From mid-June to mid-July, show time is Friday and Saturday at 8:30 P.M. Call (606) 286–4522 for information and tickets. The drama takes place inside ***Grayson Lake State Park*** (606–474–9727; http://parks.ky.gov/findparks/recparks/gl) just south of I-64 if you take exit 172. There's a large man-made lake surrounded by sandstone, a campground, a marina, and lots of fish. The adjacent Grayson Lake Wildlife Management Area is said to be home to bald eagles, among other wildlife, especially birds. Bring your binoculars.

Glamour Fish

Muskellunge, musky, *Esox masquinongy*, briartooth, water wolf . . . whatever you call a muskie, you'd better be ready for it when it hits your line. Maybe it's considered a "glamour" fish because it puts up such a fantastic fight. Maybe it's because a muskie can measure up to 50 inches and weigh more than 40 pounds. If it's because they taste so great, you may not be able to find out if you hire a fishing guide, who may insist on catch-and-release. Maybe you don't care about eating fish, but you do want to get up close and personal with a long, silver dude with a severe underbite. Call **Cave Run Muskie Guide Service** for a good time, (800) 452–1600, any time of year.

Morehead is a typical university town except that it's plopped right down in the hills of eastern Kentucky. A friend of mine chose to go to Morehead State because he loves to rock climb and sail, two sports one can't pursue in one's free time at most Kentucky colleges. Sailing and all other forms of boating and water play are available at *Cave Run Lake,* an 8,270-acre lake fed by the Licking River. If you're interested in learning about how such massive bodies of water are formed and maintained, arrange a tour of the Corps of Engineers dam and towers. If you want a less technical view, just dive in. Fishing may be the most popular thing to do at Cave Run. In fact, it's becoming known as the "muskie capital of the world." For information on fishing, camping, or anything concerning the lake, call the USDA Forest Service at (606) 784–6428.

How about seeing Cave Run Lake from an eagle's point of view? Take the Lakeview Ridge Hiking Trail, beginning at the Forest Service's visitor center (606–784–5624), on Highway 801, where you can also get maps and more information, Monday through Friday, 8 A.M. to 4:30 P.M. For about a mile the trail is merged with the Sheltowee Trace, then it goes high above the lake for another 4 miles and ends at Shallow Flats, where there is a wetland interpretive area.

And if you were wondering where all those muskies and other fish come from, tour the *Minor E. Clark Fish Hatchery,* also off Highway 801 between the lake and US 60 (you'll see signs). With 111 rearing and brood ponds on more than 300 acres, this is one of the largest state-owned, warm-water hatcheries in the United States. Admission is free, and visitors are welcome Monday through Friday from 7 A.M. to 3 P.M. Call (606) 784–6872 for more information.

At *The Kentucky Folk Art Center* (606–783–2204; www.moreheadst .edu/kfac) in Morehead, you'll find a surprising, thought-provoking, and ultimately impressive collection of carvings, paintings, assemblages, walking sticks, painted furniture, gourd creatures, and other works by folk artists from across Kentucky. The collection began in one room of the Morehead State University art department and was later moved to a small house on campus. Now an independent and fully accredited, nationally recognized museum, it is housed in a renovated historic building at 102 West First Street, near the US 60 bypass. By some definitions, folk art comprises objects that are part of everyday life and that somehow reflect the beliefs, social structure, and experiences of the people in a given region; formal training is usually not received outside the culture from which it springs. You'll understand better when you see the collection. You'll also find yourself thinking deeply and laughing your head off—great responses to art of any kind. There's also a museum store, a rare, fun place to buy birthday presents. The Kentucky Folk Art Center is open

Monday through Saturday from 9 A.M. to 5 P.M. and Sunday from 1 to 5 P.M. Admission is $3 for adults, children 12 and under are free.

At the Folk Art Center, also ask about scheduling a tour of the ***Cora Wilson Stewart Moonlight School.*** This humble one-room schoolhouse was where this dedicated teacher started the nation's first adult education night school in 1911 to combat illiteracy. She went on to receive important state and national positions in education. The building is owned by Morehead University and was moved from its original location to First Street, next to the early 1900s train depot that houses the Morehead Tourism offices.

Morehead's biggest celebration is the ***Appalachian Celebration,*** a week-long festival held in late June. Events, which take place on the university campus, include storytelling, displays by local folk artists and craftspeople, and all kinds of wonderful traditional bluegrass, country, and mountain music. Most events are free. Call (606) 783–2204 for a schedule or more information.

Down at the bottom tip of Cave Run Lake, where the Licking River begins to look like a river again, is the town of West Liberty, the Morgan County seat. Come to town the last weekend in September for the ***Morgan County Sorghum Festival.*** In the evenings people around here put on their dancing shoes. During the day someone always sets up a mule-drawn sugar cane mill at the Old Mill Park on the banks of the Licking River, so you can see how sorghum molasses is made the old-fashioned way. Call (606) 743–2300 for more information.

More Good Lodging in Eastern Kentucky

ASHLAND

Ashland Plaza Hotel
Fifteenth and Winchester Streets
(606) 329–0055
www.ashlandplaza.net
$78 to $95.

BEATTYVILLE

Travelwise Motor Inn
Highway 11
(606) 464–2225
$53 and up.

BENHAM

School House Inn
100 Central Avenue
(606) 848–3000
Country inn in restored school building. $59 to $100 for the honeymoon suite.

BLAINE

Gambill Mansion
Highways 201 and 32
(606) 652–3120 or
(800) 485–3362
www.gambillmansion.com
Room and suites in a 1923 home with spacious front porch. $100 to $150.

BUCKHORN

Buckhorn Lake State Resort Park
Highway 1833
(606) 398–7510
$60 and up.

CATLETTSBURG

The Presidents' House B&B
2206 Walnut
(606) 739–8118
www.thepresidentshouse
.com
Bed-and-breakfast in an 1847 colonial Revival mansion with four rooms and a suite, all with hot tubs. Special feature is the Murder Mystery in which the in-house writer will cater a murder mystery to a guest's choice of era, characters and suspense. $85 to $125.

HAZARD

America's Best Value Inn
359 Morton Boulevard
(606) 436–4777 or
(800) 664–6835
$55 and up.

Hampton Inn
70 Morton Boulevard
(606) 439–0902 or
(800) 426–7866
$99 and up.

Super 8 Motel
125 Village Lane
(606) 436–8888
Your basic motel. Clean. Near the business district. $57 and up.

IRVINE

Snug Hollow Farm Bed & Breakfast
790 McSwain Branch
(located on Highway 594)
(606) 723–4786
www.snughollow.com
300-acre organic farm with cabin or rooms in farmhouse. $100 to $195.

JACKSON

Jackson Inn
Highway 15
(606) 666–7551
$48 and up.

MCKEE

Lakes Creek Bed & Breakfast
350 Lakes Creek Road
(606) 287–7953
www.bbonline.com/ky/
lakescreek
A large restored 1894 log cabin. Horse boarding and trails. $85 to $95.

MIDDLESBORO

Downtown Inn and Suites
1623 East Cumberland
(606) 248–5630 or toll-free
(877) 787–1313
www.middlesboroinnand
suites.com
$55 to $60.

MOREHEAD

Brownwood
Highway 801 South in Farmers
(606) 784–8799
www.brownwoodbandb
.com
Bed-and-breakfast with one suite and a cottage. $85 to $140, plus $8 per person for breakfast.

Brownwood Bed & Breakfast & Cabins At Cave Run Lake
46 Carey Cemetery Road
(606) 784–8799
www.brownwoodbandb
.com
Four cabins near Cave Run Lake. $85 to $140, plus $8 per person for breakfast.

Holiday Inn Express
110 Toms Drive
(606) 784–5796
About $70.

PIKEVILLE

Landmark Inn
Bypass Road
(606) 432–2545
Pool, restaurant, and $69 to $73.

PRESTONSBURG

Heritage House Hotel
U.S. Highway 23 South
(606) 886–0001
$85 and up.

Jenny Wiley State Resort Park
75 Theatre Court
(606) 886–2711 or
(800) 325–0142
www.jennywiley.com
Camping, cabins, or state park lodge.

Super 8
U.S. Highway 23
(606) 886–3355
$58 and up.

SAND GAP

Mountain Springs Inn
Highway 2004, P.O. Box 24
(606) 438–7789 or
(606) 965–2789
www.mountainspringsinn
.com
Twelve guest rooms and family reunion–sized dining in a house in the woods. Horse boarding and/or trail rides on their horses. $87 to $99 includes a hearty country style breakfast.

More Fun Places to Eat in Eastern Kentucky

ASHLAND

Chimney Corner Cafe
1624 Carter Avenue
(606) 324–7500
Elegant and unpretentious. Homemade breads, fabulous dishes like crab-stuffed orange roughy, great salads and desserts. Live local music. Reasonable prices. Dinner only, Monday through Saturday.

Crisp's Dairy Treat
1816 West Ike Patton Drive (at the intersection of U.S. Highway 60 and Summit Road)
(606) 928–8193
Great hot dogs and fried apple pies. Summertime brings tangerine swirl, a local favorite. Open until late evening, later in the summer.

Katie's Corner Cafe
1450 Greenup Avenue
(606) 325–5283
Locally famous for inexpensive, great country breakfasts. Twenty-four hours, Monday through Saturday. Closed Sunday and opens at 6 A.M. on Monday.

BUCKHORN

Buckhorn Lake State Resort Park
Highway 1833
(606) 398–7510

CLAY CITY

Kathy's Country Kitchen
20 Black Creek Road
(606) 663–4179
Home cooking with daily Specials.

GRAYSON

Melini Cucina Italian Ristorante
209 South Carol Malone Boulevard
(606) 475–1521
Owned by a fabulous cook, born and raised in Italy. Ham calzone, spinach and veggie calzones, Melini stromboli, and baked lasagna. Open daily for lunch and dinner.

Tom's Pizza Family Restaurant and Dairy Bar
502 East Main Street (also Route 60)
(606) 474–6631

GREENUP

Greenbo Lake State Resort Park
Highway 1
(606) 473–7324
Variety of sandwiches, entrees, and regional specialties such as country ham and fried catfish.

HAZARD

Cliff Hagan Ribeye
200 Morton Boulevard
(606) 439–3739
Steak and barbecue meals at moderate prices.

Frances' Diner
1315 Combs Road
(606) 436–0090
Twenty-four-hour home-style country cooking "forever and ever amen."

Peking Chinese Restaurant
454 Main Street
(606) 439–5001
Downtown. Basic Chinese-style menu.

IRVINE

Cedar Village Restaurant
1100 Richmond Road
(606) 723–7777
Inexpensive country cooking, buffet or menu daily except Monday.

MIDDLESBORO

J. Milton's Steakhouse
U.S. Highway 25 East
(606) 248–0458
Steaks, chicken, and seafood.

Midnight Market
601 West Winchester Avenue
(606) 248–6950
Middlesboro's best breakfast, hands down. The biscuits alone are worth the trip. Open from 5 A.M. to 10:30 P.M., Monday through Saturday.

MOREHEAD

Melini Cucina Italian Ristorante

(see Grayson above for other location)
608 East Main Street
(606) 780–8865
Owned by a fabulous cook, born and raised in Italy. Ham calzone, spinach and veggie calzones, Melini stromboli, and baked lasagna. Select Italian wines. Open daily for lunch and dinner.

PINEVILLE

Pine Mountain State Resort Park

U.S. Highway 25 East
(606) 337–3066
Varied menu including traditional Kentucky dishes.

PRESTONSBURG

Billy Ray's Playhouse-Restaurant

101 North Front Avenue
(606) 886–1744
Down-home cooking with daily specials. Home of the Pool Room Burger and Billy Ray's Prime Roast.

Jenny Wiley State Resort Park

39 Jenny Wiley Road
(606) 886–2711

SLADE

Natural Bridge State Resort Park

Highway 11 near Slade
(606) 663–2214

ZOE

Koop's General Store

8731 Highway 11 North
(606) 464–9906
Great sandwiches. (Great town name!)

NORTHERN KENTUCKY

Like some of its most fascinating inhabitants, northern Kentucky is a bit eccentric. Places to explore range from exquisite Gothic cathedrals and puppet theaters in dense urban areas to anachronistic service stations and prehistoric museums in sparsely populated rural regions. Mark Twain once said that when the world came to an end, he wanted to be in Kentucky because it's always a good 20 years behind. Such misconceptions!

Innovation has always been at the heart of this area's delightful idiosyncrasies. Northern Kentucky boasts architecturally significant bridges, downhill snow skiing, and refreshingly creative farms that specialize in everything from irises and turkeys to maple syrup. Historic buildings and fine craftspeople round out the picture, making this relatively small area one of the most diverse in the state.

Heart of the North

Cynthiana, a small town on U.S. Highway 27 about 30 miles north of Lexington, offers classy overnight lodging at ***The Seldon-Renaker Inn,*** 113 South Walnut Street. Go downtown,

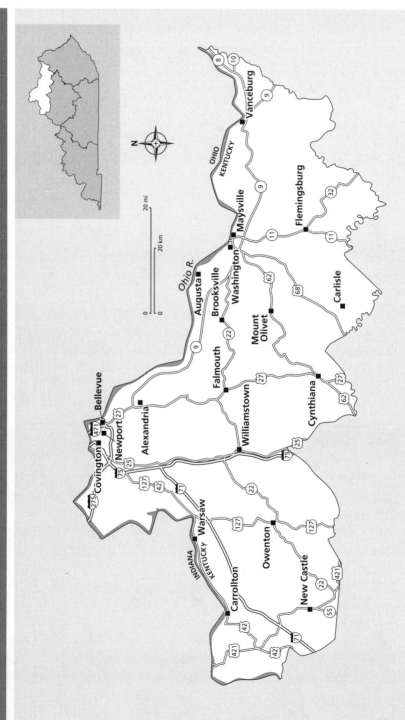

turn right on Pleasant Street, then right again onto Walnut Street, and watch for the sign on the right. The inn is a graceful Victorian house, built as a residence by Seldon Renaker in 1885 and later used as a boardinghouse, dress shop, tearoom, and doctor's office. Rooms are around $65 per night. In the morning, a full delicious breakfast is served. For reservations call (859) 234–3752.

Major events such as foundings, wars, and weather catastrophes shape the history of a community, but so do lots of smaller happenings—the first phone call, a new wing on the school, or the passing of a local "character." At the *Cynthiana/Harrison County Museum* on South Walnut Street, you can learn about both kinds of events and how they affected life in this community. You'll discover that Cynthiana was chartered as a town on December 10, 1793, and learn about the two Civil War battles, but you also can learn that the first train pulled into town on May 18, 1854; that the first dial telephone call was made at 2:01 A.M. on November 18, 1962; and that the first convenience store

AUTHOR'S FAVORITE PLACES IN NORTHERN KENTUCKY

Big Bone Lick State Park
Big Bone
(859) 384–3522

Blue Licks Battlefield State Park
Blue Licks
(859) 289–5507

Cathedral Basilica of the Assumption
Covington
(859) 431–2060

Curtis Gates Lloyd Wildlife Management Area
Crittenden
(859) 428–2262

Dinsmore Homestead
Burlington
(859) 586–6117

Mutter Gottes Kirch
(Mother of God Church)
Covington
(859) 291–2288

National Underground Railroad Museum
Maysville
(859) 564–9411

Newport Aquarium
Newport
(859) 261–7444

Pendleton County's Wool Festival
first weekend of October

Kincaid Lake State Park
(859) 654–3378

Vent Haven Museum
(of ventriloquistic figures)
Fort Mitchell
(859) 341–0461

opened in 1967. There are all kinds of artifacts, from old photos and Civil War uniforms to bonnets and hula hoops, all donated by local citizens—and nothing is refused. The museum is open Friday and Saturday from 10 A.M. to 5 P.M. Admission is free. For more information check the Web site at www .cynthianaky.com/cynthianamuseum.

In **Williamstown** there are several antiques shops to explore. If you really want to get away from it all, spend the night at **Mullins Log Cabin** in Cordova, south of Williamstown via Highway 36. There's no phone, no television, no electricity, not even running water (the old-fashioned privy is out back, about 150 feet from the house). In a nod to modern civilization, the cabin now has city water from a spigot outside the cabin. The cabin has become popular for "pioneer weddings," in which some couples even don period clothing and arrive in horse-drawn carriages. Contact owner Judy Mullins at (859) 322–3082 or www.mullinslogcabin.net for information about visiting or staying overnight.

trueblue

Main Street in Cynthiana has more cast-iron-front buildings than Chicago.

Thaxton's Licking River Canoe Rental and Paddlers' Inn near Butler, offers canoeing and tubing excursions on the Licking River. Seeing the countryside by its natural roadways can connect one to the land in a way that driving a car cannot; no road noise, no cursing at your fellow human beings for passing on a hill; nothing between your skin and the living world. In recent years customer demand to not have to drive far for overnight lodging led the Thaxtons to add cozy waterside cabins to the mix. "Our customers pretty much aggravated us into it," explained Jim Thaxton. Thus was born Paddlers' Inn, a collection of seven cabins, five at the main outpost and two at nearby Kincaid Lake. Complimentary paddling privileges are included, so you can paddle in and out, but some people come just for the getaway. Some of the cabins have kitchens and hot tubs. Thaxton's has also added tubing to its offerings. Call (877) 643–8762 toll-free or (859) 472–2000 for more information and the schedule of excursions. Cabins rent for $59.95 to $99.95 a night. Cabins are "pet friendly" with a one-time pet cleaning fee of $25. The outpost is located in Butler, about 9 miles north of Falmouth, near a bridge on US 27, a few hundred yards south of its intersection with Route 177. The Web site gives plenty of details at www.gopaddling.com.

Falmouth, located about halfway between Covington and Lexington, was founded in 1793. One of the most notable historic buildings is a handsome two-story log cabin built around 1790 called the **Alvin Mountjoy House.** It's one of the few existing 18th-century cabins with a basement. The house is not open for tours anymore, but drive by at 203 Chapel Street, which runs parallel to Main Street.

The **Kincaid Regional Theatre** is a small, professional summer theater that features new shows every season. From mid-June through the end of July, you can see Broadway musicals in Falmouth Auditorium. In downtown Falmouth go east on Shelby Street, south on Chapel Street, and look for signs. Curtain time is 8 P.M. Thursday through Saturday and 2:30 P.M. Sunday. Dinner packages are available, as are lunch packages for afternoon shows. For reservations or a performance schedule, write KRT, Route 5, P.O. Box 225, Falmouth 41040, call (859) 654–2636, or visit www.krt.citymax.com.

Every quilter I know harbors a special kind of gratitude for **The Quilt Box,** one of the largest and most comprehensive quilt shops in the state. When I first laid eyes on Charlotte Willis's marvelous quilt, *Kentucky Pride,* my initial question was, "Where did she find such gorgeous materials?" This shop has them: Natalie Lahner has made it her mission to carry every quilt-related item imaginable, including more than 5,000 bolts of 100 percent cotton fabric in colors and patterns that will make you drool, along with patterns, notions, books, and finished quilts. They also make custom quilts based on wallpaper, upholstery samples, or unusual designs.

The store is in a restored 150-year-old log structure, which is tastefully married to the Lahners' residence, a reproduction 17th-century house. (An addition was completed in 1997.) Kids love seeing the chickens on the loose.

A Right Smart Piece

When asking directions in Kentucky, you need to understand how far "a piece" is. Unfortunately, I can't give you an absolute definition. "Just a little piece" can mean a couple of miles or a few hundred yards, depending on the look in a person's eyes and the tone of the voice. If you don't imply, by your demeanor, that you will believe the directions, the direction-giver may as well lie . . . and might. A body can travel "a little piece" without completely running dry on patience. Private polling tells me "a little piece" is equivalent to "two whoops and a holler." "A far piece" is as far as language permits us to discuss distance and is, in fact, unattainable. "A right smart piece" is pretty far, but you can get there. And, finally, you must be warned about "no piece at all" or it will fool you all your life, because it sounds like you're already there, but it's farther than that. Newspaperman Allen M. Trout defined it this way: "Say you take a chew of tobacco when you start. When you have walked far enough to have chewed and spit all the flavor out, you have come no piece at all." Those who abstain from tobacco use will surely be lost.

Husbands enjoy sitting on the deck while their wives shop for fabrics. The shop hours are from 9:30 A.M. to 5 P.M. Monday through Saturday. From I–75 take the Dry Ridge/Owenton (exit 159) and go west on Highway 22. Turn right on Highway 467 or Warsaw Road, go exactly 2.4 miles, and look for the Walnut Springs Farm mailbox and the sign for The Quilt Box. Follow the gravel road 0.4 mile to the second house on the road. Call (859) 824–4007.

At the intersection of Highways 227 and 330 in Owenton sits a great new vineyard offering a wealth of reasons to visit. *Elk Creek Vineyard* has tasty wines and food, along with lovely accommodations and activities. Many folks may not know it but in 1798 Kentucky was the site of America's first commercial vineyard planted by the winemaker for the Marquis de Lafayette. By the late 1800s, Kentucky was the third largest grape and wine producer in the United States. But Prohibition dealt a severe blow to the Kentucky wine industry. Many vineyards were neglected and fell into ruin. Nestled among the rolling hills, Elk Creek Vineyards was established in 2003 and is already producing award-winning wines. The vineyard also features a deli, art gallery, cooking classes, bed-and-breakfast lodging, massage therapist, live entertainment, gift shop, and outdoor entertainment at the amphitheater during the spring and summer. Stop by for a tasting and tour. The friendly folks will make you glad you did. Summer hours are Monday through Thursday 10 A.M. to 7 P.M., Friday and Saturday, 10 a.m. to 9 P.M. Closed Sunday. Winter and spring hours close about an hour earlier on Monday through Thursday. For more information, call (502) 484–0005; www.elkcreekvineyards.com.

If sporting clays are your hobby, the *Elk Creek Hunt Club* is just down the road from the winery. The new club is popular with pros and amateurs alike. It takes about two hours to shoot a round of sporting clays. Lessons are available. A world-class facility, Elk Creek offers three separate courses—one over water—and 45 newly remodeled and paved sporting clays stations on 35 shooting fields which can be shot as 50 or 100 target rounds. Elk Creek's sporting clays courses are spread over a 2,500-acre hunting preserve. Golf carts are available for rent. Located at 1860 Georgetown Road, the club is open from 9 A.M. to dusk. Closed Monday. Call (502) 484–4569; www.elkcreekhuntclub .com.

Sanity Land

A few miles south of *Owenton* on U.S. Highway 127 sits a pink frame house in a yard full of angular alligators and stylized, wide-eyed beasts hidden in a massive bamboo forest. This is not a cubist zoo, but *Seigel Pottery,* 2545 Highway 127 South. Although Greg Seigel has a reputation for producing clay reptiles and collectible marbles, he also makes a variety of functional pots, but not without some humor. For example, a big, sturdy dinner plate glazed with a long pink spiral surrounded by blue comma-shaped dots is called *Boys and Girl*. Many of the sculptural pieces are decorated with local clays and fired in a wood-burning kiln, which produces a rich, earthy effect. The Seigels work at home, so hours are by chance. Rebekka Seigel is nationally known for her exquisite modern quilts. If you have a serious love for this art, ask to see a few of her favorites, or whatever is in progress. She also teaches seminars in quilt technique and design. You can reach the Seigels at (502) 484–2970 or www.potbaker.com.

Also in Monterey is **Larkspur Press,** sponsor of many of the aforementioned literary readings and a fine, fine little press that is Gray Zeitz's pride and joy. Larkspur books, primarily small chapbooks or broadsides by Kentucky writers, are of high quality in form and in content. All productions are done in letterpress from type set by hand and printed on paper that makes you want to touch and linger. Visitors are welcome, but call ahead, because Zeitz keeps odd hours. Write to Larkspur Press at 340 Sawdridge Creek West, Monterey 40359, or call (502) 484–5390.

To get to Port Royal from Monterey, take Highway 355 north. From the Frankfort area go north on U.S. Highway 421 a little way, then veer onto Highway 193 and go "a right smart piece." There is nothing to see in **Port Royal** but the land and the people who live by the land. That's all there is to see in many other areas of the state, but I'd like for those who are familiar with writer, teacher, and farmer **Wendell Berry** to take a good look at northern Henry County, where he makes his home. The Kentucky River forms the eastern border of the county. Here the river basin is wide, the flat bottomland soil rich, the steep hills wooded and deserted. This varied terrain insists that it be farmed in various ways. Except in the wide river bottomland, the arable areas are limited to small, odd-shaped patches, which Wendell Berry chooses to farm with a team of draft horses.

One of the truths Berry repeats is that finicky areas like these are not unique to Henry County. The idiosyncrasies of all lands must be intimately and humbly understood before we can live on them as responsible stewards, he contends. We talk of preserving the wilderness, but we don't preserve the farmland from which we feed ourselves. Farmers are, after all, people who use nature directly, not only for themselves but also for consumers, by proxy.

trueblue

People from across the nation send or bring their Christmas cards to the little town of Bethlehem, in Henry County, for a special Christmas postmark.

Wherever you live and travel, look at the land and think about the mystery of your dependency on nature and about how you can respond responsibly. Don't try this alone—talk to people and read Wendell Berry's work.

From Port Royal follow Highway 389 north into Carroll County, through the town of English, where there are ramps onto Interstate 71, and into *Carrollton.* For such a small town, it has a tremendous amount of visible remnants of its history. This National Historic District encompasses 25 blocks and includes 350 buildings, many of which are more than 200 years old. It's perched right above the confluence of the Kentucky and Ohio Rivers. A self-guided walking tour is about the best way to see the 19th-century and Victorian architecture. Start with the museum in the 1880 *Old Stone Jail* on the Courthouse Square. Some of the cells have been restored, and during the restoration work, hidden contraband was found and is now on display. The jail was actually used to detain prisoners as recently as 1969.

Afterwards, go upstairs, where female inmates were housed, to the Carrollton Visitors' Center (800–325–4290) for maps and more historic information. There is an excellent historic driving-tour booklet available. Hours are 9 A.M. to 5:30 P.M. Monday through Friday, noon to 5 P.M. Saturday. The jail is closed in winter (www.carrolltontourism.com).

There are several interesting shops in downtown Carrollton, including the *Antique Mall on the Square* and *The Craft Patch* on Court Street. You can get a sandwich at the *Mustard Seed* on Main Street.

Downtown Carrollton boasts some interesting places of lodging, especially if you're interested in history. The *Carrollton Inn* at 218 Main Street is a restored 1812 colonial inn with eleven overnight rooms (starting at $39.95) and a full dining room and lounge. While you eat, try to imagine the flatboatmen stopping here at the tavern. Today it serves Kentucky classics like "hot browns" and freshly churned homemade ice cream in the summertime. Tempted yet? The phone number is (502) 732–6905 and Web is www.carrolltoninnky.com.

Another historic tour in the area is of the *Butler Turpin House,* a very ornate Greek Revival home built in 1859 and appointed inside with period furnishings and heirlooms of the family. The stone kitchen is especially interesting. The house is located in the *General Butler State Resort Park,* just off I–71 at exit 44 to Highway 227 (signs are prevalent). Guided tours of the Butler Turpin House are given.

General Butler State Resort Park has become regionally famous for hosting mountain-bike competitions. Call "Bike Butler" at (502) 484–2998 for a seasonal schedule. There are four major competitions each year—the SunFest in June; Mud, Sweat, and Tears in July; an Off-Road Triathlon in August; and the Kentucky Open in September. It's a sport that is almost scarier to watch than to participate in. The park also has a lodge with a restaurant, cottages, and a campground. For information about either the Butler Turpin House or the General Butler State Resort Park, call (502) 732–4384 or (866) 462–8853 or check http://parks.ky.gov/findparks/resortparks/gb.

If you visit Carrollton in late winter or early spring, take a drive out U.S. Highway 42 East to *Interstate Greenhouse & Nursery,* home of fresh winter strawberries. It's all part of Kentucky's effort to diversify its agricultural efforts from tobacco. At S & W, owners Tommy Williams and Bruce Wash converted two former tobacco greenhouses into hydroponic gardens. They plant the strawberries in November and usually begin to pick in February. Planted both horizontally and vertically so they can be constantly nourished by liquids, not soil, the plants are an interesting sight, and the harvest is a delicious winter treat. The greenhouses usually yield thousands of quarts over a period of weeks, but ripening time can vary, so call ahead to see how things are progressing. The address is 3708 Highway 227; the phone number is (502) 732–8710.

East of Carrollton on US 42 is another historic house that is open for tours, the *Masterson House.* Built in 1790, it may be one of the oldest existing brick houses in this region along the banks of the Ohio River anywhere between Pittsburgh, Pennsylvania, and Cairo, Illinois. The bricks were made and fired on-site during construction. The restorers have even planted historic trees started from seedlings gathered from other pioneer homes. Admission is $2, and it is open only on weekend afternoons from 1:30 to 4:30 P.M. between Memorial Day and Labor Day. For more information call Nancy Jo Grobmyer at (502) 732–5786 or the Carroll County Visitors Center at (800) 325–4290. Ask about Heritage Days in May and September.

Just upriver a few miles is *Warsaw,* a peaceful one-traffic-light river town in the smallest county in Kentucky. There the *Gallatin County Historical Society* has restored and furnished an 1843 Gothic Revival–style home. Follow 1–75 to I–71 west and take the Warsaw exit. The person who knows it all is Darrell Maines at *Maines Hardware* (202 Washington Street; 859–567–4611). Buy some home and garden supplies and ask him a question—you'll get a good story! In town turn right by the courthouse (the second-oldest continuously operating courthouse in the state, circa 1837) at the only stoplight and look behind the funeral home for the *Hawkins-Kirby House.* To arrange a tour, ask Darrell Maines at Maines Hardware.

You don't have to call anyone to get a fabulous view of Ohio River traffic from an observation tower at the *Markland Locks and Dam,* on US 42 in Warsaw. It's a great place for a picnic, too. Any questions? Call (859) 567–7661.

Odd Bones

Eccentricity saves lives. (How's that for a bumper sticker?) The little-known **Curtis Gates Lloyd Wildlife Management Area** (859–428–2262) would not exist if the eccentric Mr. Lloyd had not written a 24-page will that thoroughly outlined the future management plan for his 365-acre farm down to every detail. The farm is now part of a 1,179-acre wild area. Before he died in 1923, Lloyd erected an enormous granite monument to himself in the woods. One side reads: CURTIS G. LLOYD BORN 1859—DIED 60 OR MORE YEARS AFTERWARDS. THE EXACT NUMBER OF YEARS, MONTHS AND DAYS THAT HE LIVED NOBODY KNOWS AND NOBODY CARES. THE OTHER SIDE SAYS: CURTIS G. LLOYD MONUMENT ERECTED IN 1922 BY HIMSELF FOR HIMSELF DURING HIS LIFE TO GRATIFY HIS OWN VANITY. WHAT FOOLS THESE MORTALS BE! A fool? Not quite. His preserve boasts one of the shamefully few stands of virgin timber in Kentucky. A forest teeming with wildlife and wilderness left to its own beautiful accord—a black walnut, 36 inches in diameter, towers over acres and acres of huge red oaks and poplars. (Please be careful during deer hunting season!) To think that I–75 is within earshot. From Crittenden follow U.S. Highway 25 south a few miles and look for the sign.

Big Bone Lick State Park is probably the only prehistoric graveyard you'll ever lay eyes on. From Florence take US 127 south (through Sugartit) and turn west on Highway 338 (Beaver Road) at Beaverlick to the town of Big Bone, then follow signs to the park. Probably during the end of the Ice Age (more than 10,000 years ago), many of the largest mammals on the continent that came to this area to lick the rich veins of salt and sulfur died, leaving their bones scattered around the massive mineral deposit. Some of the bones have been identified as belonging to the huge ground sloths, tapirs, musk

Speaking Figuratively

You know that polite-but-blank stare your children sometimes give you when you're trying to tell them something? Imagine a whole room of it, and you have an idea of what awaits you at **Vent Haven Museum** in Fort Mitchell (33 West Maple Avenue; 859–341–0461; www.venthavenmuseum.net). Vent Haven is home to more than 500 ventriloquistic figures (the world's largest known collection), left as a legacy by one William Shakespeare Berger, a Cincinnati businessman and amateur ventriloquist. Assembled between the 1930s and Berger's death in 1972 at age 94, his collection includes figures of all shapes, sizes, and heritages, some predating the Civil War; others are able to walk, move their noses, spit, and smoke cigarettes. It's a little disconcerting but fascinating, and a tour (by appointment only, May through September) will sure be something to talk about. Donation is $5 per person.

Gobble Gobble

Although thousands of people on Interstate 75 see the sign on the side of the barn daily, *Tewes Poultry Farm* is off the beaten path in spirit. The Tewes family (pronounced TOO-wis) raises and processes more than 3,000 turkeys annually, and processes more than 600 chickens every two weeks, in addition to keeping some Leghorn hens for eggs. Dan Tewes, patriarch of the 100-acre operation, and his late wife, Mary, had 18 children. There are 78 grandchildren and a growing number of great-grandchildren. Several generations of the Tewes work together to sort and wash eggs, tend to customers, and take care of the hundreds of daily tasks necessary on a "small" farm.

Way before the Interstate existed, the Teweses made final payments on their land by selling Easter chicks dipped in pastel-colored food dyes. Today I-75 cuts through the front pasture, a lumberyard sits adjacent to the house, and planes rush overhead to the Greater Cincinnati International Airport. Easter chicks would barely pay the feed bills and aren't considered ethical anymore. Despite the changes, the Teweses carry on a diverse, wholesome operation. Stop to get fresh fryers, big-breasted roasters, turkeys, bacon, eggs, and a vitamin-like dose of friendliness. The birds are dressed on Thursday or Friday, so the birds are fresh for the weekend. Tewes Poultry Farm is just north of Florence. From I-75 take the Buttermilk Pike exit and go into Crescent Springs. Turn left on Anderson Road and look for the farm about a mile on the left. They're always home and you're always welcome, but call ahead anyway at (859) 341-8844 (www.tewesfarm.com).

oxen, giant bison, and deerlike animals called cervalces, all now extinct. No one knows exactly what the cause of the worldwide destruction of these species was. Some say that glacier expansion drove animals south and created an overly dense population that eventually starved. Others blame an epidemic, unscrupulous primitive hunters, or the hand of a god.

The salt lick also was used by Native Americans and, after 1729, by pioneers who boiled down the brines to make highly valued salt. Legend has it that early Virginian settlers, who were fascinated with the massive bones, used mastodon ribs for tent poles and vertebrae for stools. Even Thomas Jefferson was intrigued. He reportedly had more than 300 specimens kept in the White House for research, but a servant pounded them into fertilizer. Not all the bones are lost, however; Big Bone Lick State Park's museum houses an incredible collection of vertebrate fossils from the area. Hours vary throughout the year. Call (859) 384-3522 or go to http://parks.ky.gov/findparks/recparks/bb/ for information.

Are you ready for a lesson in botany? Directly across the road from the state park is *Big Bone Gardens,* a six-acre pleasure garden and sales nursery owned by Mark Lawhorn and Mary Ellen Pesek. There are two big "twin" ponds, a bog area, two little ponds full of decorative aquatic plants that are for sale, and a super-duper campy concrete garden sculpture collection (baby deer and hoboes). Plant prices range from $1 to $50, and the varieties range from common native waterside grasses to Asian lotus plants. The gardens are open on weekends from early spring through July and by appointment otherwise. Park at the Methodist church across the street (but not during Sunday services, please). For an appointment call (859) 384–1949.

The tiny town of **Rabbit Hash** sits high on the banks of the Ohio River on Highway 20. It's not much of a town now, but it has an amazingly inveterate business, appropriately called the **Rabbit Hash General Store,** that has not boarded up its windows since 1831. That's more than 170 years of the screen door slamming on the funny little wooden-frame store. In addition to the usual "convenient store" items, there are locally contributed antiques and crafts. Stop by any day and have a soda. Hours are 10 A.M. to 7 P.M. daily, year-round. Located at 10021 Lower River Road, the store also has some mighty talented folks making music there on Saturday nights at 7 P.M. and Sunday afternoons at 2:30 P.M.

Kentucky has hundreds of bed-and-breakfast establishments, but this one, **Burlington's Willis Graves B&B Inn,** is one of the classiest, inside and out. The 1830s Federal-style brick home was built for Willis Graves, Burlington's county clerk for the first two decades of the 19th century. The home has been exquisitely renovated—Flemish bond brickwork and Federal mantels are all original. Unlike many bed-and-breakfasts, the furnishings are appropriate. Two rooms are available in an 1850s log cabin, now spiffed up to include fancy bathrooms and fireplaces. The inn is only a 12-minute drive to the Cincinnati/ Northern Kentucky International Airport, so it's a good option for business travelers. There's even high-speed Internet access in all the rooms. Rates range from $95 to $195 per night. Call (888) 226–5096 or (859) 689–5096, or check out the bed-and-breakfast's Web site at www.burligrave.com.

Located in a historic house, the **Tousey House Tavern** is redefining the meaning of Southern cooking. Built in 1822 by Erastus Tousey, the Tousey House has been many things over the years: a home, tavern, livery, hotel, boarding house, gift shop, consignment shop and restaurant. Former Judge Bruce Ferguson and his wife Elizabeth restored the historic property to its former beauty in 1987. Now owned by the Wainscott family, the Tousey House Tavern has a mouth-watering menu with favorites such as the Tousey Hot Brown—oven roasted turkey, Proscuitto ham, melted cheese and house-made light mornay sauce over toasted points with applewood cured bacon and tomato. Or try a dish of "Southern Comfort," also known as chicken and dumplings, featuring pan seared breast of chicken served with dumplings, carrots and cream gravy. Open Tuesday through Sunday at 4:30. Reservations recommended. Call 859–586–9900; www.touseyhouse.com.

Make a weekend of it and spend Sunday at the ***Burlington Antique Show.*** On the third Sunday of each month from April through October, a high quality antiques show fills the grounds (even some of the horse stalls!) of the Boone County Fairgrounds at 5819 Idlewild Road. People come from great distances to buy and to sell. Call 513–922–6847; www.burlingtonantiqueshow. And stop by the ***Cabin Arts and Quilt Shop*** (859–586–8021; www.cabinarts .com). They stay open on antiques show Sundays, just for you. They have everything a quilter could need (1,500 bolts of cotton fabric!) and handmade gifts and toys for the rest of us. Turn right off Highway 18 at the flashing light at the Old Courthouse corner onto Jefferson-Idlewild Road; the cabin is ¼ mile on the right.

Have a different, more adventurous notion of a vacation Sunday? Try a trail ride at the ***Little Britain Farm*** at 5307 Idlewild Road. They also give riding lessons. Total greenhorns are welcome. Call (859) 586–7990; www.little britainfarm.com.

Just 6.5 miles west of the hectic Interstate on Highway 18 is a place that recaptures life in a quieter, slower-paced time. ***The Dinsmore Homestead*** is a living-history site designed to show modern folks what daily life was like in the 1840s. The homestead includes a house, furnished with furniture and belong- ings of the family that owned it for five generations, beginning in 1839. There are numerous special events and workshops throughout the year, from basket making to an heirloom plant sale. There are also hiking trails. The homestead is open for tours from April through mid-December on Wednesday, Saturday, and Sunday from 1 to 5 P.M. Admission of $5 is charged. Call (859) 586–6117 for information or take a virtual tour online at www.dinsmorefarm.org.

From The Dinsmore Homestead, drive east on Highway 18 and turn left on North Bend Road (Highway 237). After a few miles turn right onto Peters- burg Road (Highway 20) and take it to Highway 8. Turn right onto Highway 8 and follow it to Constance, and look for the ***Anderson Ferry*** (859–485–9210), a two-boat operation in business since 1817. Today this is the quickest cross- ing from Cincinnati, via Ohio's Highway 50, to the airport on Interstate 275, especially when the bridges nearer town are choked by rush-hour traffic. Paul Anderson's two ferries, *Boone 7* and *Boone 8,* or *Little Boone,* haul passengers on demand year-round. On the Kentucky landing an old character named Arnold occasionally hangs out and "treats" customers to an endless pseudohis- tory of the boats and his life. From November through April hours are 6 A.M. to 9:30 P.M., and from May through October from 6 A.M. to 9:30 P.M. On Saturday the ferry starts running at 7 A.M., and on Sunday the start time is 11 A.M. The ferry runs about every 15 minutes. Cars are charged $4.

Metro Area

If *Covington*'s century-old *Cathedral Basilica of the Assumption* at the corner of Twelfth and Madison Streets (859–431–2060; www.covcathedral .com) were in a major coastal city or in Europe, people would rave about it. As it is, this remarkable work of French Gothic architecture is little known to the world. The building is closely modeled after Paris's Notre Dame and the Abbey Church of Saint Denis, complete with flying buttresses and fantastic gargoyles perched high on the facade. Glass is everywhere. Eighty-two windows, including two enormous rose windows, glow endlessly with the changing sun. Measuring 24 feet by 67 feet, the hand-blown, stained-glass window in the transept is said to be the largest in the world. The rich color, variety of shapes, and expressive details can leave you staggering and dizzy in the huge chamber. In one chapel are several paintings by Frank Duveneck, a Covington native who became an internationally known portrait and genre painter and sculptor. My favorite is the austere center panel of the Eucharist triptych of Mary Magdalene at the foot of the cross. To the visual strength of the space, add the music of three massive pipe organs, and you will be transported. (The basic building was constructed, beginning in 1894, for the price of $150,000, the cost of many of today's middle-American homes.)

The altar in the Blessed Sacrament Chapel reads BEHOLD THE BREAD OF ANGELS BECOMES THE FOOD OF WAYFARERS, so the faith-inspired beauty of this temple of worship is available to us worldly wanderers. The basilica is open from 9:30 A.M. to 4 P.M. Monday through Friday. Call in advance to arrange a guided tour at (859) 431–2060, ext. 17.

Adjacent to the basilica is the former chancery and the *Cathedral Museum,* where the cathedral treasures are on display. Gold and silver vessels for worship are decorated with cloisonné enamel and semiprecious stones. The chalice of the first Catholic missionary to Kentucky, Father Badin, is included in the collection. Museum and gift shop are open when the cathedral is, except on Monday.

Mutter Gottes Kirch (West Sixth and Montgomery Streets; 859–291–2288) is another of Covington's fabulous churches that is open to visitors. Call in advance for a guided tour. Started in 1870, Mutter Gottes Kirch (translated, Mother of God Church) was built in Italian (rather than French) Renaissance basilica design. Clock-bearing twin spires over the front facade seem to be held in place by the large apse dome. Inside, the lower panels of the magnificent stained-glass windows depict Old Testament promises while the upper panels depict the corresponding fulfillments. Other inspirational art includes sculpture, some by Covington artist Ferdinand Muer; Stations of the Cross; an 1876 Koehnken and Grimm pipe organ; beautiful floor tile; and large frescoes and murals by Johann Schmitt, who was once Frank Duveneck's teacher and whose work is in the Vatican.

Four galleries with new exhibitions presented nearly every month make the *Carnegie Visual and Performing Arts Center,* at 1028 Scott Boulevard, a bustling art district in itself. There's also a 750-seat theater. Call the galleries at (859) 491–2030 or the theater at (859) 655–8112 when you're in town to find out what's scheduled (www.thecarnegie.com).

Go through Covington's Riverside Drive-Licking River Historic District on the east side of town by the "Point" where the Licking River empties into the mighty Ohio. Follow Second Street east until it becomes Shelby Street and wraps around to become Riverside Drive. On the strip of land between the street and the river is the *George Rogers Clark Park,* so named because Clark supposedly stopped at the site to gather forces on his way to Ohio to fight Shawnees. In the park are a few new pieces of sculpture by George Danhires. The most fun is a bronze likeness of James Bradley, an African-born slave who worked his way to freedom, crossed the Ohio River, attended seminary in Cincinnati in 1834, and went down in history as the only former slave to participate in the famous, fiery Lane Seminary debates on abolition. Bradley is depicted as reading thoughtfully on a park bench facing the river. The piece is so realistic that passersby stop talking so as not to disturb the man.

trueblue

The only replica of the tomb of Jesus in the United States is in the Garden of Hope in Covington.

The bright blue Covington/Cincinnati Suspension Bridge, just a few blocks west of the Licking Riverside Neighborhood, has been renamed the *John A. Roebling Suspension Bridge* in honor of the engineer who designed it. When it opened in 1867, after 22 years of construction, the bridge was the longest of its kind in the world (1,057 feet) and served Roebling as a prototype for his later Brooklyn Bridge in New York City.

Take Garrard Street south and look on the right for house number 215, the *Amos Shinkle Townhouse Bed and Breakfast,* circa 1854. What was once a posh residence for one of Covington's early big businessmen, Amos Shinkle, is now an impressive bed-and-breakfast facility. Owner Bernie Moorman has taken pains to maintain such interesting features as the original murals on the walls of the front staircase. Rooms range from a master suite with a whirlpool to a converted carriage house that is ideal for families. Prices range from $95 to $175 and include a full breakfast. Call (859) 431–2118 or (800) 972–7012 (www.amosshinkle.net).

Although **Main Strasse** has been billed as a miniature German village in downtown Covington, historically the area is ethnically heterogeneous. German, Irish, and African Americans have lived in this architecturally fascinating neighborhood, which has been developed into a shopping district for tourists.

trueblue

Some scenes from the film *Rain Man*, starring Dustin Hoffman and Tom Cruise, were filmed in the northern Kentucky/Cincinnati area.

You can find everything from antiques and doll boutiques to restaurants and bakeries. At the edges of the developed area are local pubs with Irish names.

One of the best restaurants in town is not German, but Cajun and Creole. **Dee Felice Cafe,** at 529 Main Street, next to the Goose Girl Fountain, is hot. The food is spicy, and the jazz is cool. From a bowl of gumbo for about $5 to spicy blackened seafood and chicken (dinner entrees range from $15.95 to $28.95), the flavor tugs at the Southern palate. It's hard to believe that the ornate building was originally a pharmacy. No Super-X can hold a candle to these pressed tin ceilings and miniature Corinthian columns, details of which are preserved in the restaurant and painted audacious colors. Every night a live band plays Dixieland, blues, and lots of jazz on a stage behind the long bar. The founder, the late Dee Felice, was a jazz drummer in his own right; he used to play with James Brown, Mel Tormé, Sergio Mendez, and others. Lunch hours are Sunday only, from 10 A.M. to 3 P.M. Dinner begins at 5 P.M. nightly. The phone number is (859) 261–2365 and the Web site is www.deefelice.com. Reservations are suggested for dinner.

Iron horse history buffs, take note of the **Railway Museum of Greater Cincinnati** at 315 West Southern Avenue. This museum has a number of immaculately preserved items, such as a 1906 Southern Railroad open platform business car, a diner built for the Golden Rocket, several locomotives, sleeping cars, post office cars, cabooses, and more. The grounds are open year-round, Wednesday and Saturday from 10 A.M. to 4 P.M. You can watch as volunteers restore antique engines and equipment. Guided tours are given May through October, on Sunday from 12:30 to 4:30 P.M. Admission is $4 for adults and $2 for children 10 and under. Call (859) 491–RAIL for more information or check www.cincirailmuseum.org.

Unique knickknack nautical decor and more await you any hour of the day or night at **Covington's Anchor Grill** (438 Pike Street; 859–431–9498). Eating with neighborhood locals becomes a dining experience when you put a quarter in the jukebox. The mechanized C. C. doll band display comes to life in the corner of the grill while overhead a rotating ballroom star light sets the mood. Open 24 hours a day, seven days a week!

Perched high on a bluff above Covington, the Interstate, and the Ohio River is the ***Behringer-Crawford Museum*** (859–491–4003; www.bcmuseum .org) in Devou Park, a 700-acre recreational green space at 1600 Montague Road, on the west side of I–75. This unique museum houses a really impressive collection of fossils and prehistoric artifacts from the immediate region in addition to exhibits featuring Civil War relics and other artifacts from more recent history. Some of the Ice Age animal specimens were collected by archaeologist Ellis Crawford from the prehistoric site at Big Bone Lick. Hours are Tuesday through Friday from 10 A.M. to 5 P.M., 1 to 5 P.M. on weekends. Admission is $7 for adults, $4 for children three to 17.

Now that you've been high above the Ohio River and looked down at its serpentine, sparkling surface, wouldn't you like to go below it to see inside the river? The ***Newport Aquarium*** (859–261–7444, www.newportaquarium.com) has a 53-foot-long wall of clear acrylic that brings you eye level with native species of the Ohio River—big bottom-feeding catfish, nightmare-inducing gar, soft-shell turtles, shovel-nosed sturgeon, and more than you ever imagined. The aquarium is a state-of-the-art facility with exhibits focused on the rivers of the world, a shoreline museum (with an area designed for visitors to touch creatures like starfish and sand dollars), a collection of dangerous and deadly aquatic life (including electric eels and red-bellied piranha), and more. One exhibit allows you to walk through a clear tunnel through shark-filled waters. Titillating and educational, the aquarium is located in a super-modern building with nautical imagery of masts and sails. Go toward the Ohio River on Third Street until you see the Newport on the Levee complex. Open daily from 10

Wilder Spirits

Some of the wildest ghosts in Kentucky have been spotted at ***Bobby Mackey's*** (44 Licking Pike; 859–431–5588), a country-and-western club in Wilder, not far from Newport. Over the years, more than 30 people, employees, and patrons alike, have reported seeing ghosts. And these aren't your friendly ghosts—one man claimed to have been attacked by a ghost in a club restroom. Local legend has it that the hauntings are the result of the building's use for satanic worship in the 19th century and its speakeasy days during the 1920s. The owner has tried exorcism and has even posted warning signs so patrons know that not all the spirits at this nightclub come in bottles.

A.M. to 6 P.M. Admission is $20 for adults, $13 for children ages three through twelve.

Northern Kentucky ushered in the new millennium with a very visible and permanent monument. Not far from the aquarium, at Fourth and York Streets in *Newport,* is the *World Peace Bell,* billed as "the world's largest free-swinging bell." The bell weighs 66,000 pounds and is 12 feet in diameter and 12 feet high. (By comparison, the Liberty Bell in Philadelphia is a mere 2,080 pounds.) The bell was the result of a community effort led by a local business-man, Wayne Carlisle, who envisioned marking the millennium with a symbol of freedom and peace. Designed by a family-owned company based just across the Ohio River in Cincinnati, the Verdin Bell Company, the bell was actually cast in France. (The foundry in Nantes was one of the few in the world with a furnace that could melt the 100,000 pounds of bronze.) After the casting—on December 11, 1998, the 50th anniversary of the Universal Declaration of Human Rights in Paris—the bell was shipped to the United States, arriving in New Orleans in July 1999. As it traveled up the Mississippi and Ohio Rivers, the bell made stops at cities along the way to great fanfare. In October 1999 it was installed in the glass and steel pavilion that was to be its permanent home. The first northern Kentucky swinging of the bell was at midnight on December 31, 1999, to welcome the year 2000. Pictures on the bell represent significant achievements of mankind, from the Gutenberg press to the first step on the moon. If you want to see it swing and hear its deep, resonant ring, come at noon. The bell also chimes on the hour.

In the heart of Newport is the perennial favorite, *Pompilios* restaurant (600 Washington Avenue; 859–581–3065; www.pompilios.com). Established in 1933, Pompilios is a family-run restaurant and bar that has continued to provide authentic Italian food for 60 years. Even on weeknights the place is packed—people stand amicably on the sidewalk waiting to get in. Pompilios gained national notoriety when it was appeared in the film *Rain Man* with Dustin Hoffman and Tom Cruise. Remember the scene when the autistic Ray-mond counts at a glance the number of toothpicks in a box that the waitress has dropped? Oh, and people also talk about the time when the cast and crew of *Airborne*—a forgettable 1993 flick featuring then-unknown Jack Black (*Tenacious D, School of Rock*)—wined, dined, and filmed a scene at Pompilios. Open 11 A.M. to 10 P.M. Sunday through Thursday, and 11 A.M. to midnight on Friday and Saturday. Entrees range from $9.25 to $11.25.

Across the Licking River and northeast of Newport is the *Weller Haus Bed and Breakfast,* in Bellevue's Taylor Daughters' Historic District at 319 Poplar Street (2 blocks south of Highway 8). For $119 to $199 you can eat a classy breakfast and sleep peacefully amid 18th-century antiques or relax on the patio overlooking an English-style garden. Call (859) 431–6829 or (800) 431–4287 for reservations (www.wellerhaus.com).

Since 1939 *Schneider's Sweet Shop,* at 420 Fairfield Avenue (Route 8), has been *Bellevue*'s most exquisite temple of the sweet tooth. Using old-fashioned equipment and timeless craftsmanship, Jack Schneider creates truly fantastic homemade ice creams and candies. The place is famous, especially during the winter holiday season, for its opera creams, unusual little chocolate candies with rich, creamy centers, available in the tristate area only. Schneider's other famous originals include the summer top-seller, Ice Ball with Ice Cream, a scoop of vanilla ice cream with shaved ice packed around it and a healthy dose of specially concocted syrup poured over the top. They have won the award for best caramel apple in the Cincinnati area and have the popular vote for Jack's own favorite, cookies 'n' cream ice cream. This heaven is open Monday through Saturday from 10 A.M. to 9 P.M. and Sunday from noon to 9 P.M. Closing time is 10 P.M. in summer. Call (859) 431–3545; www.schneiders candies.com.

The patron saint of travelers is ready to welcome you in Bellevue. One of the most interesting and unusual bed-and-breakfasts in the area, *Christopher's Bed & Breakfast,* 604 Poplar Street, is housed in a former church. Built in the late 1800s, the 8,100-square-foot structure originally housed Bellevue Christian Church. In 1996 Steve and Brenda Guidugli purchased the century-old building and converted it into a residence. They retained all of the original stained-glass windows. Two guest rooms and one suite are available, each with private baths with whirlpools. The suite has a two-person Jacuzzi. Rates are $105 to $179 per night. Call (888) 585–7085 or (859) 491–9354 for reservations. Or be high-tech and reserve online at www.christophersbb.com.

Said to be the world's smallest house of worship, the *Monte Casino Chapel* (859–344–3309) measures just 6 by 9 feet—no better place for an intimate conversation with God. Just close the door and let fly. The chapel was built in 1910 in a vineyard on a hill just outside of Covington by Benedictine monks. In the late 1960s the chapel was moved to its present site on the campus of Thomas More College, a small liberal arts college in Crestview Hills. From I–75 take I–275 east and exit onto Turkeyfoot Road. Monte Casino Chapel is next to a large pond on the left side of the road.

Not said to be the world's smallest house of drama, the *Village Players of Fort Thomas* do, nonetheless, use a very small, intimate, three-quarter stage where plays are performed year-round except in June. The theater is located at 8 North Fort Thomas Avenue. The mailing address is P.O. Box 75082, Fort Thomas 41075. Fort Thomas is southeast of Bellevue. For a schedule and other information, call (859) 392–0500 or check www.the-village-players.com.

Buffalo Trace Area

The river towns strung along the mighty Ohio and the areas that spread away from them are usually historically significant and, for that reason, often a touch schizophrenic, caught between the stillness of the past and the fluid present. *Augusta,* in Bracken County, is one of the few such towns that has struck a happy balance while remaining scenic. From Covington or Newport, either hug the banks of the Ohio River by following Highway 8 east, or buzz along the newer "AA" Highway 546, which connects Alexandria and Ashland. If you take the AA, watch for its intersection with Highway 1159. Turn left (north) and meander around for a moment at the ***Walcott Covered Bridge,*** a 75-foot-long wooden bridge spanning Locust Creek, which was active from 1824 until 1954. Walk into the bridge and read the descriptions of bridge types, definitions of terms, and explanations for methods of construction.

The ***Beehive Tavern,*** on the north corner of Main Street and Riverside Drive, is an elegant colonial-style restaurant and bed-and-breakfast located in a 1790s row house facing the river. Drinks are served from noon until closing Wednesday through Saturday on the upstairs balcony, which has a perfect river view. Lunch and dinner are served Wednesday through Saturday. The menu changes every two weeks and includes items such as roast pork with fried apples, corn bread stuffing, and some Spanish dishes, reflecting the heritage of owner Luciano Moral, who was born in Cuba to Spanish parents. Entrees range from $11.95 to $23. Be sure to save room for dessert; the blueberry trifle cake and caramel flan are primo. Call (606) 756–2202 for information (www .shopaugusta.com or www.rosemaryclooney.com/beehive).

Directly across the street is the ***Augusta Ferry*** (606–756–3291), one of the very few functional ferries on the Ohio River. It's operational year-round 8 A.M. to 8 P.M. The ride costs $5 per car. Pedestrians on foot may ride the ferry free

Lights, Camera, Action!

You may have already seen Augusta if you watched the television miniseries *Centennial,* because the town was used to film scenes taking place in St. Louis, Missouri, in the 1880s. Because Augusta has no flood wall, Water Street (or Riverside Drive) was a ready-made set, except for a few details—the film crew put down 4 inches of dirt on the street to cover the pavement and pulled down power lines and business signs. The houses along the river were, as they always are, picture-perfect. Since then, several Public Broadcasting System (PBS) productions have been filmed in Augusta, including the classic *Huckleberry Finn.*

as long as there is a paying customer on board. Imagine yourself crossing the water when the town was new and the ferry was powered by mules.

Just a block down from the river and next to Augusta Park, at 1-2 West Second Street, is **The Parkview Country Inn,** a charming bed-and-breakfast decorated with art and antiques. The building dates to the 1830s and has served as a tavern and boardinghouse, hotel, and even a factory—in the 1960s and 1970s it housed a sewing operation that made mattresses for the U.S. Army. Current owners Larry and Shirley Mohrfield have restored it as a luxurious stopping point. There are ten guest rooms, including one that is wheelchair accessible. Rates range from $95 for a double room to $145 for a suite. There's a full-service restaurant. Call (606) 756–2603 for information and reservations (www.parkviewcountryinn.com).

The Mohrfields also operate the **Augusta General Store** on Main Street, a great place to stop for sundries and much more; the store includes a soda fountain, bakery, deli, and grill. The phone number is (606) 756–2525.

A popular event in the area is **"The Old Reliable" Germantown Fair,** held the first week in August at the Germantown fairgrounds on Highway 10. No one seems to be able to explain the "Old Reliable" aspect beyond the fact that it happens every year. Germantown straddles the Bracken-Mason county line. Thirty-three yards from that county line, in Germantown, is a classic country cooking restaurant called the **Ole Country Inn** (606–728–2912). There's nothing particularly German about the place, but fast food can't hold a candle to the speed of the cooks, and you get a real meal to boot. Hours are 7 A.M. to 6 P.M. Monday through Saturday and 8 A.M. to 3 P.M. Sunday.

Follow Highway 8 along the river to Maysville. If you arrive from the west, there is a functional **covered bridge at Dover.** Highway 1235 crosses Lee's Creek by means of this 61-foot-long Queensport truss bridge, which had a tollbooth at one end when the oldest part was built in 1835.

Maysville is the next town upriver, the site of the closest bridge to the north and the hub of activity for the whole area. To steep yourself in area history, go to the **Kentucky Gateway Museum Center** (606–564–5865; www .kygmc.org), at 215 Sutton Street, in an 1878 structure originally built to be the town's first library. Because of the historic significance of the area as an early point of access to the west, the little museum tells the bigger story of the expansion of America. Hours are 10 A.M. to 5 P.M. Tuesday through Friday, 10 A.M. to 4 P.M. Saturday and 1 P.M. to 4 P.M. Sunday. Admission is charged.

The downtown flood wall in Maysville is becoming an art gallery on a grand scale, with the creation of huge murals depicting scenes from the area's history. The larger than life **Maysville Flood Wall Murals** are privately funded and are created by Louisiana artist Robert Dafford, who has painted more than 20 murals for the city of Paducah in western Kentucky. The first three murals showed the town's pioneer landing spot, Limestone Landing, as it might have looked in the 1700s, 1800s, and 1900s, but now all have been completed. Maysville has many historic buildings and sites, from a pioneer graveyard, to the 1850s New Orleans–style homes of Mechanics Row, to the childhood home of singer Rosemary Clooney. Pick up a free walking tour brochure at the visitors bureau.

Follow Second Street past Sutton and park anywhere. On the north corner of Sutton and Wall Streets is the shop of a fine furniture maker. *Joseph Byrd Brannen & Co., Antique Furniture Reproductions* is an inspirational one-person operation. Joe Brannen is asked to make all manner of hardwood furniture, but his true love is for traditional 18th- and 19th-century American furniture in cherry, walnut, mahogany, and curly maple, a wood with delicious figuring and a mean grain from which many woodworkers keep a respectful distance. Joe does use power tools, but he finishes all of his work by hand, using planes or scrapers that are fueled by pure elbow grease. The difference is noticeable and worth the extra cost. He always has a few finished pieces of furniture on hand and welcomes visitors Monday through Friday from 9 A.M. to 5 P.M., and on Saturday from 9 A.M. to noon. For a brochure and price list, write 145 West Second Street, Maysville 41056, or call (606) 564–3642.

Drive west another 2 blocks to Rosemary Clooney Street, so named when the singer's first motion picture premiered in Maysville, her hometown. Go toward the river and you'll find the only active Amtrak station in Kentucky and a great place to eat called *Caproni's on the River* (320 Rosemary Clooney Street; 606–564–4321; www.ipro.net/users/sax/capronis). Its national fame began in the 1930s, when it was just a cafe at which eastbound soldiers

The Tables Do Turn

The Maysville-Washington area was settled by Simon Kenton, who first claimed the land. Kenton later sold it for 50 cents an acre to Arthur Fox and William Wood, who laid out the town of Washington. Like a good imperialist, Kenton had come to the area in search of sugar cane so that he could get rich making Jamaican-style rum. The hills were indeed covered with cane, but it was wild Kentucky cane, a tall, woody native grass, the only bamboo species native to North America. Nothing sweet about it. Like a good capitalist, Kenton realized his error and went on to exploit some other aspect of the land. He eventually opened a small store in a cabin in Washington; that cabin now stands next to the visitor center. Legend has it that Kenton couldn't pay his bills and was thrown into debtor's prison in Washington, the very town he founded. The tables do turn.

stopped during train layovers. Today, two long balconies look out over a wide, slow-moving part of the Ohio River. The other selling points are super food, high-quality local and foreign wines, and imported beers. The menu is diverse, with steaks, prime rib, country ham, and lots of pasta and seafood dishes. Entrees range from $15 to $25. Reservations are recommended on the weekends.

Hollywood comes to Maysville for one night every year the last weekend of September during the **Rosemary Clooney Festival.** Hot meals are served by butlers on bone china to nattily dressed tables of ten for an outdoor dinner performance in front of the historic Russell Theatre. On stage for the first few years was Maysville's native daughter, Rosemary Clooney herself. After her passing, the microphone was taken up by Debbie Boone, Michael Feinstein, Linda Ronstadt, and Roberta Flack; and George Clooney brought in musicians from the Down from the Mountain tour (after *O Brother Where Art Thou?*). It's a benefit event with profits going to restore the Russell Theatre where Rosemary made her debut in 1953. And that's just Saturday night! During the day local talent takes the stage, and on Friday there's a massive block party with regional bands and food and booths on the sidewalk. For information and reservations call Maysville's director of tourism at (606) 564–9419, ext. 322.

Another of Kentucky's few remaining covered bridges is east of Maysville in Lewis County. From Maysville take Highway 10 through Plumville and turn left (east) onto Spring Creek Road. Just as you cross the county line at the intersection with Cabin Road you'll see the **Cabin Creek Bridge** on the south side. The 114-foot-long bridge was built in 1897 and closed to traffic in 1983.

Driving the 4 miles straight uphill on U.S. Highway 68 between Maysville and Washington will take you a matter of minutes. In the 18th century, however, the climb consumed a whole day. Heavily loaded wagons and carts that had just come across the Ohio River at Maysville (then called Limestone) were worn out by the time they reached the ridge, so they stopped at Washington for a rest. I wouldn't call these pioneers tourists, but their patronage caused the town to grow from a few humble cabins into a bunch of humble cabins.

When Kentucky joined the Union in 1792, people west of the Alleghenies thought that **Washington,** population 462, might become the capital of the United States. (Obviously, the other Washington got the vote.) If time could have frozen at that moment, you probably would have seen a town much like the historic restoration that stands today. You can get a more complete story of the town and its characters from one of the tour guides at the visitor center, which is located in one of the original 119 cabins from 1790. Guided tours of the town are offered Monday through Saturday from 11 A.M. to 3 P.M., Sunday from 1 to 3 P.M. The center is closed January through March. The tours cost

$6 for adults, $3 for children. Call (606) 759–7411 for more information (www .washingtonky.com).

One of the most popular tours focuses on the area's role in the Underground Railroad. The first stop is the ***Harriet Beecher Stowe Slavery to Freedom Museum,*** where exhibits include slave manacles and collars, original slavery documents, and many items relating to Stowe and her famous 1852 book, *Uncle Tom's Cabin.* Stowe is thought to have first witnessed a slave auction during a visit to this house in 1833. Its owners at the time were the Sellmans, whose daughter Elizabeth was a student of Stowe's at the Western Female Institute in Cincinnati. The tour also includes a tour of ***Paxton Inn,*** a station on the Underground Railroad. According to local legend, slaves hid on a narrow hidden staircase until they could be moved across the Ohio River. Quilts hung on clotheslines or fences served as signs or warnings. The log cabin pattern, for example, indicated a "safe house."

Washington is full of small antiques and specialty shops selling everything from rare books to homemade candies to clocks, yarns, dried herbs, and copper lamps. To view a collection of horse-drawn carriages in the ***Carriage Museum,*** call (606) 759–7305.

Just a few miles from Washington off US 68 is the community of ***Mays Lick.*** Founded in the late 1700s, this tiny community has numerous historic buildings and churches and a couple of small shops.

US 68 follows a north-south path made by buffalo traveling to and from the salt deposit at Blue Licks. From Maysville go south on the buffalo trace to the ***Blue Licks Battlefield State Resort Park*** (859–289–5507 or 800–443–7008; http://parks.ky.gov/findparks/resortparks/bl). The place had always been one of importance to the native people as well as to the settlers who mined salt there. Its connotation darkened when in August 1792 more than 60 Kentucky pioneers were killed in a bloody Revolutionary battle against Native Americans and Canadian soldiers ten months after the British surrendered at Yorktown. All this in a 15-minute battle! A large granite obelisk at the park marks the area where the fighters, including Daniel Boone's son Israel, were buried in a common grave.

Take a hike along the buffalo trace beginning in the parking area. This 15-acre area is set aside as a state nature preserve in order to protect one of the last and largest stands of Short's goldenrod, a federally designated endangered species. Notice how the goldenrod grows thickest in the open areas. It is speculated that grazing and trampling by buffalo, now nonexistent in Kentucky, helped the plant survive; the buffalo also may have carried the seeds in their thick fur and thus spread the graceful yellow plant. (Goldenrod, by the way, is not responsible for your hay fever. Blame ragweed.) Goldenrod blooms in September, but as tempting as it is, please don't pick any.

The displays in the park museum are concerned with the cultural and geographic history of the area. Several original pieces of Daniel Boone's salt-making equipment are in the museum, donated by descendants of Simon Kenton. In 1778 Boone and a few others made a salt expedition and were taken prisoner by the Shawnees, who adopted many of the white men into their families. Boone was adopted by the chief, Blackfish. Later Simon Kenton retrieved the equipment. Today the park has fishing facilities and all the usual recreational trappings. A new lodge offers rooms from $59.95 to $129.95 per night. Cottages are also available. The lodge dining room serves breakfast, lunch, and dinner daily. Call (859) 289–5507 for information. In mid-August the park sponsors a historic reenactment of the battle during a festival that features period demonstrators and other related entertainment.

This is definitely the region of covered bridges. ***Johnson Creek Covered Bridge*** crosses the creek on the original buffalo trace just north of Blue Licks Battlefield State Park. Built in 1874, the dilapidated structure is 114 feet long and 16 feet wide, with Smith-type trusses. Take US 68 east from the park, then take Highway 165 north to Highway 1029 and watch for the bridge, which is closed to traffic.

In Fleming County, south of Maysville, there are three covered bridges. The first is the 60-foot-long ***Goddard (White) Covered Bridge,*** the only surviving example of Ithiel Town truss design in the state, a latticelike design that uses rigid, triangularly placed beams as supports. Photographers love this spot because a picturesque country church can be seen through the bridge. From Maysville go to the county seat, Flemingsburg, by way of Highway 11 south. Then follow Highway 32 east almost 6 miles to Goddard. This time, you can drive over the bridge. For more information call (606) 845–5951.

trueblue

The Franklin Sousley Monument in Flemingsburg honors one of the World War II veterans who raised the American flag at Iwo Jima.

Follow Highway 32 down the road a piece and turn right (west) on Rawlings Road, or north on Highway 1895 (Maxey Flats Road). At ***Ringos Mills*** you'll find an 86-foot-long bridge built in 1867 that was part of a large 19th-century gristmill.

A more utilitarian-style covered bridge is a few miles away near Grange City. The 86-foot-long ***Hillsboro Bridge*** is roofed and sided with corrugated tin, and the abutments are made of "red stone." The construction is of the burr truss design with multiple king posts. It's a sight! It's also a shame that it's too run-down to use. To get there from Flemingsburg, drive south on Highway 111, pass Hillsboro, and watch the right side of the road.

Seven miles south of Blue Licks is a rural community called **Carlisle,** which boasts some 350 buildings that are on the National Register of Historic Places. One of them is said to be made of the only Daniel Boone cabin logs in Old Kentuck' that haven't turned into humus—actually, the cabin is still standing. To go, take US 68 northwest of town for 3 miles and watch for the state historic marker. Tours are offered by appointment. In downtown Carlisle the **Old Nicholas County Jail** and jailer's home have been refurbished down to the dungeonlike cells. Tours are offered by appointment, and on the second Thursday of every month, a delicious four-course lunch is served for $12 per person. Reservations are required, and fill up fast despite the ability to serve 85 at a time! For information about the Boone cabin tours or the jail, call Carlisle/Nicholas County Tourism at (859) 289–5174 (www .carlisle-nicholascounty.org).

For history buffs there are several more stops to make. On Market Street you'll easily spot the **Old Train Depot,** which now houses the Historic Society. Tours are free and available any weekday. Call (859) 289–5402. **Neals Country Store** on Main Street can be toured now, despite its "in progress" status. The restored building will be a museum with a focus on area genealogy. The restored **Mozark Hall** will again be a performing arts center; restoration work revealed that the walls were plastered with old show posters from the early 1900s. Call (859) 289–4220. Just walk around the tiny town (population 1,600) and be amazed that it boasts the second-largest number of cast-iron building facades, most of which are in excellent condition. (Louisville, by the way, has the most.)

More Good Lodging in Northern Kentucky

AUGUSTA

White Rose Bed and Breakfast
210 East Riverside Drive
(606) 756–2787
Three guest rooms in an 1800 house owned by inn-keeper Bob Kelsch's family since 1917. $80 to $100.

BELLEVUE

Mary's Belle View Inn
44 VanVoast
(859) 581–8337 or
(888) 581–8875
www.bbonline.com
Two guest rooms and a suite with a great view of the Cincinnati skyline. $65 to $130.

BURLINGTON

First Farm Inn
2510 Stevens Road
(859) 586–0199
www.firstfarminn.com
Bed-and-breakfast in an 1870s home on a working horse farm. $89 and up.

CARROLLTON

Economy Inn
Interstate 71 at U.S. Highway 227
(502) 732–9301
Around $65.

General Butler State Resort Park
U.S. Highway 227 North
(502) 732–4384
www.parks.ky.gov
$45-$180.

Highland House
1705 Highland Avenue
(502) 732–5559
Bed-and-breakfast in a Mediterranean period Revival style home on the Ohio River.

COVINGTON

The Wallace House Bed & Breakfast
120 Wallace Avenue
(859) 261–2717 or
(888) 942–8177
www.wallacehousebb.com
Circa 1905 Queen Anne Victorian mansion. $109 to $139.

CYNTHIANA

Side Saddle Inn
5322 Highway 36W
(859) 234–8600
www.bridalpotpourriky.com
Guest rooms in a country setting.

DRY RIDGE

Super 8
Interstate 75, exit 159
(859) 824–3700
Around $60.

FALMOUTH

Back in Time
804 West Shelby Street
(859) 654–6100
Six rooms with private baths.

FLEMINGSBURG

Stockton Station Inn
129 West Water Street
(606) 845–0070
www.stocktonstation.com
Five guest rooms, exercise room, massage therapist available.

FLORENCE

Best Western Inn
7821 Commerce Drive
(859) 525–0090
$60 and up.

Wildwood Inn Tropical Dome & Theme Suites
7809 Highway 42
(859) 371–6300
Themed rooms, including African safari huts, an Old West room, and a '50s room where the bed is nestled into a 1959 Cadillac. $75 and up.

FORT MITCHELL

Drawbridge Inn
Interstate 75 at Buttermilk Pike
(859) 341–2800
www.drawbridgeinn.om
$70 and up.

GHENT

Ghent House
411 Main Street
(502) 347–5807
www.bbonline.com/ky/ghent
Bed-and-breakfast in an antebellum home overlooking the Ohio River.

The Poet's House
Main Street and U.S. Highway 42
(502) 347–0161
A Federal-style home overlooking the Ohio River. Guest rooms and a cottage available.

MAYSVILLE
French Quarter Inn
25 East McDonald Parkway
(606) 564–8000
$79 and up.

NEWPORT
Ash-Ley House B&B
310 East Third Street
(859) 291–1114

Gateway Bed and Breakfast
326 East Sixth Street
(888) 891–7500 or
(859) 581–6447
www.gatewaybb.com
Spacious rooms in an Italianate-style townhouse. $85.

Grace Manor Bed and Breakfast
828 Linden Avenue
(859) 491–4213 or
(877) 645–7208
www.gracemanorbb.com
1906 brick home located in Newport's East Row Historic District. Very near many attractions, including Newport on the Levee. $99 and up.

WILLIAMSTOWN
Days Inn
Interstate 75, exit 154
(859) 824–5025
$56 and up.

Red Carpet Inn
Exit 154 off Interstate 75
(859) 824–4305
$55 and up.

More Fun Places to Eat in Northern Kentucky

ALEXANDRIA
Sun Valley Pizza
5329 Alexandria Pike
(859) 635–0010
Just moderately priced carryout pizza and the like, but the steak hoagies are reputedly addictive.

BROOKSVILLE
Carbo's Cafe
113 Locust Street
(across from the county courthouse on Highway 19)
(606) 735–2091
Down home-style breakfast, lunch, and dinner.

CARLISLE
Tracks Restaurant
Highway 36, southeast of town
(859) 289–5464
Model electric train runs on tracks near ceiling while you eat.

CARROLLTON
Cooper's Restaurant
214 Park Avenue
(502) 732–4990
Catfish, barbecue, steaks, and sandwiches.

General Butler State Resort Park
U.S. Highway 227 North
(502) 732–4384
Varied menu with buffet.

Point Park
Downtown Carrollton
Naturally attractive site where the Kentucky and Ohio Rivers meet. Bring a picnic.

Welch's Riverside Restaurant
505 Main Street
(502) 732–9118
For breakfast, lunch, and dinner.

COVINGTON
Behle Street Cafe
50 East Rivercenter Boulevard
(859) 291–4100
www.behlestreetcafe.com
Eclectic lunch and dinner menu—meatloaf, salmon, shepherd's pie, Greek salad with homemade dressing. $11 to $28.

CoCo's
322 Greenup Street
(859) 491–1369
www.cocosbakery.com
Southwestern food with jazz music.

Mike Fink's Restaurant
100 Greenup Street
(859) 261–4212
www.mikefink.com
Super popular restaurant that is actually floating on the Ohio River. Great view of downtown Cincinnati lights reflected on water. The boat was put in dry dock in February 2009 for

renovations, with reopening set for fall 2009. Happy diners will probably be waiting in line for their Mike Fink fix.

Wertheim's
514 West Sixth Street
(859) 261–1233
Traditional German fare plus pasta and chicken dishes.

CYNTHIANA

Biancke's Restaurant
3 South Main Street
(859) 234–3443
www.bianckes.com
Always a big local crowd. Good Italian and American cooking for reasonable prices.

FLORENCE

Grand Cafe
7373 Turfway Road
(859) 371–9779
Fine traditional food and a great wine list.

FORT MITCHELL

Indigo Bar and Grill
2053 Dixie Highway
(859) 331–4339
Salads, pastas, and gourmet pizza.

FORT THOMAS

El Midway Cafe
1017 South Fort Thomas Avenue
(859) 781–7666
www.themidwaycafe.com
Great fajitas and other mesquite fare in a restored 1890s saloon.

MAYSVILLE

Tippedore's
(in French Quarter Inn)
25 East McDonald Parkway
(606) 564–8000
Serving breakfast only.

NEWPORT

Aoi
1 Levee Way,
Newport on the Levee
(859) 431–9400
Traditional Japanese food—sushi, sashimi, cooked entrees, and appetizers in an elegant dining room with central sushi bar. $15 to $25.

Cafe Istanbul
1 Levee Way, Newport on the Levee
(859) 581–1777
Wide range of Mediterranean food done in the Turkish manner. $12 to $21.

Hofbräuhaus
200 East Third Street
(859) 491–7200
www.hofbrauhausnewport.com
Authentic Bavarian fare (like sauerbraten and *weisswurste,* a white sausage) and beer, of course. A German beer hall *mit der gusto!* $7 to $18.

VERONA

Mr. Herb's Restaurant
2011 Verona Mudlick Road
(859) 689–7298
Locally famous fried fish dinners Thursday through Sunday.

WASHINGTON

Marshall Key's Tavern
2100 Old Main Street
(606) 759–0659
Homemade soups, sandwiches, daily specials, and pies.

SOUTH-CENTRAL KENTUCKY →

Kids aren't the only people who need to play and learn. This region's parks and large dammed lakes are like big playgrounds for adults. There are two of the world's natural wonders, Mammoth Cave, which highlights the most spectacular manifestations of Kentucky's unique karst geography, and the breathtaking Cumberland Falls, the second-largest cataract in the Western hemisphere and one of two in the world with a moonbow. South-central Kentucky is also associated with history. The north is Lincoln country and home to the state's only African-American history gallery, and the south boasts the beautiful Big South Fork National Park. *Bowling Green,* the largest city, is known, in part, for having the world's only Corvette plant. The whole region is spiced up with amusing town names, quirky craftspeople, and zany festivals.

From Caves to Culture

Being in the heart of Western Kentucky University's campus on Kentucky Street in Bowling Green, *The Kentucky Museum* is not off the beaten path, but its contents are unique. This is one of the best collections of objects pertaining to Kentucky

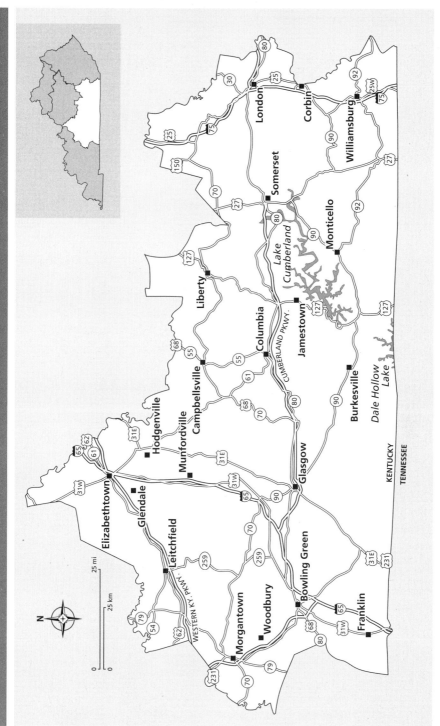

SOUTH-CENTRAL KENTUCKY

history and culture housed in one place. The museum also makes a special effort to exhibit fine traveling shows and to put together displays using borrowed objects that otherwise would never be in the public view. Traditional Kentucky quilts are the museum's forte. There's a Christmas crazy quilt made of silk hat liners, for example. During the holidays, a passel of relatives were snowbound for several weeks, so instead of flipping on the tube and watching game shows, they made a quilt together. Some of the quilts are political, such as the 1850 Henry Clay quilt with his portrait in the middle in crewel work, which was a presentation piece from Mrs. Henry Clay to the wife of Senator John Jordan Crittenden. And some quilts are downright fascinating; for example, the dizzying 66,000-piece Spectrum Quilt, which is rare in that it was made in the 1930s by a man, a jeweler who had heard that the work would

AUTHOR'S FAVORITE PLACES IN SOUTH-CENTRAL KENTUCKY

The American Cave Museum
Horse Cave
(270) 786–1466
www.cave.org

Appalachia—Science in the Public Interest (ASPI)
Mount Vernon
(606) 256–0077
www.a-spi.org

Barthell Mining Camp
Stearns
(888) 550–5748
www.barthellcoalcamp.com

Battle of Tebbs Bend Civil War Battle Site
Campbellsville
(800) 738–4719
www.campbellsville.com/civilwar

Cumberland Falls
(especially the moonbow)
Corbin
(606) 528–4121
www.corbinkentucky.us/
cumberlandfallsstatepark

Elizabethtown Historic Walking Tours
Thursday night in the summertime
Elizabethtown
(270) 765–2175
www.touretown.com/
costumedwalkingtour

Highland Games and Gathering of Scottish Clans
late May, Glasgow
(270) 651–3141
www.glasgowhighlandgames.com

The Kentucky Museum
Bowling Green
(270) 745–2592
www.wku.edu

Riverview at Hobson Grove
Bowling Green
(270) 843–5565
www.bgky.org/riverview

Wolf Creek National Fish Hatchery
Rowena
(270) 343–3797
www.fws.gov/wolkcreek

Feather Crowns

You can't help liking Curiosity Hall, a narrow hall on one side of Bowling Green's Kentucky Museum filled with unusual relics with unusual ties to Kentucky. The oddities include things such as doll heads supposedly used during World War I to transport spy messages and an item known as a "death crown" or "feather crown," a ring of feathers found inside the pillow of a deceased person. Some say that the crown means that the person has gone to heaven. Others say that the feathers form a ring slowly during one's life, and when the ring is complete, the time has come to die. A friend told me that this belief was so deeply instilled in her during childhood that, despite her logical nature (she's an accountant), she still beats her pillows every morning to fight fate and destroy the feather ring. After a year of marriage, her husband got irritated enough with the habit to ask why in tarnation she did it. When she explained, he answered, "That's pathetic, honey. These are foam pillows."

keep his fingers nimble. The list goes on. Museum hours are 9:30 A.M. to 4 P.M. Monday through Saturday, 1 to 4 P.M. Sunday. Admission is between $2.50 and $5, half price on Sunday. Call (270) 745–2592 for further information (www .wku.edu/library/museum).

Another downtown museum in Bowling Green is ***Riverview at Hobson Grove,*** which grandly overlooks the Barren River. In the late 19th century the river was bustling with commerce, so that homes facing the river had to be worthy of the attention they received. The Hobsons built a magnificent, three-story, brick Italianate mansion, which has been restored and filled with period antiques. Excellent guided tours are given for $5, from 10 A.M. until 4 P.M. Tuesday through Saturday, 1 to 4 P.M. Sunday. Riverview is closed in January. The house's many outstanding features include elaborate hand-painted ceilings in the downstairs parlors, an odd-size "thief's step" on the second floor staircase landing (designed to trip up anyone not familiar with the house), and an unusual "ocular" window beneath the cupola, which was actually part of the ventilation system. In the tour you'll also learn a little about the Hobson family history, a story full of interesting twists and turns, from how the house was saved from destruction during the Civil War to the trapeze that one young Hobson suspended from the ocular window. The house is located at the center of a city park and golf course. To get to Hobson Grove, follow Main Avenue north to the outside of the Victoria Street bypass (Hobson Lane), pass the Delafield School, and watch for the sign. Call (270) 843–5565 for more information (www.bgky.org/riverview).

Mariah's Restaurant, downtown at 801 State Street (270–842–6878; www.mariahs.com), was originally located in Bowling Green's oldest brick house, the circa 1818 home of Mariah Moore, daughter of one of the town's first white settlers. The historic house burned in 1997, and a new structure was erected using some of the original brick. The Southern-style food is very good, and the restaurant is famous for its homemade appetizers, sauces, and more than 30 variations of chicken dishes. Open from 11 A.M. to 10 P.M. Monday through Saturday, 11 A.M. to 9 P.M. Sunday.

Corvette devotees are already aware that General Motors's only Corvette assembly plant in the world is in Bowling Green. The fascinating, hourlong tour of the plant itself is offered at 9 A.M. and 1 P.M. Monday through Friday, except during model changes and on holidays. It's best to call and confirm at (270) 745–8019. Plant tours cost $5 per person. The **National Corvette Museum** at exit 28 off Interstate 65 gives fans a good look at the history and glory of the racy, powerful, best sports car made in America. There are nostalgic displays and lots of souvenirs. One thing sure to spark your curiosity is the building itself, an unusually ugly, asymmetrical, yellow, almost conical structure with a huge red spire. A query about the design to a museum employee elicited the following explanation: "Well, when the museum opened, the newspaper said that some Corvettes of the '50s and '60s had a red cone coming out of the back light. Later, someone told us that from the air, the building looked like part of the dashboard. Finally, we called the architect, who said that neither was the case; he had simply wanted to create a building that was completely different." Which it is. Admission is $8 for adults, $4.50 for ages six to 16, and $6 for ages 55 and older. There's also a one-price family admission of $20. Hours are 8 A.M. to 5 P.M. daily. For museum information, call (270) 781–7973 or (800) 53–VETTE or visit www.corvettemuseum.com.

true blue

Although Kentucky never left the Union during the Civil War, a Confederate capital was established at Bowling Green.

While you're in an automotive mood, take U.S. Highways 68/31W from the Corvette plant through Bowling Green to the intersection with U.S. Highway 231. There you'll find **Holley Performance Products World Headquarters,** a 100-year-old company that makes the carburetors for NASCAR vehicles (as well as privately owned hot rods). A free 45-minute tour shows you the engineering labs, manufacturing processes, and distribution center. Tours are usually given Tuesday and Thursday at 9 A.M. and 1 P.M. but may not be offered at certain times because of production activities. Call (270) 745–9527 for reservations (www.holley.com).

Now that you've properly paid homage to the almighty gas combustion engine, how about a little culture?

There are several downtown sites worth exploring. The **Capitol Arts Center**, 416 East Main Street, is a classic over-the-top art deco movie theater. It's been renovated and now houses the Houchen Art Gallery and is used for all sorts of cultural events throughout the year. Call (270) 782–2787 to ask what's playing or stop by the gallery, Monday through Friday from 9 A.M. to 4 P.M. (www.capitolarts.com).

A local thespian group called the Public Theater of Kentucky performs everything from drama to comedy to musical shows nearby at the **Phoenix Theatre**, 545 Morris Alley. Call (270) 781–6233 or check www.ptkbg.org for more information about shows, which are scheduled from September through June. The Sunburst Youth Theatre does children's plays with child actors and offers a popular Shakespeare summer camp for ages eight to 18.

It's designed for kids, but adults can't help but have fun at **BRIMS, the Barren River Imaginative Museum of Science**, at 1229 Center Street. The museum features some permanent and some rotating exhibits, or rather, experiential zones. Admission is $5 for "overgrown" and $4 for regular children. Hours are Thursday through Saturday from 10 A.M. to 3 P.M., Sunday from 1 to 4 P.M. Call (270) 843–9779 or visit www.brimsbg.org.

Weekdays from 9 A.M. to 3 P.M. you're free to tour the beautiful, Gothic **St. Joseph Catholic Church** at 434 Church Street in Bowling Green. Call (270) 842–2525 for details.

At 401 Kentucky Street, you'll find an unusual combination of interests. The **Depot Branch** of the Bowling Green Public Library shares quarters with what is in the process of becoming a full-fledged railroad museum. The actual depot houses the library branch, the offices of Operation Pride, a downtown revitalization group, and the offices of the Friends of the L&N Depot Inc., the nonprofit organization that owns and renovates the depot and the four railcars next to it. The library has a large early childhood center with lots of educational books and toys that circulate and a computer lab just for kids. There's also a large high-speed Internet lab for public use. They're open daily. And if you happen to need new tires at the tire store next door, you can come read while you wait. You'll immediately notice the four beautiful L&N railcars outside the depot. One is a Chessie caboose, circa 1968. One is a circa 1953 sleeper car called The Towering Pine. One is a gorgeous 48-seat diner car built in 1949 and rebuilt in 1976, called the Duncan Hines. And one is the 1911 Presidential Car, the personal car for the president of the L&N Railroad. Currently the cars can only be toured by appointment (by groups of 10 or more with at least a week's advance notice) or during one of two festivals held on site—the Duncan Hines Festival in mid-August or Rail Fest in mid-December when Santa Claus pays a visit. A full museum and gift shop are in the works, so call Operation Pride for current information at (270) 745–0090.

Another interesting Bowling Green attraction is *Lost River Cave and Valley,* where the cave is said to have the shortest, deepest river in the world and the largest cave opening east of the Mississippi River. The cave's fascinating history includes use by Native Americans as long ago as 7,500 BC, operation as the nation's only "cave mill" in the late 1700s, and use as an underground night club from the 1930s through the 1960s. Bank robber Jesse James is rumored to have hidden in the cave after robbing a bank in Russellville in 1868. A citizens' group, the Friends of Lost River, led the cave's revival as a tourist attraction. The group is exploring the possibility of restoring the waterwheel. In the meantime you can take a cave tour that begins with a short historical walk to the cave opening and concludes with a 25-minute boat tour into the cave. Before or after your tour you can explore 2 miles of hiking trails and a butterfly garden. Lost River Cave and Valley is open year-round, with tours daily, though the hours may vary seasonally. Admission to the cave tour is

Adventures in Good Eating

Duncan Hines is truly a household name, even today, 50 years after the food label was established. Today, however, the name brings to mind processed foods and, the truth be told, culinary mediocrity. Originally, however, the power of the name Duncan Hines was comparable to the power of the current star-rating system used to classify restaurants and hotels. Mr. Duncan Hines, who was born in Bowling Green in 1880, had a celebrated reputation for recommending eateries. As a young man he'd been a traveling salesman and had to eat out often. Unsanitary conditions at roadside food stands, which were ubiquitous at the turn of the 20th century, caused deadly food poisoning. As he traveled, Hines made careful notes about places that met his standards of quality.

In the early 1930s Hines and his wife traveled extensively in the United States and made a list of "superior eating places," which they mailed to friends as a Christmas present in 1935. The list was wildly popular and resulted in a book the next year titled *Adventures in Good Eating*. In 1938 they published a companion book of recommended inns called *Lodging for a Night*. A sign in front of any such establishment stating "recommended by Duncan Hines" almost guaranteed the business success with travelers.

Bowling Green hosts an annual Duncan Hines Festival in honor of this native gourmet every June. You can also drive the *Duncan Hines Scenic Byway,* beginning with a site on U.S. Highway 31 marking the Hines's former home and office. (Ask for a map at the visitor center, 352 Three Springs Road, off Interstate 65 at exit 22, or call 270–782–0800.)

between $10.50 and $15. Call (866) 274–2283 or (270) 393–0077 or visit www
.lostrivercave.com. The cave is located in Bowling Green at the intersection of
US 31W (Nashville Road) and Cave Mill Road.

If you drive the Duncan Hines Scenic Byway, you'll go through a little
town called **Smith's Grove,** 14 miles north of Bowling Green, where a short
walking tour of the 19th Century District includes a stop at the Smith's Grove
cemetery, where Patrick Henry's sister is buried. (Get a tour map at almost any
local business.) In Smith's Grove follow Sixth Street to **Cave Spring Farm Bed
and Breakfast and Caverns,** a grand antebellum house, farm, schoolhouse,
two log cabins, 1840s servants quarters, a large forested bird sanctuary, and
private cave that is 1¼ miles with spectacular 55-foot-high ceilings and prehistoric drawings on the walls that earned it the name Indian Mud Glyph Cave.
Cave tours are offered daily at 10 A.M., noon, 2 P.M., and 4 P.M. except Tuesday.
Admission is charged for nonfarm guests. Call (270) 563–6941 or visit www
.bbonline.com/ky/cavespring.

In its heyday, Woodbury was a busy little town on the Green River at the
site of Lock and Dam Number 4. After the 1841 log structure washed away in
1965, the local historical society developed Woodbury into a museum complex. What was formerly the lockkeeper's home has been transformed into the
Butler County Park and Green River Museum (108 North Church Street),
a visual history lesson about the Woodbury area with an emphasis on the
riverboat era (1840–1930). The museum is under renovation and will include
artifacts from the prehistoric era as well. Open hours vary I'd suggest making
a trip out even if the museum is closed because the site itself is beautiful and
interesting. In addition to all the buildings, there is a very early cemetery and
a dramatic overlook of the Green River and the remains of the dam and 1839
lock. To get there from Bowling Green, take the Natcher Parkway north to the
first Morgantown exit; turn right off the ramp and go into town; turn right on
Highway 403 and go 4.5 miles until you see signs for the park.

North of Woodbury on Highway 403, high on a bluff over the Green
River, is **Morgantown,** a river-dependent port town in the 19th Century District. Every Fourth of July the town celebrates with the Green River Catfish
Festival, downtown in the municipal park. River commerce brought wealth
to the town late in the 19th century, evidenced by some of the remaining
architecture, such as the **Hammers House,** a big white house with a bright
red roof at the corner of Main and Porter Streets, which was built in 1890 and
listed on the National Register of Historic Places. You can tour the house and
see the original oak stairway, "riverboat carpenter trim," and Tiffany glass.
By appointment only. Call (270) 526–4325. Make sure to ask the Hammers
House's owner about other local stories; she'll point out the house where,

during the Civil War, General Morgan spent the night and hung his flag out the bedroom window.

If you happen to be in Morgantown over the Fourth of July, join in a real small town treat, the big catfish fry in the city park.

Note: Keep an eye on the earth's undulations along the Green River near Morgantown, because there are supposed to be numerous ancient Native American burial mounds there.

If you travel northeast of Bowling Green, you will be in some of the most spectacular cave country in the world. Second to the Kentucky Derby, **Mammoth Cave National Park** is the best nationally known tourist attraction in the state, and for that reason, travelers can get information about cave history and trips anywhere within a hundred-mile radius. While definitely a well-beaten path (about 2.1 million people visit every year, and during the summer months it can be incredibly crowded), Mammoth Cave does have lesser-known aspects. Explore the cave in an old-fashioned way on a Gothic Lantern Tour. Or take a Wild Cave Tour and crawl through tight passages. Whatever tour you decide to take, if you're coming in the summer, especially on weekends, it's a good idea to reserve your cave tour well in advance. Call (270) 758–2328 or (800) 967–2283 or visit www.nps.gov/maca.

Aboveground there are more than 70 miles of wonderful hiking trails. Visit the **Old Guides Cemetery,** near the Heritage Trail near the Cave's Historic Entrance. Among those buried here is Stephen Bishop, the cave's preeminent

Kilroy's Ancestors

The **Old Simpson County Jailer's Residence** in Franklin was being renovated, and since it was expected that little if any original plaster could be repaired, workers weren't being terribly careful as they ripped out old paneling and wallpaper. Until they found, in a second-story room of the building, something that made everyone stop and stare in astonishment: drawings, possibly in charcoal, some almost life size, portraying Civil War soldiers, both Union and Confederate, including a portrait of the famous Confederate raider Gen. John Hunt Morgan. Though it may never be known exactly who created these sketches, it is known that the building was occupied by Union troops and used to house Confederate prisoners of war, and it is thought that what is left on the walls is authentic and rare Civil War graffiti. The building, now home to the **Simpson County Archives and Museum,** is at 206 North College Street, about 21 miles south of Bowling Green. Hours are Monday through Friday from 9 A.M. to 4 P.M. and Saturday from 10 A.M. to 2 P.M. Admission is free. This is an excellent resource for researching family and local history. Call (270) 586–4228 for more information (www.simpsoncountyarchives.com).

explorer in the 1800s. Bishop, like many of the people who helped map underground passages and served as tour guides in antebellum days, was a slave. His owner purchased Mammoth Cave around 1838. Bishop's many discoveries led to national renown and resulted in his freedom in 1856. He hoped to purchase the freedom of his wife and son and emigrate to Liberia but was unable to do so before his death in 1857. Mammoth Cave is open every day but Christmas.

The *American Cave Museum and Hidden River Cave* on Main Street in *Horse Cave* is an environmental education museum developed by the American Cave Conservation Association Inc. The association's worthy mission is to educate people, especially those who live on karst lands, about how the land works and about how our actions affect the health of the system. Venial sins like dumping trash in sinkholes become mortal sins in karst areas, where the whole groundwater system can easily be contaminated. Just the entrance to Hidden River Cave is accessible through the museum (for the first time since 1943). Previously, no one wanted to go near the cave and its underground stream because it carried the unpleasant stench of raw sewage.

Other exhibits in the museum include a whole wall display devoted to bats, a large cross section of a karst region, and stories and artifacts from mines, bootlegging operations, early tourist endeavors, prehistoric shelters, and ceremonial sites. For more information contact ACCA, Main and Cave Streets, P.O. Box 409, Horse Cave 42749, or call (270) 786–1466. Hours are 9 A.M. to 5 P.M. daily, with extended hours in summer (www.cavern.org).

Kentucky Repertory Theatre is one of only eight professional theaters in rural America. From late June through October, the company stages six productions per season. The range of genres is broad—Shakespeare, modern comedies, thrillers, and experimental theater by regional playwrights—and the theater thereby maintains a loyal local audience in addition to tourists. Performances are Tuesday through Saturday evening and Saturday and Sunday afternoon at the large open-thrust stage in downtown Horse Cave at 101 East Main Street. Call (270) 786–2177 or (800) 342–2177 or visit www.kentuckyrep.org.

After spelunking or theatergoing, you'll probably be irresistibly tempted to retire to your own personal concrete wigwam motel room, complete with rustic hickory furniture, color television, and fake smoke hole and tent flaps at *Wigwam Village.* Take exit 53 off I-65 and turn left; at the second stoplight, head north on US 31W and go 1 mile until you see a semicircle of 15 white wigwams with a red zigzag design on the side. In the center is the 52-foot-high office wigwam, all built in 1937, way before the Interstate existed and before concrete construction was very sophisticated. Before Americans got their kicks on the now-legendary Route 66, these maverick lodgings rose boldly from the

Funky Cave Projects and Artifacts

To date, the navigable cave system in the Mammoth Cave area is more than 300 miles long. The cave has provoked some odd projects, such as an underground hospital for tuberculosis victims. The cool, clean cave air would have been good for any victim of lung disease, but smoke from the cooking fires accumulated in the chamber where they lived and killed them quickly. What the doctors needed was more basic than holistic thinking—they needed common sense. Other cave project artifacts include leaching vats, which remain from the time when saltpeter (sodium nitrate or potassium nitrate) was extracted for making gunpowder during the War of 1812. Also make sure you hear the whole story of explorer Floyd Collins. For many years his casket was on display in the Crystal Onyx Cave, to which he had been searching for a new entrance when he died. In 1929, when local cave owners were competing fiercely for tourists, someone stole Collins's body and dumped it in the Green River because it was a popular attraction. His remains have since been reinterred in a less public place.

flat plains of south-central Kentucky. In 1935 an entrepreneur named Frank A. Redford built the first Wigwam Village in nearby Horse Cave and patented his design. The Cave City village was built in 1937, and later five more villages went up from Alabama to California. Only three remain. The other two are in Holbrook, Arizona, and Riallto, California. At the Cave City village, however, from March through November you can still sleep in a concrete tepee with original hickory and cane furnishings. Each has a private bath. Rates are very reasonable—$35 to $70 a night—but if you want to lodge in one of these little gems (now Historic Landmarks), especially on a weekend, reserve it well in advance. The main building, which houses a gift shop, stands 52 feet high and is made of 38 tons of concrete and 13 tons of steel. Call (270) 773–3381 or check the Web site, www.wigwamvillage.com.

In *Brownsville*, in the Green River Amphitheatre (call the Anderson County Tourism Office at 800–624–8687), 5 miles west of the park near where Highways 70 and 259 merge, an outdoor drama called *The Floyd Collins Story* is performed every Friday and Saturday night at dusk from late June through August. (Call 270–524–2892 for this year's dates.) Dr. Middleton buys the winning baskets and displays them at his office at 117 West South Street, along with a wonderful collection of quilts and other local crafts. His goal is to own a basket made by every maker in the area and his extensive collection has made his office almost like a local art museum. The story is based on the 1925 news event of the year, when the legendary cave explorer Floyd Collins managed to dislodge a ceiling rock and get pinned underneath it as he was entering Sand Cave. This drama is about the attempted rescue of Collins and his consequent death. More history about Collins and his death is found just by the main entrance to the Mammoth Cave National Park on Highway 70, in the ***Wayfarer Bed and Breakfast and Floyd Collins Museum*** on the site of the 1930s Mammoth Cave Souvenir Shop. Owners Becky and Larry Bull remodeled the upstairs for overnight guests who want a quiet getaway. Although each guest room has a private bath, there are no TVs or telephones in the bedrooms. Stop by to see the museum from 9 A.M. to 5 P.M. daily (admission charged). Overnight rates range from $75 to $125 and include a full breakfast. Sand Cave is just a few feet away, and you are right on the boundary of Mammoth Cave National Park. The Bulls can also get you set up for a canoeing or kayaking excursion on Green River. Day and overnight trips are offered. Call (270) 773–3366 for information about the museum, the bed-and-breakfast, or the river excursions with Mammoth Cave Canoe and Kayak (877–59–CANOE; www.mammothcavecanoe-k.com).

Just a little south of the National Park, in Park City, on Highway 255 off I–65 at exit 48, are some of the most beautiful caves in the system that are open to the public. The ***Diamond Caverns*** are particularly known for their spectacular colors. Admission is $16 adults, $8 children, and it's open daily from 9 A.M. until 5 P.M. in the summer and until 4 P.M. in the winter. Call (270) 749–2233 for information (www.diamondcaverns.com).

At the Hart of a Tradition

If you like handmade baskets, be sure to visit Munfordville in Hart County, not far from Mammoth Cave. Basket making has long been a tradition in this part of the state. By the mid-1800s numerous families in the western Hart County community of Cub Run were producing baskets and using them to barter for groceries and other goods. Shopkeepers in turn sold the baskets to customers or to traveling peddlers, and so the area's reputation grew. In the 20th century, when U.S. Highway 31W brought automobiles in force through the area, the basket makers set up stands along the road.

Although basket making in the area declined after the advent of the Interstate, in recent years the Mammoth Cave area basket industry has been revitalized. Many contemporary basket makers in the local Basket Guild create baskets in the traditional south-central Kentucky style, using white oak and making the bottommost ribs of the basket wide and flat with smaller, more rounded top ribs. Other novelty styles have also evolved; for example, basket maker Lestel Childress sometimes makes whimsical flower stand baskets, a style designed by his grandmother, Let Thompson.

In the late 1990s a family practitioner in Munfordville, Dr. James Middleton, started a basket-making contest at the Hart County Fair, usually held in late June or early July.

Kentucky was a state deeply divided during the Civil War, and exhibits at the ***Hart County Historic Society and Museum*** (109 Main Street; 270–524–0101; www.historicalhart.org) in Munfordville, 3 miles north of Horse Cave, demonstrate this point well. Among the Civil War artifacts at the museum are items belonging to two Hart County residents who fought in the conflict. Confederate general Simon Bolivar Buckner and Union major general Thomas Wood were childhood friends and West Point classmates who later found themselves fighting on opposite sides of the conflict. The Munfordville battleground site is being preserved by the county historical society at the Battle for the Bridge Preserve. Civil War reenactors perform the battle in meticulously designed costumes in mid-September, after Labor Day; the historic battle occurred on September 16, 1862. A museum staff member can guide you there. Museum hours are 9 A.M. to 1 P.M. Tuesday through Friday and 10 A.M. to 4 P.M. Saturday.

Several Amish communities are located in Hart County, and in summer months, you can buy fresh produce and other items on the courthouse lawn. Year-round, it's worth a drive out Logdson Valley Road to Anna's Kitchen. Anna Miller makes delicious jellies and relishes; stop by any day except Sunday. There's a sign by the road—just knock on the door. Call (270) 524–0820 for information.

Lost and Found

Unless I'm in a big hurry, I rarely worry about getting lost, because I know that almost any Kentucky road is going to end up somewhere interesting. And if it doesn't, well, you just turn around. So I wasn't too concerned that my directions to the Amish store near Munfordville that April Saturday were somewhat vague. "It's outside of town a little piece," said the quilter who told me about the store.

"I'm not sure which store you mean, but if you turn left at the yellow flashing light and head out of town, then turn left again after a ways, you'll come to an area where a lot of Amish people live," offered a gas station attendant. Now, that was something to go on. When I saw the sign at Logsdon Valley Road for Yoder's Harness Shop, I figured that had to be the turn.

"Look! Something's going on over there," my travel companion exclaimed. Indeed, there was. Dozens of vans, trucks—and even more horse-drawn carriages—were parked in a field, and hundreds of people, Amish and "English" of all ages, were gathered under a tent. It turned out to be a consignment auction to benefit the Amish community school, with everything from handmade bookshelves to goats going on the block. In between bidding you could fill up on just-grilled hamburgers and homemade baked goods. Best bad directions I ever had.

East of Bowling Green, the next sizable town is *Glasgow,* host of the *Highland Games and Gathering of Scottish Clans,* held near the end of May or in early June at Barren River Lake State Resort Park, east of Glasgow on US 31. The games begin with a musical extravaganza called the Tattoo, then clan and society members get together for a Tartan Ball and Scottish Country Dancing. Last but not least exciting are the athletic and battle-ax competitions, which originated as martial exercises under King Malcolm Canmore in Scotland around 1060. It's amazing to watch these manliest of manly men wearing skirts (ahem, kilts) while "tossing" logs the size of telephone poles. The best known aspect of the gathering, however, is the Ceilidh, another set of musical performances by American and international musicians—praised by Fiona Ritchie of National Public Radio's *Thistle and Shamrock* show. For more information, contact Glasgow Highland Games Inc. 119 East Main Street, Glasgow 42141, or call (270) 651–3141 or visit www.glasgowhighlandgames.com.

The *Hall Place Bed and Breakfast* is a handsome place to spend the night and have a big country-ham breakfast. From downtown Glasgow take US 31E south (South Green Street) for 1½ blocks and look for the sign on the right. Although the house was built in 1852, the three bed-and-breakfast rooms have modern, private baths, wireless Internet, and full breakfast. Rates range from $85 to $120 per night. Call (270) 651–3176 for more information (www .hallplacebedandbreakfast.com).

trueblue

Munfordville is locally referred to as Concrete Alley because it is the source of 10 percent of all commercially fabricated concrete yard-art statues made in the eastern United States.

From Glasgow take Highway 63 south to *Tompkinsville,* the Monroe County seat. Take Highway 90 to Highway 163 south of town for about 3 miles to the *Old Mulkey Meeting House.* Built in 1804 during a religious revival that swept through the region, it is not only the oldest log meeting house in the state but also probably the only example of highly symbolic log architecture. The building's twelve corners represent the twelve apostles, and the three doors are meant to be reminders of the Trinity. Daniel Boone's oldest sister, Hannah, is buried in the cemetery alongside other early settlers.

Living-History Country

"The pause that refreshes will make husband more helpful." What pause? Every experienced American consumer knows that it's Coca-Cola; the famous phrase was printed on a drink tray in 1934, when a Coke cost 5 cents. Over the years—from the early days when it was advertised as a mouthwash (and contained a small quantity of cocaine, an ingredient eliminated in 1905) to the modern era of "Classic Coke"—the famous beverage has been advertised on everything from posters to pencils to toys.

Elizabethtown is home to the world's largest private collection of Coca-Cola memorabilia, owned by the Schmidt family, who for decades owned the local bottling plant and set up a museum on the second floor. After their retirement, *Schmidt's Coca-Cola Museum* closed for a while, but it has reopened at 109 Buffalo Creek Drive (270–234–1100; www.schmidtmuseum .com) in a 32,000-square-foot museum complex all dedicated to that dastardly beverage! If you love Coke, you'll love this place. If you don't, think like a cultural anthropologist and take it all in. After all, it is America's (the world's?) most famous drink. The slick metallic building features a huge sculpted hand bursting through the exterior side wall with a bottle of Coke clenched tightly in its grasp. The collection includes a vast number of the famous serving trays and explanations of their value as collectibles. There are also other interesting items like bottles, toys, neon and metal signs, vending machines, and antique bottling equipment. And you'll learn every manner of Coke factoid you can imagine. For example, the famously shaped glass bottle was meant to look like a curvaceous woman's body and was called the "hobble-skirt" in its original 1913 form. A pharmacist from Atlanta and former Confederate captain, Dr. John Styth Pemberton, was the inventor of the original formula, which he called "the ideal brain tonic." Originally it contained wine, though he changed the kicker to extract of cola nut. His bookkeeper, Frank Robinson, came up with the name Coca-Cola and the Spencerian script that is now a recognizable trademark in any language worldwide. To get there, take exit 94 off I–65, turn right on Buffalo Creek Drive and watch for the signs. Admission is between $2 and $5. Hours are 10 A.M. to 6 P.M. Monday through Saturday and 1 to 5 P.M. on Sunday.

You'll also likely find an antique or collectible car on display at the tourism bureau as advertising for another local attraction, *Swope's Cars of Yesteryear Museum.* Bill Swope, a retired longtime auto dealer in town, has a collection of about 30 vehicles from the 1920s to the 1960s. You'll find the rest of them on display at 1100 North Dixie Highway. It's next door to the Swope dealership now run by Bill's son. The free museum is open from 10 A.M. to 5 P.M. Monday through Saturday. Call (270) 763–6175 for more information (www.swopemuseum.com).

Polarities can be wonderful teachers. Leave the Coke memorabilia and old cars and please, please, please take time to get an education at the *Emma Reno Connor Black History Gallery.* Go southeast of the courthouse on

And on That Farm She Had a . . .

I live on a farm, and people always ask, "How many animals do you raise there?" I often answer, "Several thousand" because, in addition to raising vegetable gardens, fruit and nut orchards, milk goats, chickens, ducks, a few cattle, a horse, and a passel of dogs, we're beekeepers. The bees are the only livestock that don't need fences or daily feeding. They're not pets in that I don't have an emotional relationship with them, but they are producers of the very best sweetener in the world, and they pollinate many of the plants we raise for food. We are at least the third generation in my family to buy our bees and beekeeping supplies from the **Walter T. Kelley Co. Inc.,** in **Clarkson,** about 40 miles southwest of Elizabethtown, or 4 miles east of Leitchfield on U.S. Highway 62. (The bees come through the U.S. Mail as buzzing masses in screen-and-wood boxes, and the post office calls at 5 A.M. for us to "come and get these durn things.") This company was started some 75 years ago and has a huge national customer base. It continues at its original location, where wooden beehives, supers, and frames are manufactured; beeswax is processed into comb foundation; and all sorts of other supplies are made, from stainless-steel tanks and centrifugal honey extractors to protective coveralls. Kelley's can also coordinate the sale and shipping of the gentle and hard-working three-banded Italian bees in swarms (sold by the pound) and their queens, all of which come from its bee yards deeper in the South. Visitors are welcome to stop by the office and see live bees in a glass-sided observation hive and to purchase honey and supplies. Beekeepers and educational groups can schedule full tours of the plant (by appointment only). A guided beekeeping museum is planned for the future.

Call or stop by Monday through Friday between 7:30 A.M. and 5 P.M. (except for lunch hour at noon), or on Saturday from 7:30 A.M. to noon. Call (270) 242–2012 or toll-free (800) 233–2899 for more information (www.kelleybees.com).

East Dixie Avenue, veer left onto Hawkins Drive, and look immediately for a white stucco house on the right with a sign that says BLACK HISTORY GALLERY. This was the childhood home of the late Emma Reno Connor, a teacher who recognized a disgraceful dearth of information about the lives and accomplishments of African Americans. She supplemented her lesson plans with pictures, articles, and stories of African Americans and later organized these teaching materials into museum displays.

An amateur museum that is composed of well-organized cutouts from magazines, original pen-and-ink portraits of great people, poems by Ms. Connor, and newspaper articles, this is also a powerful place full of love, knowledge, and opportunities to learn about the African-American experience. You'll enjoy learning about the lives and accomplishments of Satchmo (Louis Armstrong), Josephine Baker, Langston Hughes, Sojourner Truth, Gwendolyn Brooks, Frederick Douglass, and Martin Luther King Jr., to name a few outstanding people. Hours are noon to 5 P.M. Saturday and Sunday or as posted. On weekdays make an appointment with Charles Connor, Emma's widower, at (270) 769–5204 or with her sister Ruby Williams at (270) 765–7653. A tour of the gallery with Mr. Connor brings nationally known figures to life, and Ms. Williams knows the personal histories of local heroes. Together they could change your life. Also see www.touretown.com/blackhistorygallery.

Many towns of historic significance offer walking tours of their downtowns, but few resurrect the characters in living color. In the summer try the **Elizabethtown Historic Walking Tours,** during which you meet and see a brief "performance" by Sarah Bush Johnston Lincoln (Abe's stepmother), P. T. Barnum, Jenny Lind, Carry Nation, and eight other historical figures portrayed by local people dressed in period costumes who are well versed in their figure's history. Carry Nation, for example, runs down the street with a Bible in one hand and her famous hatchet in the other to shut down Jim Neighbor's bar. (In real life she was prevented from destroying the joint when someone knocked her out with a bar stool.) The tour covers 25 buildings and takes about an hour. Free tours are scheduled for Thursday at 7 P.M. and start in the public town square. Call (270) 765–2175 or (800) 437–0092.

The **Brown-Pusey House** (270–765–2515; www.touretown.com/brown puseyhouse) was Elizabethtown's first public lodging house for travelers. You can't stay overnight now, but you can take a free guided tour of the very stately Georgian colonial building. Gen. George Custer and his wife stayed here sometime in the 1870s. A genealogy library is also housed here. Hours are 10 A.M. to 4 P.M. Tuesday through Saturday.

Elizabethtown has another unusual seasonal event worth the trip to town. From the Wednesday before Thanksgiving until January 2 every year, Freeman Lake Park (directly behind the Coca-Cola plant on US 31W North) is transformed into a glittering wonderland during **Christmas in the Park.** Cut your headlights and take the luminaria-lined drive around the lake past more than 70 lighted Christmas displays built and donated by local businesses, including a huge swan floating in the water and Santa in a boat. The show is on from dusk until 11 P.M. nightly.

For mountain-bike enthusiasts, the Kentucky Mountain Bike Association and the Kentucky Wheelmen have developed a nice 6-mile trail system near a town called **Youngers Creek** (www.kymba.org/trails). Additional trails and a BMX-style course are planned for the field beside the pavilion and parking area so that younger kids and families can have a place to ride without having to climb the big hill. To get there take exit 10 off Bluegrass Parkway and turn north onto Highway 52. Next take a left on Highway 62 and another left onto

Old Youngers Creek Road (Highway 583). Look for Miller Road and turn right. Watch for the parking area for the trail.

From June through September in the Freeman Lake Park you can visit the **Lincoln Heritage House,** which Thomas Lincoln, Abe's father, a carpenter by trade, helped to construct, and the **Sarah Bush Johnston Lincoln Memorial,** an early-19th-century cabin that re-creates the home of the woman who married Thomas Lincoln and became Abe's stepmother when the president-to-be was only ten years old. Nearby there is also a renovated 1892 one-room schoolhouse. Hours are 10 A.M. to 5 P.M. daily during the season. Call (800) 437–0092 for information (http://www .touretown.com/sarahbush).

If you didn't get enough of old cars at Swopes, head northwest of Elizabethtown on Highway 1600 (Ring Road) to Rineyville. At Rineyville Sandblasting you'll find the **Model "A" Ford Museum,** a collection of everything from coupes to

true blue

The Squire Pates House on Highway 334 near Lewisport was the site of Abraham Lincoln's first trial. He defended himself against charges of operating a ferry across the Ohio River without a license.

antique oil cans. There are about 40 unrestored Fords from 1928 to 1931. The museum is open by chance or by appointment (call Ernest, the proprietor, at 270–862–4671), and admission is $2 for adults, $1.50 for children.

Take Highway 220 northeast of Rineyville and get on US 31W to reach Fort Knox Military Reservation, with a couple of attractions worth seeing. To America's World War II generation there was perhaps no greater hero than Gen. George S. Patton. The **Patton Museum of Cavalry and Armor** (502–624–6350; www.generalpatton.org) at Fort Knox was dedicated in the general's honor on Memorial Day 1949, four years after Patton's death. In addition to a section dedicated to Patton's life, the museum includes a display of tanks and a variety of other military items—even a section of the Berlin Wall. The museum is on Fayette Avenue near the Chaffee Avenue entrance to the base. It's open weekdays year-round from 9 A.M. to 4:30 P.M. It opens at 10 A.M. on weekends, closing at 6 P.M. May through September and at 4 P.M. October through April. Admission is free.

Not far from the Patton Museum is the **United States Treasury Department Gold Depository,** America's "Gold Vault." Although no visitors are allowed inside, you can view the building from the outside and imagine the inside, where the nation's cache of pure gold bars is stored in a two-level vault protected by a 20-ton door and armed guards.

Right at the northern edge of the Fort Knox Military Reservation in a deep bend of the Ohio River is the little town of **West Point.** Ask any local shop

trueblue

The state bird of Kentucky is the cardinal.

owner for a map showing the path of a walking tour that directs you to more than 20 buildings on the National Register of Historic Places. On the south side of town is **Fort Duffield,** a park site where Union soldiers were stationed and built earthworks in 1861. On Wilson Road, south of US 31, are two hiking trails. The Bridges of the Past trail is a 1-mile walk along the old Louisville and Nashville turnpike that takes you by three pre–Civil War stone bridges. On request you can be guided through the area by an interpreter. The walk takes about an hour. Call (800) 334–7540. Originating nearby, the Tioga Falls Hiking Trail is a 2-mile circuit that crosses into areas sometimes used for military training. (The trail is closed in that event.)

Excessive exposure to military equipment is bound to make a soul world weary. To restore some sense of faith in the world's good things, try a hike in the 730-acre **Vernon-Douglas State Nature Preserve,** located 15 miles east of Elizabethtown just off Highway 583. In the early spring the woods here are full of delicate, breathtaking wildflowers (www.naturepreserves.ky.gov/stewardship/vernondouglas).

A great place for lunch or dinner is south of Elizabethtown in a historic little railroad community called **Glendale.** Go south of town on US 31W for about 5 miles, then take Highway 222 west to Glendale. In the early 1970s, the old Glendale hardware store, which is smack-dab next to the railroad tracks on Main Street, was transformed into the **Whistle Stop Restaurant** (270–369–8586), where they now serve really, really good Southern food for reasonable prices in a cozy, depot atmosphere. Famous for its open-faced hot brown sandwich—a mountain of roast beef on bread, smothered with a rich cheese sauce—the restaurant's menu ranges from homemade soups to ham

The Heck with Straight Lines

Notice on your map how the Kentucky border bulges just a bit to the south in this area? Legend has it that when the border was surveyed and this land was to be relegated to Tennessee, the owner of this land, a farmer named Sanford Duncan, invited the surveying team to a party at the Duncan Tavern (about 6 miles south of Franklin), a popular spot for travelers on the Louisville-to-Nashville trek because of the fine food and Kentucky liquor served there. The surveyors were so appreciative (and drunk) that they agreed to survey all of Duncan's land into Kentucky. The heck with straight lines.

and asparagus rolls to fried chicken and taco salad. Desserts clarify the meaning of sin. Hours are 11 A.M. to 9 P.M. Tuesday through Saturday.

All of Glendale seems to be in a time warp. Though the village is small, it has a functional general store and several antiques and gift shops. During the first weekend in December, every building is decked out for a ***Christmas in the Country*** event, open to the public. Or come to Glendale on the third Saturday in October for the ***Glendale Crossing Festival***, when the spirit of the old-time trading days pervades the town.

In the midst of this pretend atmosphere is an 1870s farmhouse with a big, inviting front porch. This is the ***Petticoat Junction Bed & Breakfast*** (223 High Street; 270–369–8604; www.historicglendale.com). Six overnight rooms are available, three of which have private baths (one bath has an old-time claw-foot tub and the other two state-of-the-art Jacuzzis). Two rooms are in a small, private cottage out back. Rates range from $85 to $95.

Another place that works to generate Glendale's nostalgic charm is ***Tony York's on Maine***, owned and operated by chef Tony York, which serves gourmet food in a supper-club setting. The current building was reconstructed after a 2008 fire. The building had been an old farmhouse dating to the early 1900s that was moved to the site by Sonny Hatfield after the original train depot burned down in the 1930s. (The original train station may have been one of the many that were robbed by Jesse James.) The diverse menu is a tribute to Kentucky traditions, as is the Depot's motto: "Never rush a supper-club experience—we won't." The motto seems to prove true the old joke that if you want someone from the south to hurry up, you are just gonna have to wait a minute. The Depot is located downtown on Main Street next to the railroad tracks and serves lunch and dinner daily. You can call (270) 369–6000 for reservations or more information.

For Amish crafts and goods including quilts, baskets, and flavor-packed fruit preserves, watch for horse-drawn wagons set up as roadside shops in and around town. Whether or not you are interested in buying, just stop in and enjoy a lazy stroll under the shade trees downtown. Or if you prefer to stroll on the Web, have a look at www.historicglendale.com.

Just down the road in Sonora is the Thurman Phillips Historical Home, which now houses ***Claudia's Tea Room and Guest House***. The Victorian–era home was originally built in 1897 by Josiah Phillips Jr. and was recently restored by its current owners, the Thurman family. The Thurmans have done an excellent job maintaining the home's stately look by filling the house with antiques, including an impressive private library of antiquarian books. Although the home is reason enough to visit, a tea at Claudia's is not a thing to be missed. Come hungry because "tea" involves a nine-course feast of finger foods and sweets! All the goodies are made by chef York at The Depot (above), but the recipes are said to have come from the Elmwood Inn in Perryville (now closed). Seatings are at 1 P.M. and 3 P.M. Thursday through Saturday. There are no clear markings on the building and no signs advertising its services. Nonetheless, Claudia's serves tea to thousands of folks who are in the know every year. In addition to delectable food and teas, the home offers seven bedrooms for overnight accommodations and can be rented for large parties and receptions. Call (270) 949–1880, www.claudiatearoom.com for tea or lodging and event reservations.

About seven miles outside of Sonora on the corner of U.S. Highway 720 and Melrose is the *Flint Hill General Store,* also known as Cardin's Grocery (270–369–7633). Thought to be one of the oldest working general stores in Kentucky, Flint Hill is located in a former one-room schoolhouse circa 1900. Although it doesn't look like much from the road and only boasts a single gas pump, the place is almost always packed with folks trying to pick up a few essentials for the kitchen or to catch the latest gossip from the store's owners and operators Jo Ann and Wesley Cardin, who have been at the heart of this hive of activity for almost 35 years. Speaking of hives, note the 200 hornet nests that hang from the ceiling (all fortunately unoccupied) or just drop some peanuts in your Coke and kick your feet up. Either way, the Cardins will be happy to see you.

You've always tried to avoid places that are lame, but once you hear this, you'll want to set foot in a place that's limp—well, that's called Limp. From the Elizabethtown or Glendale area, take U.S. Highway 62 south. Just past Big Clifty, take Highway 720 to the right (north), then Highway 920 (Salt River Road) to the right and look for the *Three Springs Farm Orchard* on your left. This fruitful place is the home of Dale and Yvonne DePoyster and their family. The DePoysters grow all kinds of beautiful flowers as well as delicious things to eat, from berries in the summer to apples, pears, cider, and pumpkins in the fall. The greenhouse at the farm is open in early spring for flowers and plants. To enjoy the rest of the harvest, visit the DePoysters' country-style store, Three Springs Farm Store (270–360–0644) in Leitchfield. The store is located at 618 East Dixie in Elizabethtown. Hours are 9 A.M. to 6 P.M. Monday through Saturday and, in April, May, September, and October, noon to 5 P.M. Sunday. Call the store to see what's in season.

The *Official Kentucky State Championship Old-time Fiddling Contest* is an event for beginner and virtuoso musicians or for anyone who just likes to listen to bluegrass music. Fifteen to 20 different contests, including harmonica, flat-top guitar, mandolin, banjo, bluegrass band, and even jig dancing, are held annually at *Rough River State Dam Park* in northern Grayson

County during the third week in July. This is a recommended place to have a breakdown—take your choice of "Tennessee Breakdown," "North Carolina Breakdown," "Straw Breakdown," or "Cheatum County Breakdown." When the region's hottest fiddlers compete in the Governor's Cup Fiddle Off, you'll want to cry at the music's sweetness—but the wind from the musicians' lightning quick bow action will dry your tears before they can hit your cheeks. Camping is available, and folks are invited to come early for the informal jam sessions that go on all week prior to the main contest. For more information about the park or the contest, call (270) 257–2311 or check www.kentuckyfiddler.com. Also ask about the park's other special events such as the "Dulcibrrr" in February, a weekend for fans of lap and hammered dulcimers.

In the town of *Leitchfield,* 18 miles southeast of the State Resort Park, you can make an appointment to tour the *Jack Thomas House,* the oldest house in the county and a grand Federal-style mansion. The original two-room house, built in 1815, became the south wing of the expanded building. Tours are given Tuesday through Friday from 10 A.M. to 4 P.M. Admission is charged. For information and tours, call the Grayson County Historic Society at (270) 230–8989 or check the Web site, www.graysoncokyhistsoc.org.

Not everything in the area is caught in the past. John and Lisa Brittain of the *Nolin River Nut Tree Nursery* have become famous for performing nutty modern-day miracles. Of the more than 100 varieties of nut trees grown in their nursery, most are grafted. You're not supposed to be able to graft most nut trees because the sap tends to run so much that the grafts don't take—that is, heal and fuse to the rooted tree—yet these growers make expert use of an obscure method called a coin purse graft. They also are able to dig and ship nut trees up to 5 feet tall—that's 4 feet taller than the "rules" claim to be possible without fatally damaging the taproot.

The Brittains can probably answer any question you have about nut trees and sell you just about any variety your heart desires. They now have more than 175 varieties available, plus 15 kinds of persimmons and four varieties of pawpaw. For between $16 and $68 per tree, you can choose from a number of walnuts, heartnuts, butternuts, chestnuts, hickories, pecans, and hicans (a cross between hickory and pecan). Order as far in advance of spring as possible, and call if you plan to visit. For a catalog, write Nolin River Nut Tree Nursery, 797 Port Wooden Road, Upton 42784, or call (270) 369–8551. Or check out their Web site at www.nolinnursery.com. Be sure to call ahead if you want to visit.

Abraham Lincoln has put *Hodgenville* on the map and kept it there. From Elizabethtown take Highway 61 south to Hodgenville and follow signs to the *Abraham Lincoln Birthplace National Historic Site* (270–358–3137; www .nps.gov/abli), just south of town. A humble log cabin like the one in which

Abe was born on February 12, 1809, is enshrined in a huge, stone-columned building prefaced by 56 steps, which represent the years of Abe's life. The park is open from 8 A.M. to 4:45 P.M. daily, with hours extended until 6:45 P.M. in summer. Go through town on US 31E to visit **Knob Creek Farm,** Lincoln's boyhood home. There is a replica of the cabin where young Abe's first memories were formed; this was the last place he lived in Kentucky. The farm is open year-round, with a ranger on-site to answer questions April through October. The buildings are closed for safety reasons. Call (502) 549–3741 for more information.

Downtown on Lincoln Square near the bronze statue is the small **Lincoln Museum** (270–358–3163; www.lincolnmuseum-ky.org), open Monday through Saturday from 8:30 A.M. to 4:30 P.M., Sunday from 12:30 to 4:30 P.M. Admission is $3. The museum features twelve scenes from Lincoln's life (with wax figures) and a display of memorabilia. Ask about the **Lincoln Days Celebration** held in town during the second weekend of October. The festival features a few odd events, including Lincoln look-alike contests and a very manly rail splitting tournament. Call the LaRue County Chamber of Commerce at (270) 358–3411 for more information.

Lakes and Knobs Region

Going east from Glasgow, the high road leads to Columbia, the low road to **Burkesville.** Take Highway 80 or the Cumberland Parkway to **Columbia.** Few people know that on April 29, 1872, Jesse James and his gang held up the Bank of Columbia and killed a cashier, R. C. Martin. Nor do most know that Mark Twain's parents, Jane Lampton and John Marshall Clemens, were married in Columbia in 1823. Fewer still realize that Maxwell House coffee was developed by a Burkesville boy named Joel Owsley Cheek. After a brief career as a traveling (by horseback) salesman, Cheek started experimenting in the late 1870s with roasting and mixing blends of coffee that were usually sold to the stores green and unground. The first place to sell the expensive blend was the Maxwell House hotel in Nashville, Tennessee. The rest is history.

On the campus of Lindsey Wilson College in downtown Columbia is an architectural treat worth taking a side trip to see, wherever you're going. The **John B. Begley Chapel,** at 210 Lindsey Wilson Street, was designed by E. Fay Jones, a Frank Lloyd Wright disciple who is said to be the world's foremost chapel architect. It looks like two silos made of brick with glass domes, and, in fact, was inspired by farm silos. But few farms could afford silos made using 180,000 bricks! It's open to the public Monday through Friday from 8 A.M. to 4 P.M. You're welcome to attend the services held for students at 10:30

A.M. every Wednesday. For more information call (270) 384–8400 or visit www .lindsey.edu.

North of Columbia, just off Highway 55, is the **Green River Lake State Park** (270–465–8255; http://parks.ky.gov/findparks/recparks/gr) and the starting place for a self-guided tour of sites associated with the **Battle of Tebbs Bend,** fought in early July 1863. This battle marked the beginning of Confederate general John Hunt Morgan's daring campaign, known as the Great Raid into Indiana and Ohio, which ended later in July when he and his men were captured in Ohio. The battle at this site ended when the Confederates were demoralized by what they mistakenly thought to be Union reinforcements arriving. The Union commander, Col. O. H. Moore, had fooled the Rebels into thinking backup troops were arriving all night by having his men go back and forth over a bridge crossing the Green River. One other fascinating deception in this battle was revealed afterward when one of the Union wounded turned out to be a 16-year-old girl named Lizzie Compton, from London, Ontario, who was posing as a man. There have been reenactments of the battle in years past, but they were suspended a few years ago after, as one observer put it, "the North and the South *really* got into it with each other." Disagreements over whether to stage the battle authentically or to have the Rebels win led to the event's demise. You can get information about the battle at the park or at the Taylor County Tourism Commission, 107 West Broadway. The commission's phone number is (800) 738–4719.

In the park, stop by the interpretive center and request the key to the **Atkinson-Griffin House** (www.campbellsvilleky.com/historical), 1½-story double-pen log building used by the Confederates as a hospital after the battle, which now houses some Civil War exhibits and even has bloodstains on the upstairs bedroom floor. Also, get the little map and list of other battle sites.

The next major town to the north is **Campbellsville,** in which there are two relatively obscure historic sites that are worth a stop. At 1075 Campbellsville Bypass, visit the **Jacob Hiestand House,** an exquisite Federal-style stone house built in 1823 by a German tanner who had moved to Kentucky from Pennsylvania. The house that is there now was moved (try to imagine that task!) from its original site because it was endangered by sprawling development. Though there are many stone houses in this state, this one was particularly well crafted. The house is open 9 A.M. to 5 P.M. Monday through Saturday and 1 P.M. to 5 P.M. Sunday. Admission of $2 is charged. Call (270) 789–4343 for more information.

Another building that was moved from its original location for the sake of preservation is the **Friendship School,** a humble little one-room schoolhouse built in 1918 and now located behind the Taylor County High School at 300

Ingram Avenue. People are welcome to visit the schoolhouse on Sunday after-noon between 1 and 4 P.M. from July through December, or by appointment (800–738–4719). This little school is a classic example of Kentucky's one-room schoolhouses, which were built inexpensively and run by teachers who were legendary for their level of devotion and self-sacrifice. The Friendship School, like many of its kind, had a class size of between eight and 40 students, ranging in grade from first to eighth. Like the current hours Friendship School is open, the school year ran from July through December from 8 A.M. to 4 P.M. regardless of weather conditions. Such tiny schools were located within walking distance of a few families who could pay the teacher. (This may come back into vogue and would certainly be considered radical.)

trueblue

When Taylor County's Friendship School was built in 1918, there were 7,067 one-room schools operating in Kentucky. Most had closed by the 1950s.

Campbellsville is a great place to visit if you're in the market for fine hand-made cherry furniture. There are three companies in town that manufacture the furniture: *Campbellsville Cherry Reproductions, Inc.,* on Saloma Road (270–465–6003); *Campbellsville Hand Made Furniture,* on the Water Tower Bypass (270–789–1741); and *Gary Humphress & Sons,* on East Main Street (270–465–2786; www.humphressfurniture.com). All welcome visitors and have showrooms of beautiful beds, chests, tables, and other pieces. If what you want is not in stock, you can order it and have it shipped. "Campbellsville cherry" graces houses all over the world.

In a little town called *Mannsville,* east of Campbellsville about 8 miles on Highway 70, is *Penn Country Hams,* at 8812 Liberty Road, a place that might be familiar to a ham fan since it sells more than 50,000 a year. You can tour the facilities and do some taste testing before you purchase. Call (270) 465–5065 for information. Hours are 8 A.M. to 6 P.M. Monday through Saturday.

West of Campbellsville about 13 miles in the town of *Greensburg* stands the oldest existing courthouse west of the Alleghenies. It was built in 1803 and now houses a regional museum. Around town you can see a number of other historic buildings, many of which are on the National Register of Historic Places, including a log cabin, circa 1796; an old railroad depot; and a 445-foot-long pedestrian bridge. You can see the area like the early pioneers did, from the water. Take a guided or an unguided canoe trip (from May through September only) down the Green River near Greensburg for $30 to $45 per canoe. There are even some Class I rapids occasionally. Call *Canoe Kentucky* (Green River) to schedule a trip at (800) K–CANOE–1 or visit www.canoeky.com.

South of the Campbellsville/Columbia/Greensburg area is **Dale Hollow,** a large man-made lake that straddles the Kentucky-Tennessee line. Take Highway 61 to Burkesville and watch for signs. The area is full of small marinas, motels, and fishing camps. It is said to be one of the cleanest lakes in the state, and since there are myriad inlets and islands, Dale Hollow is good place to swim. Dale Hollow Lake Resort Park has a lodge and offers horseback riding and hiking. Call (270) 433–7431 or (800) 325–2282, or visit http://parks.ky.gov/findparks/resortparks/dh for reservations or information.

Northeast of Dale Hollow is **Lake Cumberland,** one of the largest fabricated lakes in the United States; its peak surface area is more than 55,000 acres. It is also said to have more walleye, bass, and crappie than any other American lake.

Although there are water-oriented businesses all around the lake, you may want to stop by the headquarters of the Lake Cumberland State Resort Park (off U.S. Highway 127 just south of Jamestown; 270–343–3111; www.lakecumberland.com) to get specific information. If you boat around the big, clear lake, you'll find endless little coves to explore, places to swim, fossils over which to ponder, and almost no commercial development to distract you. The park also has a lodge with a restaurant, cottages, an indoor pool, campgrounds, and a marina.

Don't you want to know where all those fish in the lake come from? (Well, not all the fish—birds transport some.) Follow US 127 south from the park and watch for signs for the **Wolf Creek National Fish Hatchery** (270–343–3797; www.fws.gov/wolfcreek), where thousands of rainbow and brown trout are raised. Auxiliary pleasure begins if you take time to watch wild birds, such as the ever-so-svelte great blue heron or the sassy belted kingfisher, feast on the easy pickings. Deer feed near the dam daily at dusk. The hatchery has some interpretive displays that explain the process of mass-raising fish. Open from 7 A.M. to 3:30 P.M. daily.

Starting from the state park, take Highway 1058 west, then Highway 379 south through Creelsboro; when the road almost touches the Cumberland River, watch for signs for the **Creelsboro Natural Bridge.** Though there are many rock bridges in Kentucky, this

trueblue

Besides Dale Hollow lake, another thing shared by Kentucky and Tennessee is a little town with a rowdy reputation called **Static,** which sits directly on the border where U.S. Highway 127 goes through. Kentucky says Static belongs in Tennessee, and Tennessee says the town is all Kentucky's. With a town name that means "showing little change," it's no wonder no one claims the place. To make things worse, legend has it that Static was named after a local farmer's one-eyed bulldog.

75-foot arch has been designated a National Natural Landmark because it is limestone rather than the more common sandstone.

A town named *Touristville* makes a person suspicious, and rightly so. Some chamber of commerce type was on the ball that hot summer day in 1929 when the post office was named. For a time Touristville did profit from the flow of vacationers through nearby *Mill Springs,* which sits very near what is now Lake Cumberland. *Dunagan's Grocery & Supply* in Mill Springs now serves as post office for both towns. The anachronistic store really is an attraction for nostalgia buffs and curiosity seekers. In 1935 Everette Dunagan's father moved the store to its present site from about a hundred yards across the road, employing one pair of mules, a bunch of logs used as rollers, some cable, and two days' worth of ingenuity. Since then precious little has changed. He carries a little bit of everything, as a good country store owner must; there's even a great little photo postcard of Dunagan's. Take your own picture or make a sketch. The place has been painted by several artists. Mr. Dunagan keeps his place open from 8 A.M. to 5 P.M. every day but Sunday. To visit, take Highway 90 to Highway 1275 and go 1 mile west. Trust me—you'll love it.

To get to Mill Springs, go to Monticello in Wayne County and follow Highway 90 to Touristville. Turn west on Highway 1275 and you'll see signs for the *Mill Springs Mill,* "largest overshot waterwheel in the world." That's a slightly overrated waterwheel, but as it turns out, the wheel is 40 feet, 10

The Bigger Apple!

Fast-food restaurants really weren't the first to "supersize" it. As evidence, there's the annual *Casey County Apple Festival,* held in Liberty the last full week in September.

This festival has been an annual event since 1974, often attracting up to 50,000 visitors. Undoubtedly they follow their noses to this small south-central Kentucky town, because cookin' big is a centerpiece of the event.

The folks in Casey County, you see, have a special supersize oven, and they set it up in the city parking lot at festival time. The feasting begins Wednesday night, when they bake a giant chocolate chip cookie. Then on Thursday night, guests can share in a giant pizza. All of this is just a warm-up, however, for the main course, which gets under way Saturday morning when volunteers start assembling "the world's largest apple pie." Mix 30 bushels of apples, 200 pounds of sugar—you get the idea. The result: a 1,200-pound pie with a buttery crust 8 feet in diameter. (It takes a forklift to get it into the oven.) The pie bakes and bakes until noon Saturday, when it is scooped into bowls for the drooling crowd. Got a major sweet tooth? Call the Casey County Chamber of Commerce at (606) 787–6670 for more information about this all-American feast.

Mysteries of Dark Skies

If you happen to be driving along Kentucky Highway 78 near Liberty after dark, take a few moments to glance skyward. You are at the site of a true unsolved mystery. It happened on January 6, 1976. Three Casey County women, two of them grandmothers and all avid churchgoers, were returning from dinner at a Stanford restaurant. Between Hustonville and Liberty, they saw what they thought was a plane about to crash. Next thing they knew, it was an hour and 25 minutes later and they were 8 miles down the road, with severe headaches and burnlike red marks on the backs of their necks. The car's electrical system was malfunctioning, and the paint on the hood was blistered. Shaken and confused, the women returned to Liberty, where a neighbor asked them to draw what they had seen, and their aircraft looked suspiciously like a UFO. Soon, a veritable army of UFO investigators, and the national tabloids, descended upon this small Kentucky town. Under hypnosis the women told a story that seems almost commonplace today, but was then quite rare: They had been taken aboard a spacecraft and examined by creatures with huge, pale blue eyes. Later they even passed a polygraph test. These unlikely UFO abductees have long since moved away from Liberty, Kentucky; they grew tired of hearing the ridicule and laughter. The case, however, remains unsolved, a mystery to be pondered by those who gaze upon the night skies of Casey County.

inches in diameter, making it the third-largest in the nation and among the top 10 in the world. It may be the only one of the biggies to still be functioning as a gristmill. The first cereal grinding mill was built around 1817 at this site, where 13 springs gushed out of the hillside. The waterwheel also powered a cotton gin, carting factory, and wagon production line. After a fire and several remodelings, in 1908 the Diamond Roller Mills's 40-foot wheel was installed. Today the mill is open at no charge to the public from May through October, 9 A.M. to 5 P.M. daily. On weekends cornmeal is ground with the old equipment. For specifics call (606) 348–8189.

The mill is the site of a tide-turning Civil War battle in January 1862. Confederate general Felix Kirk Zollicoffer set up camp at a house near the mill, the Metcalfe House. Zollicoffer lost the Battle of Logan's Crossroads and thereby left the first gap in what was a long, strong Rebel defense line in Kentucky. Just west of Somerset on Highway 80 in a town called Nancy are the **Mill Springs Battlefield** and the Zollicoffer Park and burial site, where more than a hundred rebel troops are buried under one stone, all from the Mill Springs battle. Driving tour maps of the battlefield are available at the park. From the cemeteries you can see (and smell and taste and climb) the fruit trees at the adjacent **Haney's Appledale Farm** (606–636–6148; www.haneysappledalefarm.com, one of the state's best and largest apple and peach orchards, located 1 mile east of the battlefield (west of Somerset 8 miles) at 8550 West Highway 80. July through Christmas the orchard is open Monday through Saturday from 9 A.M. to 5:30 P.M. and on Sunday afternoon. Some of the time "U-pick" is available, and you're always welcome to buy any quantity of fruit you want—the owner says, "Heck, I'd even cut an apple in half if that's all you wanted."

If you venture into **Somerset,** you'll not be excited by the seemingly endless strip-type development, but there is one place that may be worth stopping: Call (606) 677–6000 for a schedule of performing arts events at the **Center for Rural Economic Development** at 2292 South Highway 27 (www .centertech.com).

When you leave Jamestown, you leave the lake area and enter the Knobs again. Take US 127 north into Casey County, known as the **Gate Capital of the World.** Most gates, truck racks, and round-bale feeders are made of tubular steel, a concept first developed in 1965 by Tarter Gate in Dunnville, the first and largest of the gate companies in the county, producing more than 1,000 gates a day.

Due to the isolation and beauty of this hilly country, a large number of Mennonites have moved into the area. It's always inspirational to see their neat, well-tended farms, but these people are not interested in intrusion from the outside world. This community has two businesses that are open to the public. Going north on US 127 from Russell Springs at Highway 80, turn southeast on Highway 910. Go about 3½ miles and turn east onto South Fork. This is a beautiful drive past both secular and Mennonite farms (watch for "shocked" corn and draft horses in the field). It's hilarious to see the contrast in styles: Watch to the right side of South Fork for the gaudiest house in the world; the obviously secular yard is thick with whirligigs, holiday yard art, and endless junk.

At the other extreme and just a few miles away, **Bluegrass Wood and Leather Craft** (furniture, chairs, tables, harnesses, and leather goods) is a

The Underwater World of "Atlantis"— in Kentucky

Burnside, just south of Somerset on U.S. Highway 27, is not only the only town on Lake Cumberland—it is the only town under the lake. In the late 1940s the U.S. Army Corps of Engineers moved the entire town to higher ground because the lake area was being impounded. The durable remains of old Burnside become visible during the winter when the lake's level lowers. It's eerie seeing foundations, porch steps, and sidewalks emerge from the mud and debris.

remarkable place run by remarkable people. The store is a large building on the right filled with furniture (mainly in oak) upstairs and leather goods downstairs, all of excellent quality. Because the Mennonites in the area do much of their farming with horses and mules, the leather items are primarily horse-related, but there aren't many limits to these craftsmen's abilities. The fellows in the shop are more than willing to answer questions, and if you're serious about a purchase, they are glad to take a special order as long it falls within their way of working. There's no phone, but they are usually open on weekdays during business hours.

Back on Highway 910, go "just a little piece" farther south to **Dutchman's Market,** a small Mennonite general store in the basement of their community elementary school. To remain apart as much as possible from the corrupt aspects of today's culture, these Mennonites often employ low-technology methods for farming, building, and living in general. So, if you are in search of something unusual, a modern instance of an old model of any kind of equipment, like a hand pump for your cistern, inquire about it at Dutchman's. Let me also recommend the local sorghum molasses. Alan Oberholtzer, the local molasses meister, keeps this store well stocked. You'll want to speed home to make a mess of biscuits just to have an excuse for draining what promises to be the first of many jars.

Head south again and make your way toward Somerset. Along the way, if you want to stop for lunch or dinner, try the **Yosemite** (pronounced YO-sehmite) **Country Store.** The homemade chili is hot—a liquid atomic fireball. This is one of those groceries that makes its own pickled eggs. What's funny is that the homemade eggs are kept next to a jar of commercial eggs, which are dyed a sickening hot pink. The manager told me it increases sales of the homemade ones. Smart. Yosemite is on Highway 70 going southeast from Liberty. You can stay on Highway 70, which becomes Highway 635 and runs into US 27, which leads into Somerset.

trueblue

The last stagecoach line in Kentucky ran the 20 miles between Monticello, a town named for Thomas Jefferson's home, and Burnside.

Nearby in **Burnside,** on US 27 south of Somerset, is **General Burnside Island State Park,** a 430-acre island that's right in the middle of a deep bend in the Cumberland River as it's widening into lake status. You can camp here, launch a boat, even play golf. What the heck?! You're on an island in Kentucky! Call (606) 561–4104 for any information (http://parks.ky.gov/findparks/recparks/ge). At Christmas the park sponsors a lavish 3½-mile drive-through light show with several hundred displays and more than a million lights. Lucky for them electricity is cheap in Kentucky.

If you're not a camper, you can enjoy luxurious lodging at Raintree Inn Bed & Breakfast, located on Lake Cumberland south of Somerset. Take US 27 south to Highway 90; turn right and go 3¼ miles; turn right on Old Highway 90 Loop #3 and watch for the sign. This beautiful antebellum home with huge columns looks like something out of a movie—and it is. The place takes its name from the movie starring Elizabeth Taylor and Montgomery Clift and was one of the Kentucky locations where the film was shot. Owner Gwen Ison has lovingly restored the home and filled it with antiques. Three guest rooms in the main house, as well as the carriage house and guest rooms in the barn, are available for $90 per night ($145 for the carriage house). A full country breakfast is served. On the property you can also explore a real tobacco barn and remnants of an 1800s stagecoach stop. Call (606) 561–5225 for reservations or information. You can also write: 3314 Old Highway 90 #3, Bronston 42518 or visit www.bbonline.com/ky/raintree.

The ***Natural Arch Scenic Area*** was once Cherokee country and is now a beautiful place to take a few short but spectacular day hikes. (If you're feeling energetic, you could actually cover all the trails in one day.) From Somerset take US 27 south for 21 miles, then turn right (west) on Highway 927 and follow the signs for 4 miles. The natural arch for which the area is named is a majestic 50-by-90-foot span of sandstone that curves above the forest below. Short trails go to some spectacular overlooks and fertile deep valleys. Early spring is a great time to go; every week brings a different set of wildflowers, including the rare lady's slipper. For trail maps or trail condition reports, contact the Somerset District Office, 135 Realty Lane, Somerset 42501, or call (606) 679–2010.

The Shortest Creek in the World

Stab, a short name for a small town with a short creek, is 10 miles east of Somerset along Highway 80 near the Pleasant Run Baptist Church. Short Creek emerges from a hillside cavern at an impressive width of about 25 feet. It flows in a semicircle for maybe 150 feet and ducks back underground in a small cave. There's no doubt, this is the shortest creek in the world. The family that owns the creek says that there was a gristmill at one end and that the creek formerly was used for wintertime baptisms because the water is always 54 degrees Fahrenheit. The Taylors own the small grocery at Stab, too. Stop by their store and ask permission to have a picnic by the creek. You may hear some good stories.

You absolutely must pay a visit to some or all of the Appropriate Technology Demonstration centers owned and operated by ***Appalachia—Science in the Public Interest,*** or ASPI. Make your way toward Mount Vernon via Interstate 75, exit 59; U.S. Highway 150; or any of the small but beautiful and navigable roads that wind that way. This place marks the western edge of one of North America's most diverse eco-regions, the Mixed Mesophytic Forest, a highly varied hardwood forest. This also marks a theoretical borderline into the foothills of Appalachia, a region much beset by economic and ecological abuse. ASPI's vision is to demonstrate and promote the economic and political power found in self-sufficient living, simple living that is healthy for people and for the environment. Although Appalachia desperately needs this vision, the sustainable practices promoted by ASPI apply to everyone in every situation: Use locally available materials and apply good science in order to live compatibly with your natural surroundings. In the 1970s there were many demonstration sites like this across the nation. This is one of the few remaining centers, and it's more active than ever.

Downtown Mount Vernon is ASPI's main headquarters and houses a small-town demonstration site with a wonderful intensive garden nestled surprisingly right in the midst of asphalt parking lots. The office is open from 8 A.M. to 4 P.M. on weekdays. Call ahead to make an appointment to visit the demonstration center; (606) 256–0077; www.a-spi.org.

Cumberland Falls is not really off the beaten path, but it's such a flamboyant, unusual cataract that it must be recognized. Follow I–75 to Corbin, get off on U.S. Highway 25W, veer west on Highway 90, and follow the signs to ***Cumberland Falls State Resort Park*** (606–528–4121 or 800–325–0063; http:// parks.ky.gov/findparks/resortparks/cf).

trueblue

Cumberland Falls near Corbin is the second-largest waterfall east of the Rockies (only Niagara is bigger).

The wide, humble Cumberland River explodes dramatically as it crashes over the curving precipice and becomes the largest American waterfall east of the Rocky Mountains, except for Niagara. When the entire disk of the moon is illuminated and the skies are clear, a long moonbow arches from the top of the falls to the turbulent waters below. The only other moonbow in the world is at Victoria Falls along the Zambezi River in southern Africa. The Cumberland Falls is so powerful that the mist fans way out and above the water; when the wind is right, you get a gentle shower on the rocks at the top. More than 65 feet high and 125 feet across, the waterfall is believed to have retreated as far as 45 miles upstream from its original position near Burnside. In a process that takes many millennia, the water wears away the soft sandstone under the erosion-resistant lip at the top.

The park, which is open all year, has another smaller but beautiful falls called *Little Eagle Falls.* If it's hot, the pool below Little Eagle Falls is a divine swimming hole. Ask for information at the park lodge about hiking trails, rooms, cabins, and special events. Within the park is a state nature preserve left to its wild state. It boasts more than 15 species of rare plants and animals including endangered mussels and plants like the box huckleberry, brook saxifrage, goat's rue, and riverweed. A guided hike can be a real education.

Another way to "get into" the river, and to have a rip-roaring good time, is to hook up with a guided canoeing or white-water rafting trip down the river. Write to *Sheltowee Trace Outfitters,* P.O. Box 1060, Whitley City 42653, call (800) 541–RAFT, or visit www.ky-rafting.com.

The other big playground in this region is at the *Big South Fork National River and Recreation Area* (www.nps.gov/biso) in McCreary County and below the border. Take US 27 or I–75 south to Highway 92 and go west to Stearns. If you're arriving via US 27, check out the natural rock bridge just off Highway 927, which goes to Nevelsville. You can also get to Big South Fork on Highway 700, which intersects US 27 near Whitley City. The latter route brings you directly to *Yahoo Falls,* Kentucky's highest at 113 feet. The designation is a little misleading, though. Yahoo is by no means a massive waterfall. In fact, it's just a thin stream of water that drops a great distance. In dry summers it virtually disappears. But water quantity aside, the hike to the bottom is pleasant and well marked.

The whole Big South Fork area is beautiful. Deep, jagged gorges are frequent surprises, and the variations in the landscape, from cool woods to hot, high, open-faced rocks, are endlessly pleasing. That the area was once extensively logged and mined is apparent. From early April through the end of October, the USDA Forest Service operates the *Big South Fork Scenic Railway,* which takes visitors on a three-hour trip through the Stearn Coal and Lumber Company's former logging and mining empire, now mostly second-growth woods. Call (800) 462–5664 or check www.bsfsry.com for information and excursion times. You can also drive or take the railway to an abandoned coal mining camp called *Blue Heron,* or Mine 18. This isolated company town was built in 1937 and nearly abandoned by the late 1950s, and the original buildings were ingeniously rebuilt as "ghost structures" in 1989. Life-size photographs of miners and their families occupy the skeletal structural and corrugated-steel spaces, and recorded voices depict life in the camp through a kind of time-delay oral history. The walk across the coal tipple bridge is breathtaking—you can't help but appreciate the engineering. More information is at www.nps.gov/biso/bheron. Another camp, circa 1910, called the **Barthell Mining Camp,** is accessible only by train. You can even lodge overnight in one of the mining cabins. The appointments have improved over the days when miners slept here, however: Each cabin includes two bedrooms with queen-size beds, and kitchens with microwaves. Rates are $95 to $125 per night, depending on the season. Call (888) 550–5748 for information (www .barthellcoalcamp.com).

At the peak of a hill in Stearns is the **McCreary County Museum** (606–376–5730; www.mccrearycountymuseum.com, located in the nearly century-old former Stearns Coal and Lumber Company office building. The history, depicted by displays, begins with pre-European Native American culture and ends in the present with a gallery devoted to local contemporary artwork. The museum is open Tuesday through Saturday from mid-April through October.

Take exit 11 off I–75 and keep an eye peeled for a new brick colonial-style building on the campus of Cumberland College in **Williamsburg.** This is the **Cumberland Museum, Inn, and Center for Leadership Studies.** Students work in the facility to help pay for their tuition and to learn real-world skills in hotel management. The restaurant and lodgings have a great view of the surrounding mountains. Rates are around $94; call (606) 539–4100 for information (www.cumberlandinn.com). Among other things, the eclectic Cumberland Museum has an Appalachian lifestyle exhibit, a Native American artifacts col-

trueblue

In 1818, while drilling for salt along the Big South Fork, workers inadvertently discovered oil. So began the first commercial oil well in America.

lection, a very unusual collection of more than 6,000 Christian crosses, and a "life science" collection that consists of actual, preserved animal specimens, such as polar bears and shrews, shown in displays that mimic their natural habitats. There is an admission charge. For more information call (606) 539–4050. Hours are 11 A.M. to 6 P.M. Monday through Friday and 10 A.M. to 6 P.M. on Saturday.

Jellico, Tennessee, just across the border on I–75, is (or was) the number one place for underage Kentuckians to get hitched. In Jellico they do it fast, legal, and without parental or priestly consent: "I do, and he does, too."

Just east of Williamsburg is **Friendship Mountain Crafts,** one of many fruitful mountain craft cooperatives in the Appalachian region. Because this one is near a beaten path, the folks are prepared to show visitors around. For example, women who regularly quilt together often have some beauties for sale at the center. Activities change, so call ahead at (606) 549–1617. From

Williamsburg go 9 miles east on Highway 92, turn right (southeast) on Highway 904, and watch for the sign. Hours are 10 A.M. to 5 P.M. The co-op is closed Wednesday, Sunday, and the entire month of July.

Corbin sits on the adjoining corners of Whitley, Laurel, and Knox Counties and serves as the commercial hub for the whole area. Although Corbin is not famous the world over, its native son, Col. Harland Sanders, is. From Tokyo to Moscow to London, England, and London, Kentucky, the Colonel's red-and-white portrait, complete with the almost sinister goatee, smiles out on chicken consumers everywhere going through the doors of Kentucky Fried Chicken. Corbin is the home of the original restaurant—it's even listed on the National Register of Historic Places. At The *Harland Sanders Cafe & Museum,* see Harland's kitchen as it was in the 1940s and eat in a dining area restored to resemble the original restaurant. To get there, go north of Corbin and take US 25E south; turn right at the second traffic light. Hours are 10 A.M. to 10 P.M. daily. Call (606) 528–2163 or check www.chickenfestival.com/sanders for information.

London, the next town to the north, is trying to get in on the chicken action, too, and holds an annual World Chicken Festival downtown at the end of September. In addition to the usual festival activities, all the great cooks in town compete for coveted cook-off prizes. The real winners are the tasters. Call (800) 348–0095 for specifics.

If you think the Interstate near London looks busy now in a postindustrial, highway-laced world, ponder the years between 1775 and 1800, when more than 300,000 people came into Kentucky from the east through this area when it was wild. The *Levi Jackson State Park* is situated at the intersection of the Wilderness Road and Boone's Trace, the two main frontier "highways." The park is just 2 miles south of London on US 25. The Mountain Life Museum gives newcomers to the area a glimpse of pioneer history with a reproduction pioneer settlement stocked with period furniture and Native American artifacts. Also at the park is McHargue's Mill, a completely operational restored gristmill, circa 1812, that serves as a kind of mill museum and has what may be the

trueblue

The world's largest collection of millstones is found at McHargue's Mill near London, Kentucky.

world's largest collection of millstones. On park grounds is the only marked burial ground along the Wilderness Road (though historians believe that there are many other cemeteries lacking headstones). For questions about hiking, camping, or any park information, check http://parks.ky.gov/findparks/recparks/lj.

Ask at the area visitor center, off I–75 at exit 41 (800–348–0095), about **Camp Wildcat Civil War Battle Site.** The Battle of Wildcat Mountain, as it's also called, was four days of skirmishing that took place October 1861. Collectively, the encounters are considered the first major battle and Union victory in Kentucky. The battle site off Hazel Patch Road includes various monuments and rough terrain.

The Rockcastle River, the lower part of which has been designated a Kentucky Wild River, runs through some gorgeous country in the Daniel Boone National Forest. Riding its currents is probably the perfect way to see the land in this area. No matter what your skill in a canoe or kayak, you will be challenged. Between March and October three area outfitting companies offer trips along the Rockcastle, which, by the way, has rapids rated between Class I and IV. **Sheltowee Trace Outfitters** (800–541–RAFT) offers guided trips for between $20 and $35 per person. **Rockcastle Adventures** (606–864–9407) rents canoes and kayaks for self-guided trips along the river, Buck Creek, or Wood Creek Lake with shuttle service and primitive camping for between $30 and $50 per person.

The next town to the north is **Mount Vernon.** Mount Vernon is considered a kind of gateway to the Knobs, the serious hills that skirt the Appalachian Mountains. For a double delight—beautiful mountains and wonderful people—take a drive straight uphill from the caution light in downtown Mount Vernon at the junction of US 150 and Highway 1249. Exactly 10 miles later you'll find yourself on a hillside in front of a redbrick ranch house on the left, home of **Betty Thomas Teddy Bears.** Betty works at home and welcomes visitors but requests that you call first at (606) 256–5378 to see her fine dolls and stuffed animals—everything from realistic Canada geese and goslings, decoy-size mallard ducks, debonair foxes dressed in traditional hunt clothing and hard hats, Old World–style teddy bears, mice, cats, dogs, unicorns, soft-sculpture baby dolls, and on and on. Most of her pieces have hinged joints, and all are stuffed so tightly that they stand independently; all are made of high-quality wool, satin, or cotton in delicious colors.

Ms. Thomas's patience, persistence, and skill with her hands come by her honestly. Her parents raised 13 children in a log cabin in a holler (hollow) just across the road from her present home. Her father, William McClure, is rightfully considered a kind of legend among folk-culture enthusiasts. For years his handmade wooden roof shingles were in constant demand in all the surrounding states, as were his handsome carved dough bowls. You can see some of his work on the roof of the Aunt Polly Hiatt house at Renfro Valley (coming up next). They say that although that roof has gaps in it so big you can see sky through them, it doesn't leak a drop. Long live the McClure family!

Here's the lineup: "Banjo Pickin' Gal," "Winking at Me," "Chicken Reel," "Cackling Hen," "Barbara Allen," "Poor Ellen Smith," "Tramp on the Street," "Matthew 24," and "Old Shep." These could be the names of thoroughbreds in the starting gate at the Derby but are, in fact, some of the best country songs ever written and some of the first ever performed at Renfro Valley, Kentucky's Country Music Capital. Many folks in the region remember when they first heard John Lair's silk-smooth voice in 1939 broadcasting an all-country-music radio show live from his big tobacco barn in Rockcastle County. Those humble beginnings have led to the establishment of a large complex of buildings and traditional music and entertainment programs at Renfro Valley; the radio shows are now transmitted to more than 200 stations in North America. In addition to performance events in the auditorium (a luxury barn), there are on the grounds a craft village with mountain craft demonstrators, a gift shop, the Renfro Valley Museum, a bakery, a hotel, and a restaurant. Go north from Mount Vernon a few miles on US 25; for the more scenic route, to the Renfro Valley exit. For more information, show tickets, or reservations, call (800) 765–7464 or check www.renfrovalley.com. Renfro Valley is open March through mid-December.

Next door to Renfro Valley is another attraction sure to get your toes tapping. And along the way you just might learn something about Kentucky history. The ***Kentucky Music Hall of Fame and Museum*** opened in 2002 to honor the state's musical heritage from country to classical. Exhibits include costumes from Kentucky stars such as Loretta Lynn, The Everly Brothers, and Rosemary Clooney; a time line with fascinating and beautiful antique instruments; and a hands-on area where you can explore pitch, tempo, and timbre. The museum also hosts special performances and offers weekly music lessons and an on-site sound studio for aspiring inductees. The museum is open 10 A.M. to 6 P.M. Tuesday through Saturday and 9 A.M. to 5 P.M. Sunday. Admission is $7.50 adults, $4.50 children (877–356–3263; www.kentuckymusicmuseum .com).

More Good Lodging in South-Central Kentucky

BOWLING GREEN

Best Western Motor Inn
Interstate 65, exit 22
(270) 782–3800 or
(800) 343–2937
$69 to $100.

1869 Homestead Bed & Breakfast
212 Mizpah Road
(270) 842–0510
www.1869homestead.com
Historic home on 55 acres, with three guest rooms and numerous hiking trails. $79 to $99.

BRANDENBURG

Doe Run Inn
Highway 448, northwest of Fort Knox
(270) 422–2982
www.doeruninn.com
Rustic country inn decorated with antiques. About $50 per night.

BURKESVILLE

Cabin Fever
630 Davidson Road
(270) 358–4415
www.kvnet.org/cabinfever
Bed-and-breakfast in wooded setting.

CORBIN

Best Western
2630 Cumberland Falls Road
(Interstate 75, exit 25)
(606) 528–2100
About $75 per night.

Cumberland Falls State Resort Park
Highway 90 southwest of Corbin
(606) 528–4121
Rustic stone lodge and 16 cabins; open year-round. $50 to $195.

GLASGOW

Four Seasons Country Inn
Scottsville Road
(270) 678–1000
Twenty-one guest rooms with private baths. $126 per night.

JAMESTOWN

Lake Cumberland State Resort Park
off U.S. Highway 127
(270) 343–3111
Two lodges and 30 cabins; open year-round. About $46 to $135 per night.

LEITCHFIELD

Rough River Dam State Resort Park
Highway 79
(270) 257–2311
Lodge and cottages.
$50 to $130 per night.

MAMMOTH CAVE

Mammoth Cave Hotel
Mammoth Cave National Park
(270) 758–2225
www.mammothcavehotel.com
Rooms and cottages; pet kennel available. $36 to $90.

RADCLIFF

Best Western Gold Vault Inn
1225 North Dixie Highway
(270) 351–1141
$60 to $80 per night.

SMITHS GROVE

Victorian House Bed and Breakfast
110 Main Street
(270) 563–9403
www.bbonline.com/ky/victorian
Four rooms with private baths and fireplaces; located in antiques district 10 miles north of Bowling Green. About $105 per night.

WILLIAMSBURG

Cumberland Inn
649 South Tenth Street
(606) 539–4100
www.cumberlandinn.com
About $85 per night.

More Fun Places to Eat in South-Central Kentucky

BOWLING GREEN

Brickyard Cafe
1026 Chestnut Street
(270) 843–6431
Italian trattoria in an 1860s brickyard building.

440 Main Restaurant and Bar
440 East Main Avenue
(270) 793–0450
Elegant dining in a restored historic home.

Judy's Castle
1302 US 31W Bypass
(270) 842–8736
Country cooking. Well loved breakfasts and daily plate specials—meat-and-three-veggies classics.

BRANDENBURG

Doe Run Inn
Highway 448, northwest of Fort Knox
(502) 422–2982
Country ham, skillet-fried chicken, and other regional favorites.

CAVE CITY

Water Mill Restaurant
Highway 70
(270) 773–3186
Large buffet or order from the menu.

Sahara Steak House
413 Happy Valley Road
(270) 773–3450
Steaks, seafood, and country-ham dishes.

CORBIN

Cumberland Falls State Resort Park
Highway 90, southwest of Corbin
(606) 528–4121
Wide variety of sandwiches and seafood entrees, plus regional specialties such as country ham, served in a family atmosphere.

Dale Hollow Lake State Resort Park
Highway 1206, south of Lake Cumberland
(270) 433–7431
Variety of American dishes and regional special-ties. Dinner buffet Friday through Sunday.

ELIZABETHTOWN

Ginza Japanese Restaurant
1705 North Dixie Highway
(270) 737–5536
Japanese food in casual setting. Popular lunch.

Stone Hearth Restaurant
U.S. Highway 62
(270) 765–4898
Home cooking.

LEITCHFIELD

Rough River Dam State Resort Park
Highway 79
(270) 257–2311
Buffet and regional specialties.

LIBERTY

Bread of Life Cafe
5369 South Highway 127
(4 1/2 miles south of town)
(606) 787–6110
Pennsylvania Dutch-style cooking. Proceeds go to the Galilean Children's Home. Freshly based bread, rolls, desserts. Buf-fet and menu. Except Sun-day, open daily for all three meals.

RENFRO VALLEY

The Lodge Restaurant
Interstate 75, exit 62
(800) 765–7464
Country cooking, with great soup, beans, chicken and dumplings, and chocolate pie.

SCOTTSVILLE

Harper's
3085 Old Gallatin Road
(270) 622–7557
Three meals a day served Wednesday to Sunday, but it's the catfish that has made this second-generation family-owned place popular for almost 30 years.

WESTERN KENTUCKY

The sky seems bigger in the vast, open land of this western region. Sunsets are beautiful, and you can see a storm coming for hours. There's plenty of room for everyone, and everyone's here, from coal miners and bluegrass musicians to Amish farmers and master quilters. There must be something in the soil here because legendary figures have sprung up like weeds: Robert Penn Warren, Edgar Cayce, Casey Jones, Jefferson Davis, and John James Audubon, to name a few. Western Kentucky also boasts some of the best museums in the state, such as Shakertown at South Union, the most southern of all Shaker communities; the Museum of the American Quilter's Society; and the Owensboro Museum of Fine Art.

Most dear to Kentuckians is the Land Between the Lakes, a clean, gorgeous, wild land surrounded by Lake Barkley and Kentucky Lake, a double paradise for fisher folks. There must be more resorts and marinas per square mile around the Land Between the Lakes area than anywhere else in the state. Stop and ask about camping, cottages, fishing, restaurants, or anything else your heart may desire. American bald eagles also find this region attractive and make their homes here and along the shore of the Mississippi River in the far southwestern region.

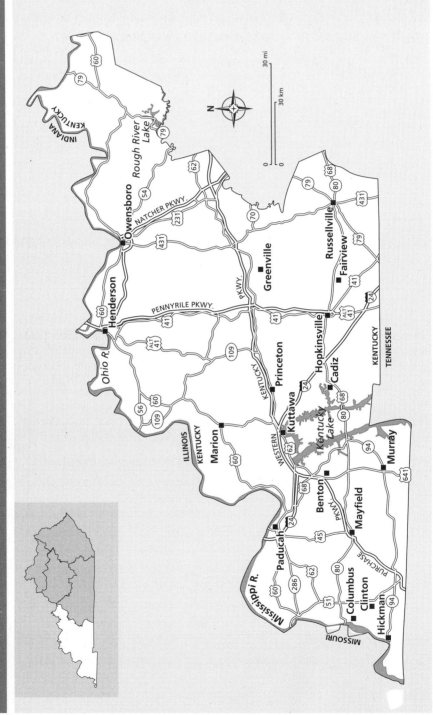

WESTERN KENTUCKY

You'll find western Kentucky quiet, not overdeveloped, yet full of fascinating surprises. The fact that people here have uniquely open spirits gives the traveler a chance to absorb and deeply enjoy the culture of this place.

Jackson Purchase

On the fourth Sunday in May, if you are anywhere near **Benton,** west of the lakes on U.S. Highway 641, plan to attend **Big Singing Day,** the only American singing festival that uses the 1835 *Southern Harmony Book* of shape note tunes. (Shape note singing is a traditional form of a cappella that represents the four notes—mi, fa, sol, la—on the staff by a different shape; i.e., diamond, triangle, circle, square, respectively.) This wonderfully nonhierarchical group singing event has been happening here since 1843. There is no leader and no instrumental accompaniment, and the songs, usually traditional Welsh hymns, are arranged in parts such that no one sings beyond his or her range. Weather permitting, the singing happens outdoors on the courthouse lawn.

AUTHOR'S FAVORITE PLACES IN WESTERN KENTUCKY

American Quilter's Society National Quilt Show and Contest
late April, Paducah
(270) 898–7903
www.aqsquilt.com

Ben E. Clement Mineral Museum
Marion
(270) 965–4263

The Homeplace 1850
Land Between the Lakes
(270) 924–2000 or (800) 525–7077

John James Audubon State Park
Henderson
(270) 826–2247

Paradise Steam Generation Power Plant Tour
Paradise (near Drakesboro)
(270) 476–3301

Seaman's Church Institute
Paducah
(270) 575–1005

Shakertown at South Union
South Union (near Auburn)
(270) 542–4167

Trail of Tears Intertribal Pow Wow
the weekend after Labor Day
Hopkinsville
(270) 886–8033

Wickliffe Mounds Research Center
Wickliffe
(270) 335–3681

The other big event is Benton's **Tater Day,** held on the first Monday in April since 1843 and one of the world's few events dedicated to the delectable sweet potato. Pay your homage to a great food and enjoy a friendly small-town festival. Activities run the whole weekend, leading up to the day itself. For information on Big Singing Day or Tater Day, call the Marshall County Tourism Office at (800) 467–7145 or visit www.kentuckylake.org.

Just outside Benton in **Draffenville,** the music continues. On any Saturday night of the year and on Friday in June, July, August, and December, a live country music show is performed by Clay Campbell's **Kentucky Opry.** Locals love this show, so if you're serious about getting to know this region, you've got to stop by and "give a listen." It's a family-oriented place, so children are welcome but alcohol is not. The specialties are country, gospel, and some really hot bluegrass. Regular admission is $11 for adults and $5.50 for kids, although tickets for celebrity concerts might be higher. Call (270) 527–3869 or (888) 459–8704 or go high-tech and log onto www.kentuckyopry.com.

Going south on US 641 brings you to the peaceful town of **Murray,** which Rand McNally ranked the "number one retirement location in the country" because of the proximity of outdoor recreational areas, the low crime rate, and the low cost of living.

Rudy's Restaurant (270–753–1632), on the west side of the courthouse square at 104 South Fifth Street, is so crowded at lunchtime that you may have to sit with a stranger if you're determined to have a fresh hamburger and homemade onion rings. This little place has been open since the early 1930s, when the original Rudy made it famous for its consistently good country cooking and cutting-edge gossip. Rudy, a short, roly-poly fellow whose lip never knew the absence of a cigar, collected money and spread the news of the day from a stool behind the big brass cash register. Monday through Friday breakfast starts at 5 A.M., and lunch ends at 2 P.M.

trueblue

Kentucky is one of only four states to use the designation *commonwealth*, meaning government based on common consent of the people.

Potter Wayne Bates is known throughout the region for his meticulously crafted sgraffito porcelain vessels. My own favorites are the striking black-on-white radial designs on wide bowls, but he also makes use of brighter colors. You can see a wide selection of his pieces and usually watch him at work if you visit his studio and showroom called **Gallery 121.** Because he works and lives at the same site, he's usually open daily, but it's a good idea to call ahead at (270) 436–5610. To get there from Murray, take Highway 121 South

Authentic to the End

Civil War reenactors (and Kentucky has a slew of them) often take their reenactment quite seriously, insisting on meticulous detail and authenticity in their uniforms and accessories and often adopting the total identity of soldiers from the past. Carrying this thought to its ultimate conclusion was one of the inspirations for **Bert & Bud's Vintage Coffins,** of Murray. Roy "Bud" Davis, the former director of the Clara M. Eagle Art Gallery at Murray State University, creates 19th-century "toe pincher–style" and other unique coffins at a studio in his garage. So far, business hasn't been exactly lively, but one Murray antiques buff ordered a coffin for use as a coffee table, and a Nova Scotia customer plans to use one in a theatrical production. Meanwhile, he is looking at lighter sidelines. He also built a whimsical coffin that looks like a dollhouse for his wife. "She has no intention of using it for a long time," he noted. "Our market is really not for people who need a coffin now, but for people who want something different and tend to plan ahead." Give Davis a call at (877) 371–9279 or (270) 753–9279 if you're interested in stopping by while you're in Murray. The Web site is fascinating too: www.vintagecoffins.com.

(in town it's Fourth Street South); drive 8.3 miles (if you measure from the courthouse square) and watch on the left for his gallery sign. He has a great Web site at www.waynebates.com that shows the work and gives information about upcoming events at the studio and so forth.

Take Highway 94 east from Murray and go about 8 miles. Look for a sign that says *Alfred Duncan House of Willow* (270–759–9595). Go another mile and turn right on Old Newburg Road and look for a sign that says *George Beard's House of Willow* (270–436–5084). In either place you'll probably see curving bent willow chairs in the yard by the signs. Each man has a workshop by his house. Each man is carrying on a "stick furniture" tradition that was probably started by the gypsies who sold willow chairs in this area in the 1930s. George Beard taught Alfred Duncan the craft and approves of his student's work so much that he claims he can't tell their work apart. Both men are extraordinary, thrifty chair makers. Regardless of the fact that this style of outdoor furniture is in vogue at the moment, this craft has lasting integrity. These chair makers go to riverbanks in Kentucky and all over swampy areas of the South to gather red and white willow branches that they bend and nail into place while still green. Nothing is wasted; the large stock is used for heavy supports, thin branches are twisted into decorative backs or armrests, and the very thinnest trees, some as young as six months, are used as "benders," pliable pieces that make accommodating seats. Sit in any chair, love seat, or rocker and your body will understand that the Shakers couldn't have designed them better. The choices of branch size and spacing create a simple and visually stunning effect. Beard has become something of a regional treasure. In 1978 the Smithsonian bought one of his hooded chairs in red willow for its permanent collection; a dark red Indian willow love seat is in a museum in Utah; and the Kentucky Museum in Frankfort exhibits a settee and child's chair. These are craftsmen not to miss and nice folks to boot. They're usually around, but if you'd like to make sure they have some furniture in stock, call ahead.

Hazel, just south of Murray on US 641, was one of the towns that sprang up in the 1890s as the railroad connected western Kentucky with the rest of the world. The town may have been named for the daughter of the conductor of the first through train, although other Hazels are also in contention. Samuel H. Dees, who founded the Hazel Post Office, also had a daughter named Hazel. Some think the name refers to the thick hazel groves that grow in the area. In more recent times, Hazel has made a name for itself as an antiques lovers' haven. The town's charming turn-of-the-20th-century storefronts are now home to dozens of antiques malls and shops; one count placed more than 250 dealers active in the community. So bring your measuring tape, your magnet, your price guides, and your checkbook, and plan to spend all day wandering from shop to shop. Charlie's Antique Mall on Main Street also has an old-fashioned soda fountain. Call mall owner Ray Gough for information about any of the antiques stores at (270) 492–8175, or visit www.charliesantiquemall.com.

Get back on Highway 94 and head west toward the Mississippi River and the little town of Hickman. If you're inclined to take a bizarre little side

SELECTED SOURCES OF TRAVEL INFORMATION FOR THE JACKSON PURCHASE AREA

Kentucky's Western Waterland Tourist Information Center
721 Complex Drive
Grand Rivers 42045
(270) 928–4411
Stop by in person by taking exit 31 off Interstate 24 at Grand Rivers and following the signs. (Note the small herd of buffalo on the opposite side of the highway.)

Mayfield Tourism Commission
201 East College Street
Mayfield 42066
(502) 247–6101

Paducah/McCracken County Convention and Visitors Bureau
128 Broadway, Paducah 42001
(270) 443–8783, (800) PADUCAH
www.paducah-tourism.org

Murray Tourism Commission
(800) 651–1603

trip, take a brief detour onto Highway 97 south toward Bell City and watch for **Murdocks' Mausoleum,** a semiunderground building with a sign on the top that reads, STOP SEE A ROAD MAP TO HEAVEN. Who wouldn't stop? On the wall of the porch is a large painted sign describing how one can get to heaven—the gospel of John is heavily quoted. Behind a decorative iron door and window one can view the burial area. The graves of two women take up perhaps a sixth of the burial space, leaving the rest free for future occupants.

As you pass through Cayce, know that this was the home of the legendary daredevil railroad engineer John Luther Jones (better known as Casey Jones), who was "yanked-up" here. When he got his first job with the Illinois Central, there were so many Joneses that his boss nicknamed him "Cayce." The legend that developed around him after his death somehow also corrupted the spelling to "Casey," but folks here haven't forgotten.

In downtown **Hickman,** next to the chamber of commerce, is the shop of **J. M. Cooper,** Old World–style tinkerer extraordinaire. Although he makes and repairs guns and jewelry, Cooper is best known for his work on clocks. The shop is filled with all kinds of modern and antique clocks, some of his own, some belonging to townspeople (the mayor told me that J. M. has had at least ten of her clocks for at least a decade), but his pride and joy—the courthouse clock—rises high above everything else on the bluff. In 1974 J. M. completely rebuilt the innards of the old Seth Thomas, originally installed in 1904. The clock parts weigh almost 2 tons, the bell about 2,800 pounds, and the striking hammer a hefty 40 pounds. Few such clocks are in operation, and fewer yet are still wound by hand; every eight days "Coop" climbs the long stairs of the clock tower and winds. On slow days, when he's feeling up to it, he'll take people up. His shop hours are by chance, so call the chamber ahead at (270) 236–2902 to find out if J. M. is in.

trueblue

Mark Twain called Hickman "the most beautiful town on the Mississippi."

The **Warren Thomas Black Museum,** 603 Moulton Street, preserves history of the town's African-American community. The building itself is one of the most significant artifacts; it's an 1890 church, Thomas Chapel, founded by former slaves. The chapel was named for "Uncle Warren" and "Aunt Sally" Thomas, who gave the land for the building. Warren Thomas was the congregation's first minister. In 1895 the original building burned and the present building was built to replace it. For decades it served as a school and center of community life for African-American citizens in Hickman. The old Thomas

Where, Oh Where Did Wolf Island Go?

Hickman County is missing a tooth. Sometime between 1820 and 1870, a channel of the Mississippi River shifted to the east, leaving a 9,000-acre chunk of Kentucky land stranded in Missouri, nearly a mile west of the rest of the county. Despite its new location, in 1871 the Supreme Court awarded the land, now called Wolf Island, to Kentucky, thereby denying the big daddy of all waters the power to move official boundaries.

Chapel building became a Kentucky Landmark in 1978. Tours are given by appointment; call (270) 236–2423.

From Hickman you can take the ***Hickman-Dorena Ferry*** across the Mississippi River to Missouri. The ferry runs daily except Christmas Day. The first run of the day is at 7 A.M. from the Kentucky side, 7:30 A.M. from the Missouri side, with the last run at 6:15 P.M. from the Kentucky side and 6:30 P.M. from the Missouri side. During the day, runs are made by demand. There's a button to push on the telephone pole near the ferry entrance to signal the captain that you want to cross. Fare for an automobile is $10 one-way. Save your ticket and you get half fare for the return trip. Call the ferry boat itself at (731) 693–0210 or the main office at (731) 285–0390 for information (www .dorena-hickmanferryboat.com).

From Hickman you can also follow Highway 94 southwest to ***Reelfoot Lake.*** The part of the lake that is in Kentucky (most is in Tennessee) is wild, beautiful swampland. During the winter of 1811–12, a series of earthquakes along the New Madrid fault shook the whole region so violently that the tremors made bells ring as far away as Pittsburgh, Pennsylvania. Reelfoot Lake was created when the quakes caused the Mississippi River to run backwards; when it returned to its usual flow, it straightened out and left behind one of its old curves. Look at your map and the abandoned bend will become obvious. Admire the large stands of bald cypress trees. Their lower trunks are broad, flaring like upside-down flying buttresses; the needles are feathery and fine; and they're surrounded by their own "knees," or cone-shaped roots, which seem to emerge from the water independently. These roots make it possible for the large trees to remain upright in the muddy soils. Follow Highway 94 southwest to the Reelfoot Lake National Wildlife Refuge and talk to the rangers about the local wildlife.

The only way to go farther west in Kentucky is to drive down Highway 94 into Tennessee, where it becomes Highway 78. From Tiptonville, Tennessee, follow the signs to the Madrid Bend, also known as Kentucky Bend or Bessie

Bend. A few families have the peninsula to themselves to farm however they please.

North of Hickman and "inland" a bit, on U.S. Highway 51, is the town of **Clinton,** home to the new **Hickman County Museum,** which is a testament to the spirit of local devotion to local history. Volunteers and a museum board renovated an 1870s house (once belonging to Capt. Henry Cruse Watson, who fought with the Confederate army) at 221 East Clay Street. Each of nine rooms presents thematically grouped artifacts (all of which were donated), from the College Room to the Medical Room. Items on display range from historic military uniforms, an early 1900s fire-hose cart designed to be pulled by two men on foot, political mementos associated with "local boy" Alben W. Barkley, pottery made by prehistoric peoples called Mound Builders, and all sorts of agricultural tools. Hours are 1 to 4 P.M. on Wednesday and Saturday, or by appointment. Admission is $1. For more information call (270) 653–6566 or (270) 653–6587.

In the center of the Jackson Purchase region is the town of **Mayfield,** known to outsiders for **The Wooldridge Monuments,** "the strange procession that never moves," in the cemetery. The entrance to the Maplewood Cemetery is in town at the intersection of the U.S. Highway 45 overpass and North Seventh Street. The 18-figure group in sandstone and Italian marble was erected in the late 1890s by an otherwise inconsequential bloke named Henry G. Wooldridge. Though he is the only person buried on the site, the figures represent him on his favorite horse, Fop; him standing by a podium; two hounds, a fox, and a deer; and his three sisters, four brothers, mother, and two great-nieces, one of whom, rumor has it, actually resembles Henry's first love, Minnie, who died in her youth. Legend has it that when the statues were en route from Paducah, a drunk climbed

trueblue

Alben W. Barkley was born in 1877 in Graves County and raised there in relative poverty before his steady political climb from law clerk to county attorney to U.S. congressman, senator, and finally, in 1949, to vice president in the second administration of President Harry S. Truman.

on the flat railcar and mounted the stone horse behind the stone Wooldridge to ride into Mayfield, the drunk king of a mute parade. For information call the Mayfield/Graves County Chamber of Commerce at (270) 247–6101.

If you aren't sure whether you are really in the South, you will be when you encounter another memorial in town right in the center of town square, because it's dedicated to Mayfield's Confederate dead. More local history is explained just blocks away in the **Western Kentucky Museum** at 120 North

Bobbie Ann Mason

Mayfield is the hometown of Bobbie Ann Mason, one of America's most perceptive and powerful writers. If you've read her work, you'll feel you've been in this region before. Her fiction is intensely crafted and rich in realistic detail, and her characters seem familiar, not at all larger-than-life. Mason says, "Like me, these characters are emerging from a rural way of life that is fast disappearing, and they are wondering where they're going to end up." Her novels include *Feather Crowns*, *Spence + Lila*, and the powerful work about the effect of the war in Vietnam on rural Americans, *In Country*, which was made into a well-loved movie by the same title. She has written many short stories and recently published a selection of her favorites called *Midnight Magic*, which will make you seek out all her short fiction. Mason lives in Kentucky and still has family in Mayfield.

Eighth Street, at the corner of West North Street. The museum of artifacts dating back to the late 19th century includes lots of regional business and agricultural paraphernalia, particularly pertaining to tobacco. Also housed in the restored icehouse is the **Graves County Art Guild,** which showcases local paintings and sculptures. Both are open Tuesday through Saturday from 10 A.M. to 4 P.M. For more information call (270) 247–6101.

Stanley Boekout has built houses and furniture all of his life. Upon retirement, however, he switched scales and now builds dollhouses. He even creates custom-built miniature replicas of real-world homes, complete with miniature furniture, carpets, kitchen accoutrements, lamps that plug into outlets (yes, he can wire them for electric service), and birdhouses for the yard. His shop, **Wood 'n Crafts,** is attached to his house, just south of Mayfield at 1312 Highway 303, and he welcomes visitors. Most every day the shop is open from 8 A.M. to 5 P.M. Custom orders are welcome, so bring blueprints.

A great place to eat in town is the **Hills Barbecue** (270–247–9121). Coming from Murray by Highway 121 north, it's on the left at the Y intersection of Cuba and Paris Roads, next to McDonald's. In business since 1949, the place is known for homemade pies and any-way-you-want-it sandwiches. It has a big porch for summer eating, a drive-in window, indoor tables, and a long sociable counter. The decor has definite allure. I tried, in vain, to buy an old tin John Ruskin cigar sign—best and biggest. Hours are 7 A.M. to 10 P.M. Monday through Saturday.

Fiery debates and pit barbecue are at the heart of the **Fancy Farm Picnic,** perhaps the sole survivor of grassroots political-campaign picnics in America. *The Guinness Book of World Records* lists it as the world's largest one-day picnic, not surprising when more than 15,000 pounds of fresh pork and mutton are cooked annually. The first Saturday in August at 10 A.M., games and enter-tainment begin, country-goods booths go up, and local, state, and national political figures rile the crowds, one way or another. Speeches are given from a red, white, and blue bunting-covered flatbed wagon, just like in 1880, when the picnic was established as the last opportunity for candidates to meet before the August primaries. Because the primaries are now held in May, the picnic functions as a debate forum for the final candidates. Fancy Farm is 10 miles west of Mayfield on Highway 80, at its junction with Highway 339.

Does talking politics make your head reel? Try reeling in a live fish instead. (Though both can emanate less-than-delicate aromas.) West of Fancy Farm, near Arlington at the corner of Highway 80 and County Route 1130, is **Grogan's Pay Lake** (270–655–2470). If your luck leaves your line empty, bring a catch home anyhow from the Fresh Fish Market.

Due west on Highway 80 in Hickman County is the low-lying river town of **Columbus.** Slightly upriver, between Columbus and Clinton, the **Columbus-Belmont Battlefield State Park** (270–677–2327; http://parks.ky.gov/findparks/recparks/cb) perches on 200-foot-high palisades. The park marks the Civil War site of the westernmost Confederate fortification in Kentucky. Rebel soldiers installed a whopping mile-long chain, held afloat by wooden

A Festival Whose *Ap-peel* Is Remembered

Fulton, Kentucky, a fence-sitting town on the Kentucky-Tennessee border (South Fulton is in the Volunteer State), reminds me of that old song, "Yes, We Have No Bananas." Once, Fulton had plenty of 'em. For decades, wholesalers from all over the country came to Fulton to buy bananas, which were shipped from South America via New Orleans to the largest icehouse in the United States in, you guessed it, Fulton. In 1962 the town started the annual International Banana Festival, which featured the "world's largest banana pudding." One year the publicly made pudding topped two tons in order to make it into *The Guinness Book of World Records*. Changing times, however, were catching up with Fulton, and in the festival's last years, the town had to practically beg for bananas. So in 1992 the festival was disbanded. In a way, though, you can still experience it, in a children's illustrated story published online by Indiana author and illustrator Jerry Jindrich. Through tales and drawings, Jerry and his wife, Susan, have created an educational fantasy world online called the "Island of Meddybemps, home of Chateau Meddybemps." One of the stories, titled "But That Wasn't the Best Part," was inspired by the International Banana Festival, which Jerry attended one year. Wonder what the best part was? Visit www.meddybemps.com and find out a little about a Kentucky town's festival that will always *ap-peel* to the imagination.

The Most Debated Place Name in Kentucky

If you've become hooked on digressions, here's an opportunity to indulge. Continue from Barlow on US Highway 60 east to La Center and take Highway 358 north, then go west on Highway 473 through Ogden (once called Needmore) to *Monkey's Eyebrow,* the most debated place name in the state of Kentucky. There is no post office, hence no official name, but we argue nonetheless. Journalist Byron Crawford submits the idea that, if one looks at the shape of the northern boundary of Ballard County, the Ohio River forms a rough profile of a monkey in such a way that this community is just where the eyebrow would be. Others say that there was a store owned by John and Dodge Ray, the brothers who settled the sandy loam ridge in the late 19th century, and behind it was a berm that resembled a monkey's eyebrow because it was covered with tall grasses. New theories are welcome fuel for the fire.

rafts, across the Mississippi River to prevent Union gunboats from moving south. Each link of the chain weighed 15 pounds, and the anchor attached to it was six tons. Cannons were lined up on the face of the bluffs. Shortly after the fortification was complete, Union forces led by Ulysses S. Grant took the town in 1861 when Confederate forces were crumbling everywhere. The park's high bluff is a pleasantly dizzying picnic and camping site. The huge anchor with its chain is still on display, along with some cannons. Civil War buffs will also enjoy walking along the earthen fortifications and visiting the small but interesting Civil War Museum with its exhibits of cannonballs, documents, and other artifacts. The park is open year-round, but the museum is open April through October. There's a small admission fee.

Follow Highway 123 north to Bardwell, then take US 51 north to Wickliffe. Every Memorial Day weekend from Wickliffe to Fulton, on the Tennessee border, US 51 is lined with flea markets and yard sales. If you can't find junk to your heart's desire on that weekend, you ain't never gonna find it.

Go through Wickliffe as if you were crossing the river to Cairo, Illinois, and look for signs to the *Wickliffe Mounds Research Center* (270–335–3681). You'll understand why the Mississippian Indians chose this site as a town or ceremonial grounds when you stand on the highest mound and look out toward the wide sparkling junction of two massive rivers, the Ohio and the Mississippi. The scene is exhilarating. In addition to the intact, four-sided, flat-topped ceremonial mound, three excavation areas have been preserved and interpreted for the public.

One of the most significant displays is in the cemetery. Without being eerie or morbid, the space is moving. The bodies were buried close together, each surrounded by a few significant belongings, each facing east as if to remain in contact with the cycle of days and nights. The display explains how archaeologists determine diet, illnesses, typical injuries, and physical appearances by analyzing the remains of people who weren't radically different from us. All the actual human remains and burial goods have been replaced with plastic replicas in their original positions. This seriously self-examining display deals with various points of view, including a Native American view, about the appropriate study and treatment of human remains. The curators and Native American advisers are working toward making Wickliffe Mounds into a ceremonial site, as it was thousands of years ago. Hours are 9 A.M. to 4:30 P.M. daily from March to November. Admission is $5 for adults, $4 for children. Write to the Wickliffe Mounds Research Center, P.O. Box 155, Wickliffe 42087.

About 6 miles northeast of Wickliffe on U.S. Highway 60 is the town of Barlow, and in it a museum called the *Barlow House Museum,* on the corner of Broadway and Fifth Street, which pays tribute to the early history of Ballard County by preserving the home and belongings of a family that helped settle the region. In 1849 Thomas Jefferson Barlow bought land but didn't want to farm, so he opened a general store and started selling lots for houses. Like many an American town, that's how Barlow was born. The fully restored 1903 Victorian home belonged to Thomas's oldest son, Clifton J. Barlow, and remained in the Barlow family until 1989. The house is open to the public for tours Monday, Friday, and every other Sunday from 1 to 4 P.M., or by appointment, and also for meetings, receptions, and so forth. Contact Della Johnson for more information at (270) 334–3010 or (270) 334–3691, or visit www.ballard conet.com/barlowhouse.

To get in touch with nature, go east on US 60 until you reach Future City. Turn left (northeast) on Highway 996 and go almost 6 miles to where the road ends in a strange swampy landscape. The Kentucky State Nature Preserves Commission has purchased *Metropolis Lake* in order to protect this intriguing, naturally formed, little body of water and the surrounding river floodplain from destructive development. Fishing is permitted here because anglers drool over the lake's population of fish and because people take good care of the area. Although the lake area used to be a developed commercial recreation area, today it is more pure, an enchanted dreamscape with bald cypress and swamp tupelo trees casting strange shapes against the sky and even stranger reflections on the water. Beavers, kingfishers, wildflowers, and seven rare aquatic species are among the many living creatures that share this special space. If you have questions call the commission at (502) 564–2886; www .naturepreserves.ky.gov/stewardship/metrolake.

Stay on US 60 and go east into **Paducah,** the urban center of the Jackson Purchase region. As you near the downtown area, look for Noble Park on the west side of the road. Stop when you come across an enormous, haunting sculpture of a Chickasaw Indian. The piece, called **Wacinton,** or "to have understanding," was carved from a 56,000-pound red oak tree by Hungarian-born sculptor Peter "Wolf" Toth in 1985. Toth donated the piece to the city of Paducah and the state of Kentucky in honor of the Native American people who lived in the area before the Jackson Purchase, in 1818. In 1972, at the age of 25, Toth decided to carve a giant Native American sculpture for every state in the Union. He refuses pay. His "trail of whispering giants" is his gift to our national conscience. He identifies with the suffering of Native Americans because he and his family lost everything when they fled Hungary in 1956 just before the communist revolution. Paducah's *Wacinton* is Toth's 50th sculpture. After the United States, he says he'll be carving in Canada, then Mexico.

The people of Paducah have renovated and preserved a once-dilapidated Classical Revival mansion by making it into the **Whitehaven Welcome Center,** south of town on Interstate 24, and filling it with antique furniture from the area. Get travel information here, or call the center at toll free at 800–PADUCAH, or check www.paducah-tourism.org. The lobby and information area are open 24 hours, with tours of the house offered from 1 to 4 P.M. daily.

In downtown Paducah between Broadway and Kentucky Avenue is the Market House, the hub of business and trade since 1836. Today the building houses three arts organizations. The **Market House Museum** (270–443–7759) is a regional history museum that includes the reconstructed interior of an 1877 drugstore. Hours are noon to 4 P.M. Tuesday through Saturday from March through December. Admission is $1.50. The **Yeiser Art Center** and gift shop (270–442–2453) hangs traveling exhibits of contemporary and traditional art. Hours are 10 A.M. to 4 P.M. Tuesday through Saturday. Admission is $3 for adults, $1 for children. Also in the building is the **Market House Theatre** (270–444–6828; www.mhtplay.com), a not-for-profit community theater—check its busy production schedule.

trueblue

Paducah was founded in 1827 by William Lewis (of Lewis and Clark).

Across the street, the **Paducah Harbor Plaza** is a five-story yellow brick building with stained-glass windows and ornate sandstone cornices. Beverly McKinley has opened a bed-and-breakfast on the second floor, making accommodations available in high style as they were when the place was called the Hotel Belvedere. For between $85 and $150 a night, one or two people get a renovated bedroom appointed with antiques and handmade quilts, and a continental breakfast. In the morning, guests get first crack at the apparel, jewelry, and accessories at So Cool, a store on the first floor of the plaza. For lodging information call (270) 442–2698 or (800) 719–7799 or visit www .phplaza.com.

When people think of Kentucky crafts, quilts are often the first things that come to mind. Since April 1991, Paducah immediately comes to mind as the quilt capital of America, thanks to the *Museum of the American Quilter's Society,* downtown at the corner of Second and Jefferson Streets. Those of us who have grown up around (or under) handmade quilts and have taken them for granted can't help but be awestruck with the beauty and variety of the quilts in the museum. Unlike many collections in the region, this museum is primarily devoted to the modern quilt. Those who appreciate abstract painting may find a new passion in the bold shapes and colors of these "canvases."

In addition to the main display area of more than 150 quilts from the permanent collection and the two additional galleries with quilts from traveling exhibitions, the 30,000-square-foot building has a climate-controlled vault, classrooms, a gift shop, and an excellent bookstore that features more than 400 books pertaining to quilting and textiles. The museum is open Monday through Saturday from 10 A.M. to 5 P.M. year-round. From April through October it is also open Sunday from 1 to 5 P.M. and Monday from 10 A.M. to 5 P.M. Admission is $8 for adults, $6 for children. For more information call (270) 442–8856. Three-day quilt-making workshops taught by renowned quilters from across the country are offered every year. For schedules write MAQS/Workshop Program, P.O. Box 1540, Paducah 42002-1540 or check www.quiltmuseum.org.

Also contributing to Paducah's position as Quilt City USA is the annual *AQS National Quilt Show and Contest,* sponsored by the Paducah-based American Quilter's Society. This national quilt extravaganza is held in late April at the Executive Inn Convention Center in downtown Paducah. More than 400 quilts from all over the world are displayed and judged to win a part of the $75,000-plus in cash awards. During that week the whole city is overflowing with quilts. Special workshops and lectures are offered, quilt supply vendors set up shop, and there's even a fashion show and contest. Hotel space is at a premium during the show, so plan ahead. For show information, write to AQS, P.O. Box 3290, Paducah 42002-3290, or call (270) 898–7903. Or visit the Web site at www.americanquilter.com.

Within sight of the Museum of the American Quilter's Society are two other sites not to be missed by quilt aficionados. Look for a huge painted mural of a quilt on the side of a building at 119 North Fourth Street. Inside is *King's Quilting Studio* (270–444–7477; www.paducahquilts.com), the showroom, studio, and classroom of Sara Newberg King. In addition to fine quilts, you'll find hand-dyed silk scarves and other wearable art by King. Ask about special classes and lectures. And if you're saturated with looking and ready to get to work, continue up the street to 420 North Fourth Street, where **Quilter's Alley** offers a plethora of quilting supplies and gorgeous fabrics. Classes are offered regularly, and these knowledgeable folks can make appraisals. For more information call (270) 443–5673 or visit www.quiltersalleypaducah.com.

Right in the hub of old downtown Paducah at 118 Second Street is the business you wish was next door every day. Five generations of German bakers have titillated taste buds at **Kirchhoff's Bakery and Deli** since it was established in 1873. Traditional as the skills are, the owners have stayed current and now offer a range of gourmet market items, deli cheeses, and fresh vegetables, as well as to-die-for breads and pastries. Lunch is served daily from 11 A.M. to 2 P.M., and the calzones go fast. Hours are Monday through Friday from 7 A.M. to 5 P.M. and Saturday from 8 A.M. to 4 P.M. The phone number is (270) 442–7117; www.kirchhoffsbakery.com. One of Paducah's most unique and geographically relevant institutions is the **Seamen's Church Institute/ Center for Maritime Education Paducah** at 111 Kentucky Avenue, which is perched just to the dry side of the confluence of the Tennessee and Ohio Rivers. The Seamen's Church Institute began in the early 1800s as a floating church serving keelboat captains and other river workers. Today the Center for Maritime Education trains barge and riverboat captains and pilots to navigate freshwater inland rivers. In addition to the educational component, there is a nondenominational ministry based here that serves river workers in a variety of ways, from providing Christmas and Easter gifts to running a crisis hotline and coordinating services with "river-friendly" churches. Call (270) 575–1005 or visit www.seamenschurch.org.

The **River Heritage Museum** is located next door at 117 South Water Street. This museum is housed in a beautifully restored 19th-century bank building, thought to be the oldest surviving structure in downtown Paducah. The museum's exhibit hall tells the story of inland navigation history through artifacts, maps, video, and interactive computer stations. The focus is on the cultures of the region shaped by the Ohio, Tennessee, Mississippi, and Cumberland Rivers, from the early indigenous peoples and their bark canoes to life and industry on the river today. Hours are 9:30 A.M. to 5 P.M. Monday through Friday year-round, and on Sunday from 1 to 5 P.M. from April through November. There's no admission charge, but a $2 per-person donation is suggested. For information call (270) 575–9958 or visit www.riverheritagemuseum.org.

When you step outside the front doors of the museum, you're facing the confluence of two of the four rivers, the Ohio and the Tennessee. You're also facing a marvelous artistic vista that was created along the city's flood walls—some 22 murals showing scenes from Paducah history. The **Paducah Flood Wall Murals** were all created by Robert Dafford, a Louisiana artist noted for his large-scale public works in the United States and Europe.

Downtown Paducah seems somewhat larger than life itself during the summer **After Dinner Downtown Paducah** events. Each Saturday night, from the first Saturday in May through the second weekend in October, is like a mini festival, with music on the street corners, antique car displays, carriage rides, and late shop hours. The events attract lively crowds. Contact the tourism office at (800) PADUCAH for more information.

Even when it's not Quilt Festival or After Dinner time, downtown Paducah is a lively and enjoyable place to be. There are numerous antiques shops and restaurants within easy walking distance of the museums and flood wall murals. In fact, the downtown revitalization has been so successful that city leaders are using it as the model for the revival of another city neighborhood, **Lower Town.** LoTo, as locals call it, is a historic district bordered by Park Avenue, Jefferson Street, Fifth Street, and Ninth Street, with houses from the 1820s through 1920s in various stages of renovation. An organization was founded in Paducah to foster this area as an arts district, and the city has advertised special incentives, from low-cost mortgages to marketing support, to attract both local and nonlocal artists.

Civil War buffs, take heed! The taking of Paducah by the Union in 1861 marks a significant moment in the war—when Kentucky finally lost its neutrality. The Union was responding to the recent Confederate victory at the nearby Mississippi River town of Columbus. This and other war stories are explained through artifacts, documents, and photographs at the **Tilghman Civil War Museum,** at the corner of Seventh and Kentucky Avenues. The restored house was once home to a Confederate general, Lloyd Tilghman, who defended the Tennessee and Cumberland Rivers and

trueblue

Both Civil War presidents—Abraham Lincoln and Jefferson Davis—were born in Kentucky, one year and 100 miles apart.

was finally killed in action near Vicksburg. The center is open Friday from noon to 4 P.M. and Saturday from 10 A.M. to 4 P.M. or by appointment. Call (270) 575-5477. Eight other relevant Civil War sites in downtown Paducah can be seen on a free walking tour. Stop by the visitor bureau at 128 Broadway for a map.

For a worthwhile side trip from Paducah, head south of town on Highway 994, then east on Highway 348 toward the town of Symsonia where you'll find the **Henson Broom Shop Museum.** With a few simple pieces of equipment, three generations of skill, piles of sticks, heaps of broom straw, and lots of energy, Richard N. Henson makes hundreds of graceful, functional brooms. His grandfather, also Richard N. Henson, started making brooms in 1930 when the American economy was faltering and the family needed more income. The elder Henson liked to say, "A Hoover put me into business, and a Hoover put me out of business," referring to the president and the vacuum cleaner, respectively.

Today the third-generation broom maker is rarely out of work. During the summer and fall, Henson converts his horse trailer into a portable workshop, dons a costume, and travels to festivals where he does historic craft reenactment, educating the public while he works. (He has been winning blue ribbons for his craftsmanship all over the country.) Brooms have changed very little during the past hundred years. If you used to watch the television show *Dr. Quinn, Medicine Woman*, you probably saw Henson's brooms for sale in the show's general store and in use by the characters. To his array of old-fashioned kitchen, shop, whisk, cabin, colonial hearth, Shaker, and parlor brooms, Henson has added a fancy, twisted-handle design he calls the Jane Seymour Broom in honor of the show's star. Prices range from $5 to more than $50. He's glad to have visitors, so stop by anytime. You can call him at (270) 851–8510, write him at 1060 State Route 348E, Symsonia 42082 (http://www .hensonbrooms.com).

Pennyroyal Region

Tennessee Valley Authority's (TVA) *Land Between the Lakes* national recreation area is considered the "crappie fishing capital of the world," not to mention the huge populations of largemouth and smallmouth bass—an angler's dream come true. The Tennessee River was dammed to make Kentucky Lake, and Lake Barkley was formed from the mighty Cumberland River. Together they comprise 220,000 acres of clean, safe water and form a 40-mile-long peninsula, which the TVA has developed for recreation and education.

For bird lovers, Land Between the Lakes, or LBL, is one of a scant handful of places where one can get a glimpse of wild bald eagles. In the 1960s poaching and the use of chemicals such as DDT reduced the number of breeding eagles to fewer than 600 pairs, making our national mascot nearly extinct on this continent. The wildlife management people at LBL successfully got the numbers back up by returning raptors to

trueblue

Kentucky Lake and Lake Barkley together form one of the largest engineered lakes in the United States.

a natural habitat with very little human contact. Ask about eagle and wildlife programs at the Woodlands Nature Center. During the winter, eagle field trips are scheduled for the weekends (www.lbl.org).

Photographers can get close-up pictures of these marvelous creatures in captivity at the nature center or, if you're lucky and very patient, in the wild. Throughout the year there's plenty for nature enthusiasts to see and do. In addition to plenty of lake access ramps, there are great hiking trails, ranging from 0.2 to 65 miles in length. (The easy **Center Furnace Trail** goes past a historic iron furnace.) You can also rent a bicycle or a canoe. One of the natural programs has been an effort to reintroduce endangered wildlife species. LBL is home to the nation's largest public herd of bison, and in 1996, elk were released into the area. You may be able to see these animals along a self-guided driving tour of the **Elk & Bison Prairie.** At the Golden Pond Visitors Center, there's a small planetarium. And if you drive to the southern end of LBL (actually in Tennessee), you can walk around **The Homeplace 1850,** set up as a working 19th-century homestead. Enter the park from any direction—U.S. Highways 68 and 641, Highway 94, or I–24, or in Tennessee, U.S. Highway 79 or Tennessee Highway 76—and go to the North, South, or Golden Pond Visitors Centers for directions and information about the park. For information about any of the attractions in Land Between the Lakes, call (800) LBL–7077 or go online at www.lbl.org.

If you're hungry and caught smack-dab between a lake and a wet place, pull into **Patti's 1880s Settlement,** home of the Mile-High Meringue Pie, the 2-inch-thick pork chop, and bread baked in a flowerpot. With five gift shops, two restaurants, a miniature-golf course, and an animal park, Patti's seems like a continuation of the dream that a young multimillionaire, Thomas Lawson, had for the town in the 1880s when he found it nestled between the Cumberland and Tennessee Rivers. Lawson changed the town's name from Nichols Landing to Grand Rivers and built himself a resort town with the theme of Southern hospitality. Now that the rivers have been dammed, it should be renamed Grand Lakes, but . . . Patti's Restaurant, owned by the Tullar family, and a perennial favorite with both seasonal and 12-month diners, is open year-round from 10:30 A.M. to at least 9 P.M. every day. Other activities vary some. Call (270) 362–8844 or (888) 736–2515 or visit www.pattis-settlement .com for specifics. Dinner reservations are strongly recommended. Patti's is usually packed.

true*blue*

The Land Between the Lakes area was once known as the Moonshine Capital of the World.

Living near the Pokey?

If you stand on the lakeside near Kuttawa and look across the water, you will see a massive monolithic stone fortress perched on a peninsula that is reminiscent of Alcatraz. This is the Kentucky State Penitentiary at Eddyville, Kentucky's only maximum-security prison. Growing up, whenever kids were reprimanded, someone would say, "Keep that up, and we'll be coming to visit you in Eddyville." A woman who actually grew up in Eddyville in a house just up the hill from the pen told of being in the kitchen and hearing prisoners bang chains against their bars as a form of protest and seeing the men hang white sheets out prison windows with written pleas to the outside world stating their dire need for a new warden. It spooked her to think that the prisoners could see their free neighbors and were bold enough to attempt communication. She also remembered the more trusted old lifers being allowed to sell trinkets by the front gate on Sunday afternoon. One old man gave her a shellacked peach-pit necklace because she reminded him of his own little ones far away.

At the Grand Rivers exit, number 31 off I–24, Kentucky's Western Waterland regional tourism information center (270–928–4411) is an important spot to stop and gather information. While you're there, look carefully at the pasture across the highway—there's a small herd of buffalo just like those that roamed these plains in the hundreds of thousands before European settlement.

An interesting loop drive in this area is along a bit of Lake Barkley's shore. Go to *Kuttawa,* a town with a name that means "beautiful" in Shawnee: From I–24 take exit 40, turn south on U.S. Highway 62, then turn south on Highway 295. You'll curve along the rim of the lake (gorgeous at sunset) toward Kuttawa. Just as you get to town, look for a public parking area on the lakeside and, if it's summer, stop for a little walk along the "Kuttawa cliffs," where you may be lucky enough to watch daring locals do some cliff diving into the deep water. In downtown metropolis Kuttawa there's a beach, marina, and harbor with a restaurant famous for its generous "Rudyburger." To complete the loop, stay on Highway 295 until it intersects with US 62, at which point you can go whichever direction your trip is taking you. Both the Western Kentucky Parkway and I–24 are nearby. For more information, try the Kuttawa Chamber of Commerce at (270) 388–5300 or www.kuttawaky.org. If you're ready to get off the highway and get out of your car, you could try climbing in the saddle and hitting the trail. Happy Trails Riding Stable offers guided tours through the woods. Call (270) 871–4370 or (270) 853–8664 for directions and more information.

The *Davis House,* a bed-and-breakfast in Kuttawa at 528 Willow Way, offers lodging overlooking the lake. The house is named for the family that bought it in 1953 and moved it to its present location when the lake was created. Current owner Betty Dixon bought the 120-year-old house in 1989. There are five guest rooms, along with a lakeside patio and nearby boat dock. Rooms are $75 per night. Call (270) 388–5585 for reservations (www.thedavishouse.com).

One bed (no breakfast) that is worth a visit ranks among Kentucky's most unusual grave markers. Stay on Main Street (also Highway 295), going north until the road splits into separate high and low lanes, and look to the left for the entrance to the city cemetery. When the cemetery driveway forces you to go either right or left, go right. In about 100 feet you will reach a grave that is on the left under a large oak tree and next to a tall obelisk. The marker is a life-size double-bed frame made of stone, beneath which are buried Eliza Jane and Charles Anderson. Married for 60 years, they moved to this marriage bed in 1901 and 1895, respectively. It's a beautiful marker and eerie, too. You'll see.

Due north of Eddyville, if you were to drive aboveground on US 641, you'd pass through Fredonia and Crayne before entering the busy little town of **Marion.** If you were to drive several hundred feet underground, you might just pass through sparkling veins of the amazingly beautiful mineral, fluorspar. Unlike diamond, fluorspar is beautiful in its natural state, just as you'd find in the walls of the underground highway on which you're traveling. Fluorspar, the industrial name for fluorite, the nonmetallic mineral calcium fluoride, is the primary source for tooth-decay retardant, as well as an important material used in the production of aluminum, zinc, some ceramics, and a whole range of chemicals. During and after World War II, Kentucky was the largest producer of the mineral in the United States.

For an actual tour (not virtual or imaginary) of some of the most interesting and varied samples of these crystals to be found anywhere, head down Main Street in Marion, then right on First Street, and watch for the signs to the **Ben E. Clement Mineral Museum,** 205 North Walker Street, in a former elementary school building. Year-round hours are 10 A.M. to 3 P.M., Tuesday through Saturday, and admission is $3 to $5. Someone knowledgeable will be on hand to guide you through this stunning array of fluorite crystals as well as other minerals and geological and archaeological specimens (petrified dinosaur dung, eggs, Mastodon teeth, and so forth) collected by Ben Clement over his 60-year career in the mining business. Most unforgettable is the room full of optical fluorite mounted in vitrines that light the crystals from beneath. For more information call (270) 965–4263 or visit www.marionkentucky.us/clementmineralmuseum.

Another little museum in town deals strictly with objects made and used by the human hand. The **Crittenden County Historical Museum** at 124 East Bellville Street, just downhill from the Crittenden County Public Library, is open from April through October, Tuesday through Saturday from 10 A.M. to 3:30 P.M. or by appointment. Admission is free. Next to the white concrete-block building that houses an enormous range of regional artifacts is a reconstructed log cabin with period implements. It's delightfully out of sync with the rest of the neighborhood. Call (270) 965–9257 for more information (www .marionkentucky.us/historicalmuseum).

The region north of Marion and south of the Ohio River has been settled in recent years by Amish families whose farms and houses might not strike you as much different than the surrounding non-Amish farms, but for a few subtle signals—and not just black buggies, either. See what you notice. For an interesting driving loop, take US 60 north, then turn left (northwest) onto Highway 654 at the community of Mattoon. On the left is a very large, active Amish farm where there is a harness shop that's open to the public. Look across the road for a sign that says MOST FAMILY BAKED GOODS and definitely stop if it is open. Continuing north (watch for a flock of emus at a farm on the right with a sign in the yard for RAY'S SMALL ENGINES), make another stop 1 mile beyond the Mount Zion Church Road at The Dutch Way Store, a tiny, family-run general store that's primarily stocked with goods for Amish use: inexpensive footwear; spices; all sorts of dry, bulk foods; and plenty of sewing supplies. It's open from 8 A.M. to 5 P.M. every day but Sunday. One overall-clad, non-Amish man shopping there bought two pounds of powdered sage leaves. He was slaughtering hogs and thinking about sausage spices. Seasonally, you can dig your own mums at the farm next to the store. Other signs along the way might alert you to the availability of lye soap or sorghum, fresh eggs or apple butter.

To continue the loop, go back and take the Mount Zion Church Road west and turn left (south) onto a tiny gravel road called Turkey Knob. When you meet Fords Ferry Road, either turn left (south) to get back to Marion or turn right, then right again onto Highway 91 and head toward Illinois. To cross the wide and mighty Ohio River, you'll have to ride the **Cave-in-Rock Ferry,** unless the water's high, in which case you're up a creek. There's no place to cross closer than Paducah. The ferry runs daily from 6 A.M. to 10 P.M. The ride is free.

trueblue

The Albany, New York, setting of the movie *How the West Was Won* was filmed in Smithland, Kentucky, in 1961 by Metro-Goldwyn-Mayer.

There was no way to cross the mighty waters in the bitter winter of 1838 when thousands of Cherokee traveled on foot during the forced march from their homelands in southern Appalachia to what would eventually become reservation lands in Oklahoma. This devastating march, known as the Trail of Tears, included a winter spent at a site called **Mantle Rock.** Now owned by The Nature Conservancy and preserved for its rare biological community as well as for its historic importance, this gorgeous site is open to visitors year-round. From Marion take US 60 southwest to Salem, then turn north on Highway 133. Continue through the community called Joy; when you have passed the junction with Highway 1436, go exactly 1.1 miles and look on the left for a bronze historical marker with the number 1675 painted on the post. It's very easy to overlook. If you pass the Cave Spring Church, you passed Mantle Rock. Park your car and take the short (¾-mile) hike in to the most dramatic natural feature of the preserve, a 30-foot-high sandstone arch with a 188-foot span and some fabulous honeycombed weathering patterns. It was here that the Cherokee waited for the ice in the river to melt. Over 4,000 died of cold and starvation, since they were not prepared for winter. In the spring they finally crossed into what is now Galcouda, Illinois.

Preceding this bleak event by almost 10,000 years, Archaic peoples camped on this site. Between AD 600 and 800, Lewis peoples, who were hunter-gatherers, had a village here. Archaeologists have discovered more than 100 stone burial mounds. Today the site is home to some rare and fragile plants, like June grass. The site is lush and quiet and so isolated that you might be able to let your mind travel to other times. If you want more information about the site or would like to arrange guided tours of the fragile glades (normally off-limits to hikers), contact The Nature Conservancy, 642 West Main Street # 1, Lexington 40508, or call (859) 259–9655; www.nature .org. You are also welcome to visit the new **Mantle Rock Native Education and Cultural Center** at 110 South Main Street in Marion (270–965–5882; www.mantlerock.org).

The first major town east of the lakes on Highway 68 is **Cadiz** (pronounced KAY-dizz), named, perhaps, after the hometown of an early Spanish surveyor. Since the creation of Land Between the Lakes, people say that the name means "gateway" in Spanish, since Cadiz is at the southeastern entrance to the area. Saxophone lovers pay homage here to the inimitable Boots Randolph, who was born in Trigg County. (The question is, should a golf course be named after a musician? Poor guy.) Ham lovers must have a meal in town; prize-winning hams are served everywhere. During the second weekend in October, follow your nose to the **Trigg County Country Ham Festival,** which features the *Guinness* record holder for the world's biggest ham and biscuit. Non-Southerners may learn that not all country ham can be safely compared to the salt-drenched tongue of your big brother's hiking boot. Call (270) 522–3892 for festival information.

In downtown Cadiz, visit the ***Janice Mason Art Museum,*** 71 Main Street. A former post office building has found new life as an arts center, thanks to

trueblue

Musician Boots Randolph was
born in Trigg County, Kentucky.

the efforts of a dedicated group of community volunteers. There are changing regional exhibits in various mediums, as well as a small gift shop. Hours are 10 A.M. to 4 P.M. Monday, Tuesday, and Thursday through Saturday, and 1 to 4 P.M. Sunday. The museum is closed Wednesday. Call (270) 522–9056 to find out what's on display (www.jmam.org).

For more information about local attractions, including walking tours of historic homes and the Little River area, stop by the log cabin tourist center on Main Street downtown, call (270) 522–3892, or go to www.gocadiz.com.

There is something eerie and irresistible about stepping into a person's space and looking at the way that individual's daily life is shaped and revealed by his or her personal belongings. The *Adsmore Museum* in *Princeton* draws visitors into the lives of its early-20th-century residents in that almost taboo way by presenting the house intact, changing detailed decorations and personal accessories eight times a year, and building the tour around stories of the family. The interpretive staff reenacts weddings, birthday parties, and wakes (complete with wailing mourners dressed in period clothes). Details make this place a treat. That the Victorians in Europe were not morally able to utter the phrase "chicken thigh," for example, comes as no surprise when you find that the piano's legs, like a lady's, were always chastely covered with a shawl.

Built in grand late-Victorian style in 1857, Adsmore was fully restored in 1986 by the local library board to which Katharine Garrett, the last family resident, donated the building and its contents. Adsmore could have also been called "Collectsmore," for it is furnished lavishly with items from all over the world. Also on the grounds is the Ratliff Gun Shop, a restored 1844 cabin filled with antique tools. The museum and grounds are open Tuesday through Saturday from 11 A.M. to 4 P.M. and Sunday from 1:30 to 4 P.M. Admission ranges from $2 to $7, according to age category. Group rates are available. Call (270) 365–3114 or visit www.adsmore.org. Adsmore, at 304 North Jefferson Street in downtown Princeton, has been called the Natchez of West Kentucky because of its grand homes. From Cadiz the quickest route is Highway 139 north. From the Land Between the Lakes, take US 62, or take exit 12 from the Western Kentucky Parkway.

Princeton's oldest building, the circa 1817 Federal-style Champion-Shepherdson House at 115 East Main, has been renovated and is now home to the *Princeton Art Guild*. Like so many early settlements, Princeton began with a general store located near a big, dependable spring. A lean-to money counting room, also used by fur traders, is now an artist-in-residence studio. The main building houses a gallery, a gift shop, and space for special events and workshops. Hours are 11 A.M. to 4 P.M. Tuesday through Saturday. For more information, write the guild at P.O. Box 451, Princeton 42445, or call (270) 365–3959.

In the not-so-distant past, the change of seasons was reflected in retail stores, and not just by "fall fashions" or seasonal decorations. Nowadays we often are offered the same things year-round. Not so with **Newsom's Old Mill Store** at 208 East Main Street. Garden plants are available in the spring and fresh produce is available as it comes in during the growing season. Gifts and specialty foods are offered year-round, with a special emphasis on country ham. The Newsoms sell their own aged hams, bacon, sausage, and, the favorite, hickory-smoked barbecue ham. The barbecued ham sandwich is a local favorite. Store hours are 9 A.M. to 4:30 P.M. Monday through Saturday. Call (270) 365–2482 for mail-order information.

For a historic picnic spot, stop just 1 block south of the Princeton courthouse at **Big Spring Park,** the original settlement's water source and a site where the Cherokees camped on the Trail of Tears. Also noteworthy is the Black Patch Tobacco Festival, which Princeton hosts in early September to commemorate the times when dark-leaf tobacco was harvested in the area in massive quantities. Accompanying this event is a dark and touchy history

Fire?

Early one morning, during recent travels through western Kentucky, I was driving down an old highway in that trancelike state of the traveler. Moisture was rising like liquid smoke from low places, and silver frost traced grassy meadows where shadows lingered. Everything was beautiful and slightly surreal. My eyes snapped wide open at the sight of a tall, skinny barn from which real smoke was pouring out of every crack as if it was about to lift off its rubble stone launch pad foundation and head to Mars. It was sided with a hodgepodge of corrugated roof tin, galvanized here, rusted or painted there, and long boards were leaning at steep angles against any panel that opened or was loose enough to flap in the wind. Nearly driving off the road, I looked hard. The structure was not burning, but it sure as heck was smoking. Throughout the day I saw dozens more tall skinny barns made of just about anything, uniformly and calmly smoking away. These, I realized, were curing barns for dark-fired tobacco, unfamiliar to a bluegrass resident for whom Burley tobacco, which is air-cured in sievelike open-slatted black barns, is standard. Dark-fired tobacco is hung in these tall barns and carefully dried by use of slow-burning, smoldering fires usually built in pits in the floor. This year, late October was curing time. And for the traveling outsider, time not to call 911 at every puff of smoke.

involving tobacco price wars and the night riders, a movement of farmers (made nationally famous by writers such as Robert Penn Warren) who turned to a sophisticated form of organized violence to ensure the viability of their way of life. Local historians explain the events during the Black Patch tour.

Take Highway 91 south from Princeton to downtown **Hopkinsville.** In the grand old Federal-style post office building at the corner of East Ninth (US 68) and Liberty Streets is the **Pennyroyal Area Museum** (270–887–4270; http://www.hoptown.org/museum), an impressive regional-history museum.

The main display area is in the huge mail-sorting room. Notice the enclosed catwalks overhead, secret vantage points from which postmasters watched postal workers handle the mail, not to enforce efficiency (it is after all, a federal institution), but to prevent workers from stealing cash from the envelopes in a pre-checking account era.

The museum's displays address many facets of the Pennyroyal region's history, from agriculture and the Black Patch wars to reconstructed pioneer bedrooms and an 1898 law office. In the middle of the room sits a beautifully preserved original Mogul wagon, made just 2 blocks away in a large factory that manufactured every imaginable type of wagon. Mogul Wagon Company's ads in the 1920s read EASY TO PULL, HARD TO BREAK and BUY A MOGUL AND WILL IT TO YOUR GRANDSON. Railroad and early automobile artifacts compete for your attention with a miniature circus made by John Venable, which is said to have inspired Robert Penn Warren's *The Circus in the Attic,* the title piece of an early collection of short stories. Museum hours are 8:30 A.M. to 4:30 P.M. Monday through Friday and 10 A.M. to 3 P.M. Saturday. Admission is $1 for children under twelve and $2 for adults.

The Edgar Cayce exhibit is one of the most popular in the museum. The display case contains a few photographs and significant personal objects, like Cayce's dog-eared desk Bible. Cayce, who was born in 1877 in southern Christian County near Beverly, was a "strange" child who preferred meditating on the Bible to playing baseball. In 1900, after a severe illness, Cayce mysteriously lost his voice. When put under hypnosis by "Hart—The Laugh Man" in 1901, Cayce diagnosed the problem and restored his own voice by using a treatment he discovered during hypnosis. That was the beginning of his career as an internationally known clairvoyant, "the sleeping prophet." He gave 14,256 psychic readings in which he diagnosed medical problems and predicted world affairs, including natural disasters and economic changes. Today the Association for Research and Enlightenment, based at Virginia Beach, Virginia, where Cayce spent the last 20 years of his life, continues "The Work," as Cayce called it, by providing a library and educational programs related to his readings.

Many of Hopkinsville's visitors from the west, passing through town en route to Virginia Beach, stop to see the place where Edgar Cayce and his wife, Gertrude Evans, are buried in the Riverside Cemetery on the north side of town, just east of North Virginia Street. Seven miles south of town on the Lafayette Road (Highway 107) in Beverly are Cayce's church, the Liberty Christian Church, which is open to the public at no charge, and his school, the Beverly Academy, which is now on private property. If you're a Cayce fan, ask at the museum about other significant sites.

Hopkinsville has done more than any other town in the state to pay tribute to the Native American people who were forced to move from their southeastern homelands across the Mississippi River to Oklahoma on the infamous Trail of Tears during the winter of 1838–39. More than 13,000 Cherokees camped in Hopkinsville and received provisions for their forced migration, during which thousands of people died.

The Trail of Tears Commission Inc. has developed the ***Trail of Tears Commemorative Park*** at Ninth Street and Skyline Drive on the west edge of town. The park includes impressive, larger-than-life statues of Cherokee chiefs White Path and Fly Smith, who are buried on the property. Near the banks of the Little River is a log cabin that serves as an education center.

Although the Cherokee people fought alongside the colonists during the American Revolution and later with Andrew Jackson in the War of 1812, Jackson, as president in the late 1820s, insisted that Native Americans of numerous tribes yield and leave their homelands east of the Mississippi. The forced removal spanned a decade, causing tremendous loss of lives in the process and leaving the survivors a legacy of hardship on barren reservations in the West. It should also be noted that gold was discovered on Cherokee land in Georgia in 1828, 10 years prior to the Native Americans' forced migration. The park includes a heritage center. Hours are Monday through Saturday from 10 A.M. to 4 P.M. from April through October, and Tuesday through Saturday from 10 A.M. to 2 P.M. November through March (www.trailoftears.com).

The ***Trail of Tears Intertribal Indian Pow Wow*** has become an annual event, held the first full weekend in September. Although the recent history of the Native American people is tragic, this public festival is meant to commemorate the beauty and integrity of their culture. The pow wow features Native American crafts, food, storytelling, blow-gun demonstrations, and a very competitive Indian dance contest. Contact the Trail of Tears Commission Inc., P.O. Box 4027, Hopkinsville 42240, or call (270) 886–8033 or (800) 842–9959, or check www.kyfestivals.com.

Ferrell's Snappy Service, 1001 South Main Street (270–886–1445), is a local landmark and a great place to get a classic grilled burger and fries. David

Amish Ingenuity

Just to illustrate how the Amish in the area (there are many kinds of Amish communities) adjust their lives to both the community rules and the modern world, let me tell you how Betty Miller gets to work at Schlabach's Bakery every morning. Her community uses tractors and horse-and-buggy rigs, but not cars or bicycles. If she were male, she might hop on her Massey Ferguson and drive; if she were a child, she might sprint. Instead, she gets on her small tractor (a ride-on lawn mower) and commutes through yards and along the shoulder of the highway. Some churches won't allow use of any vehicle with rubber tires, so the members own steel-wheeled tractors. Other churches allow cars and trucks but insist they be painted black, even the chrome parts. Others allow congregation members to have cars and attend graduate school. And, at the other extreme, very orthodox communities use only horses and oxen.

S. Ferrell and his wife, Cecil Doris, opened the restaurant in 1936. Originally it offered curb service. Although Ferrell died in 2001 at age 87, his famous burger with pickles and onions continues to be one of Western Kentucky's most delicious traditions. Ferrell's is open 24 hours Monday through Saturday, but closed Sunday.

South of Hopkinsville, on the Tennessee border, is a small portion of the large Fort Campbell Military Reservation. Generally it's a private, no-trespassing kind of place, but the public is welcome to visit the **_Don F. Pratt Memorial Museum,_** a showcase of sorts for the history of the 101st Airborne "Screaming Eagles" Division (Air Assault), which is based here. Indoors one can see exhibits from the Civil War through Desert Storm, a restored World War II Cargo Glider, and other war-related artifacts. Outdoors are a number of army aircraft, including helicopters. Admission is free, and the hours are 9:30 A.M. to 4:30 P.M. Monday through Saturday, except Christmas and New Year's Days. To get there from U.S. Highway 41A, go through the fort's main gate and stop at the visitor center, where you have to get a pass. Then continue on the same road, turn right on Tennessee Avenue, and left into the museum. For more information call the museum at (270) 798–3215 or visit http://www.fort campbell.com/pratt.php.

As soon as you drive east from Hopkinsville, you are in an area heavily populated by Amish and Mennonite people. Nationally there are about 85,000 Amish, many of whom live in Pennsylvania, Ohio, and Indiana in communities that are being encroached upon by rapidly widening urban edges. Rural Kentucky has become a popular place for Amish families to relocate because the land is beautiful, isolated, and relatively inexpensive. When you visit Amish and Mennonite businesses, keep in mind that they are committed to their way of life in part because they want isolation from the rest of the world. Respect their privacy. Observe their work practices, for they are good stewards of their land and of all their resources. We could stand a little education.

About 6 miles east of town on US 68, at a big farmhouse with rock pillars by the driveway, Henry Hoover runs an unadvertised bulk food and farm supply business primarily meant to serve an orthodox community known as Horse and Buggy Mennonites, folks who have no cars or telephones. He will sell to the public, so stop in if you need flour, cereals, bread, cheese, and so forth. It's a great way to avoid excessive packaging and higher prices due to expensive advertising. Hours are by chance.

Pete's Custom Saddle Shop is an orderly, productive (secular) one-man leather operation at 9728 Jefferson Davis Highway (Old Highway 68) about 8 miles east of Hopkinsville. In addition to making and refurbishing more than a hundred saddles a year, Russell (Pete) Harry makes holsters, halters, and bridles, not to mention guns, tomahawks, and an occasional painting. Although he's geared primarily to custom work, there are always a few items for sale in the shop that will knock your socks off. Pete's original saddle designs range from a sleek bird hunting saddle to variations on Civil War styles to a western pleasure show saddle with special braces for a local woman who is paralyzed below the shoulders. One claim to fame is that he has built maybe 80 percent of the sidesaddles used in the United States, most of which are distributed by a company called Hundred Oaks. Even if you are not in need of tack, his stunning work and positive spirit are unique and inspirational. Because his hours are not regular, call him at (270) 886–5448 before visiting. www.petes customsaddles.com.

About a mile and a half past Pete's is ***Fairview,*** a tiny rural town you can't miss, thanks to the ***Jefferson Davis Monument State Historic Site*** looming overhead at a height of 351 feet. From miles away in any direction, the incongruous tower, said to be the tallest concrete-cast obelisk in the world, is visible poking into the sky. During summer months you can ride an elevator to the top for an impressive view of surrounding countryside. The obelisk has recently been renovated. You can also tour the visitor center, which includes a variety of exhibits on Civil War Kentucky. Davis, the first and only president of the Confederate States of America,

trueblue

The Jefferson Davis monument in Fairview is the fourth largest concrete obelisk in the world (351 feet).

was born in March 1808 in a house called Wayfarer's Rest in Fairview. The house was located on the site of what is now the Bethel Baptist Church. The

Jefferson Davis Monument is located on US 68E. Call (270) 886–1765 for hours and information (http://parks.ky.gov/findparks/histparks/jd).

Adjacent to the monument is the *Zimmerman Farms produce stand.* From late May to mid-October, you can buy delicious, organically grown fruits and vegetables. You can trust the Amish when it comes to wholesome, flavorful produce.

At *Elkton,* 8 miles east of Fairview, take Highway 181 south for about 10 miles and look to the right for *Schlabach's Bakery* (270–265–3459), an Amish bakery specializing in satisfaction. Its sourdough bread, sweet rolls, pies, cakes, cookies, and yes, even granola are delicious and always fresh. Hours are 8 A.M. to 5 P.M. every day but Thursday and Sunday. Although the owner is Abe Schlabach, you'll be more likely to meet one of his bakers, who live nearby.

Another mile or so south, at the intersection of Highways 181 and 848, is the *Penchem Tack Store* (270–483–2314), a large Amish tack and farm supply store also patronized by the general public. John H. Yoders and his sons work in the leather shop in the basement while another family member tends to retail sales upstairs. It's a great place to browse, especially if you're in the market for good functional suspenders, straw work hats, Redwing shoes, veterinary supplies, tack (commercially and locally made), or just a soft drink and candy bar. Hours are 8 A.M. to 5 P.M. Monday through Saturday.

If you are in the area in early summer and get that unbearable craving for strawberries (it's best to gorge), call one of (there are several!) the local *strawberry kings* like Tommy Borders near Elkton (270–265–5770), to see if they are open for picking. They'll direct you to the field on which you may sweetly graze.

Due south on either US 79 or 41, nestled right next to the Tennessee border, is the town of *Guthrie,* birthplace of Robert Penn Warren, poet laureate of the United States and Pulitzer prize winner for both poetry and fiction. For those who have read his work, it is enriching to walk the streets and drive by the endless fields, an environment that obviously influenced his writing. Once in town, if you want details or if you'd like to tour the *Robert Penn Warren Museum,* the house in which Penn Warren was born, contact Mrs. Dean Moore at (270) 483–2683. Tours are given 11:30 A.M. to 3:30 P.M. Tuesday through Saturday and 2 to 4 P.M. Sunday. The house is at the corner of Third and Cherry Streets. For a biography or to read some of Penn Warren's work, check www.poets.org. You can even hear him read from his work in his amazing voice.

In Daysville the place to be on Saturday night is *Libby's Entertainment Center.* This country music showcase hosts local entertainers and talent

Stick 'Em Up

The **Southern Deposit Bank** in downtown Russellville, on the corner of Main and Sixth Streets, was the scene of a great crime, the Jesse James gang's first out-of-state robbery. Prior to that day the gang was just a handful of local hoodlums. On May 20, 1868, the gang held up the bank for $9,000, shot and wounded bank president N. Long, and galloped away to join the ranks of America's famous federal fugitives. (What old Jesse didn't know was that there was an additional $50,000 in the vault.) Today the building has been restored into a classy apartment building.

contests as well as Nashville performers, dances, and other special events. The folks who got their start here include Tracey Lawrence and Aaron Tippen. The doors open at 6 P.M., and the show starts at 8 P.M. Admission is charged, and concessions are available. It's a family-oriented spot with no alcohol served. Daysville is located between Elkton and Russellville, at the junction of US 68 and Highway 1309.

If you need a place to spend the night in **Russellville,** try the restored 1824 home of George Washington's third cousin, John Whiting Washington. The **Washington House** is a bed-and-breakfast with three lodging rooms, each fully furnished with antiques that are for sale. The first week in October is a great time to visit town and this bed-and-breakfast because of the Logan County Tobacco Festival; or try the weekend before Thanksgiving, when gorgeous old houses in town participate in the Christmas Open House. Prices are between $85 and $125. Contact Chuck and Regina Phillips, 283 West Ninth Street, Russellville 42276, or call (866) 850–9282 or (270) 726–1240, or check www.bbonline.com/ky/washington or www.washingtonhousebb.com.

In Russellville an impressive four-story brick building houses the **1817 Saddle Factory and Museum** (South Breathitt Street at East Fourth Street; 270–726–4181). The structure is considered one of the earliest industrial buildings constructed in Kentucky. Historic records show that by 1820 there were 44 people living and working at the factory, most of whom were slaves and indentured servants. The museum exhibits objects that they manufactured—saddles, bridles, saddlebags, girths, suitcases, shoes, and so forth. You can see the workers' living quarters in the attic; there's graffiti on the plaster walls that somehow makes one's skin crawl. One object with West Kentucky mythic status is the weathervane in the shape of a fish, which was supposedly shot in 1868 by a member of Jesse James's gang. Tours begin at the Historic Russellville Visitor Center (280 East Fourth Street) and cost $2 per person.

Three miles east of Auburn on US 68 is **South Union Shaker Village,** now a wonderfully curated museum marking the site of a once-thriving village comprising more than 6,000 acres and 200 buildings. Members of the United Society of Believers in Christ's Second Appearing, more commonly known as Shakers, lived at the South Union community from 1807 until 1922. They supported themselves with sophisticated enterprises in garden seed, fruit preserves, fine colorful silk handkerchiefs, and farming. They also ran a large, steam-powered mill, hired out some of Kentucky's first purebred bulls for stud all over the state, and built and leased out (to "the World") a train depot, post office/general store, and tavern.

The 40-room building that now serves as the main museum was the Center House, a dwelling complete with kitchen, communal dining room, and bedrooms—men on one side, women on the other. The structure fulfills your basic expectations of a Shaker building, but in a slightly showier way—some of the trim boards are beaded, there is a nook for a clock, the first-floor window casings flare, and arches abound. From the woodstoves to the cooking utensils to the hat molds, South Union is filled with original Shaker objects, not reproductions. Even the brick dust and mustard-ochre stains on the woodwork are original (let's hear it for organic paint!). This Shaker museum also boasts the largest collection of western Shaker furniture in the United States.

The museum and gift shop are open from March 1 through December, Thursday through Saturday from 10 A.M. to 5 P.M. and Sunday from 1 to 5 P.M. Admission is $6 for adults and $2 for children ages six to twelve. Children age five and under are admitted free. Call (800) 811–8379 or (270) 542–4167, or write South Union Shaker Village, P.O. Box 30, South Union 42283, for information and a schedule of events. This and other info is also available at their Web site, www.shakermuseum.com. One mile east of the museum is Highway 73. Turn right (south) and go ½ mile to the **South Union Post Office** (270–542–6757), established April 1, 1826. This was the last building constructed in the Shaker community.

Directly across the road from the post office is the **Shaker Tavern Bed and Breakfast,** an ornate Victorian tavern the Shakers had built to house the overflow of railroad travelers stopping at the village for lodging. The tavern was always run by non-Shakers and still is. The tavern is a combined restaurant and bed-and-breakfast and given this place the sparkle it deserves. Six classy bed-and-breakfast rooms are available for between $70 and $80 per night, and the chefs guarantee a full Southern breakfast in the morning. Guests also get a tour of the museum at South Union Shaker Village. Call (270) 542–6801 for reservations or more information (www.bbonline.com/ky/shaker).

Yellow Banks, Green River

Daddy, won't you take me back to Muhlenberg County,
Down by the Green River where Paradise lay.
I'm sorry, my son, but you're too late in askin',
Mr. Peabody's coal train has hauled it away.

John Prine's famous lyrics give us a glimpse of Muhlenberg County's history, while traveling through the area gives us an update. ***Paradise*** is an enormous steam-generating power plant, the largest of its kind when it was built in the late 1950s. The county has not been hauled away completely, but you may think they're trying to do so when you see some of the monstrous earthmoving machines in the surface mines visible from several major roads. (The term strip mine is taboo.) Just driving through will convince you that this was the largest coal-producing county in the United States for 23 consecutive years until Environmental Protection Agency (EPA) regulations reduced the market for the area's high-sulfur coal. Seeing Paradise for yourself is worth the effort. From Central City (at U.S. Highways 431 and 62), take Highway 70 south to Highway 176 and go east until you get there.

Don't worry, you'll know it because the landscape changes dramatically as you approach the Green River. First, there are the long train tracks with car after car of coal. There are the strange swampy lowlands, some of which are reclaimed mining areas. If you follow some of the side roads, you'll see eerie little pockets of undisturbed areas, mostly cemeteries, where no mining was allowed. Eventu-

true blue

The first commercial mine for bituminous coal in the entire state was opened near Paradise, in Muhlenberg County, in 1820. From 1973 to 1987 Kentucky led the nation in coal production.

ally you arrive at the power plant, announced by massive, curving cooling towers and a horizontal sulfurous yellow cloud, on still days. Tour availability varies depending upon what's going on at the plant, so be sure to call (270) 476–3301 in advance if you're interested. The engineering is spectacular, as is the altered landscape.

Aside from coal, great country music is this area's claim to fame. In front of the City Building in ***Central City*** is a monument to the town's native sons, Phil and Don Everly. Every Labor Day weekend the Everly Brothers and more than 10,000 fans come to town for a benefit concert called the ***Everly Brothers Central City Music Festival,*** the proceeds of which go to music scholarships and other community projects. One of the favorite events is the

One Interesting Town Mascot

What do bluegrass music, Scottish taxidermy, and barbecued mutton have in common? The Owensboro area. If you are approaching the area by the Bluegrass Parkway and still need convincing that Kentucky is far from mundane, head north on the Green River Parkway and take exit 69 to the tiny town of **Dundee.** When you get into town, keep your eyes to the sky. Standing stiffly above the Masonic lodge is a stuffed goat, imported almost 100 years ago from Dundee, Scotland. The town, which was once called Hines Mill, changed its name to commemorate this oddity.

International Thumb Picking Contest in honor of Merle Travis. Travis, who was born in Muhlenburg County in 1917, was the son of a tobacco farmer and miner. According to music legend, he became friends with two coal miners, Mose Rager and Ike Everly (the Everly Brothers' father), who taught him how to use his thumb to play the bass strings while playing melody on the treble strings. Travis took the style and made it his own, becoming one of the first country players to demonstrate that a guitar could be a lead instrument. Pickers in the area continue to carry on his "Western Kentucky thumb picking" style. Call (270) 754–9603 for festival information; www.centralcitykytourism.com.

Greenville, just south of the Western Kentucky Parkway on US 62 or Highway 189, is home to several unique attractions. One is the **House of Onyx,** a mega mart of gemstones that promotes investment in precious rocks and discourages trust in the banking system. Beyond inventory and prices, its literature consists of an odd combination of claims that the House of Onyx is a real, honest business and fortune cookie–type moralistic quotes. One's curiosity is piqued. The business is primarily geared toward the wholesale and mail-order markets, but if you are in town on a weekday between 9 A.M. and 4:30 P.M., call ahead for a tour of the retail showroom. The mind boggles at the sight of rows of cases of rubies, sapphires, pearls, and myriad other stones. Though there is no sign, the office is in the Aaron Building at 120 North Main Street. Ring the doorbell and explain your interest, or call ahead for an appointment at (270) 338–2363; www.centralcitykytourism.com.

A little-known fact: Greenville is the home of the **State Championship Washer Pitching Playoffs.** Washer pitching is the rural American version of the ancient game of quoits and is related to horseshoes. In the heat of late summer, the playoffs are held at the Greenville Municipal Ball Park. You'll get a schedule for the event if and when you win a district blue ribbon.

Fishing is fantastic in the **Lake Malone State Park.** The 788-acre lake is surrounded by a 388-acre park laced with middle-aged pine forests and sandstone bluffs and caves where the Jesse James gang supposedly hid out. (Jesse James is to Western Kentucky what Daniel Boone is to the central and eastern parts—both hid everywhere, carved their initials on every historic tree and building, and are still receiving royalties for their freely interpreted deeds.)

This popular fishing lake is stocked with largemouth bass, crappie, bluegill, and channel catfish. Amenities include boat dock rental, camping, a swimming beach, picnicking, and playgrounds. Lake Malone is 22 miles south of Central City. From the Western Kentucky Parkway exit at Central City and take US 431 to Kentucky 973 to the park. From Greenville take Highway 181 south to Highway 973 and go 5 miles to the park. The park is open from early April until the end of October. For more information, call (270) 657–2111.

Barbecue Doesn't Get Much Better

In mid-May Owensboro comes alive for the *International Bar-B-Q Festival,* during which time the local folks compete fiercely for culinary titles. A friend's father, "Pop Beers," concocted a darn good recipe for barbecued chicken that has won three festival championships. Because this generous soul has given me permission to pass on to you his secret recipe, I hereby command you to sensitize your palate before participating in the festival. I quote:

Bring the following ingredients to a rapid boil on medium high heat:

1 stick butter

Juice of 1 big lemon

1 tablespoon Worcestershire sauce

1 tablespoon soy sauce

5 shakes Tabasco sauce

1 teaspoon black pepper

1 teaspoon paprika

1 teaspoon garlic powder

1 teaspoon Accent meat tenderizer

1 teaspoon poultry seasoning

Cook until a brown scum forms and then goes away. Let cool and use. Won't spoil if kept. Makes enough for three 3-pound chickens. To use, cut fat (not skin) off chicken. Grill chicken on one side for 30 minutes, turn and repeat, then turn again, baste, and grill for 15 minutes; turn again and repeat. Eat!

On to the self-proclaimed **Bar-B-Q Capital of the World** and the third largest city in the state, **Owensboro.** In this town, where there's smoke, there's barbecue. Initiate yourself by eating at one of the many "smoking" restaurants, ranging from a humble joint called **George's Bar-B-Q** (1362 East Fourth Street; 270–926–9276), where you can sample one version of honest-to-goodness Kentucky burgoo (a super-hearty meat-and-veggie stew that originated in Wales and came here via Virginia with the pioneers), to the famous **Moonlite Bar-B-Q Inn** (270–684–8143), a huge restaurant west of town on Parrish Street where the barbecue is all hickory-pit cooked. George's is open 8 A.M. to 8 P.M. Monday through Friday and 8 A.M. to 9 P.M. Saturday. Hours at Moonlite are 9 A.M. to 9:30 P.M. Moonlite's famous buffet is available from 11 A.M. to 2 P.M. and from 3:30 P.M. to closing Monday through Saturday and 10 A.M. to 3 P.M. Sunday.

My favorite landmark in Owensboro is a **sassafras tree** in the front yard of E. M. Ford & Company on the corner of Frederica and Maple Streets. At a height of 100 feet and a circumference of 16 feet, this 250- to 300-year-old droopy-armed beauty is registered by the American Forestry Association as the largest of its kind in the country and probably in the world. A Mrs. Rash saved the tree from the merciless highway department by planting herself at the base of the trunk with a shotgun in hand. She then pulled political strings, and the governor immediately installed a retaining wall and lightning rod. (I'll bet Earth First! would recruit Mrs. Rash.)

The **Owensboro Area Museum of Science and History** (122 East Second Street; 270–687–2732; www.owensboromuseum.com) is a natural science and history extravaganza containing everything from live reptiles to a 100-plus-seat planetarium, a tobacco-store figure of Punch, dinosaur replicas, and artifacts illustrating events in Kentucky history. Kids and uninhibited adults love the hands-on science exhibits called *Encounter* and *The Owensboro Rotary Playzeum*. Though it is said that the museum started in a church building in 1966, the truth is that it began somewhat earlier in local storyteller and natural historian Joe Ford's backyard playhouse, where he stockpiled insects, rocks, and snakeskins, some of which are still in the museum collection. Open Monday 10 A.M. to 8 P.M., Tuesday through Saturday 10 A.M. to 5 P.M., Sunday 1 P.M. to 5 P.M. adults, $10 for a family.

Western Kentucky is almost as famous for bluegrass music as it is for barbecue. In fact, the Father of Bluegrass Music, Bill Monroe, was born and is buried in the little town of Rosine, one county over from Owensboro. The **International Bluegrass Music Museum** (117 Daviess Street, in Owensboro's RiverPark Center; 270–926–7891 or toll-free 888–MY–BANJO; www.bluegrass-museum.org) honors Monroe and other bluegrass stars. The museum features vintage photographs along a time line of bluegrass history, instruments and interactive exhibits, and a Hall of Honor. Hours are 10 A.M. to 5 P.M. Tuesday through Saturday and 1 to 4 P.M. and Sunday. Admission is $5 adults, $2 children.

One of Kentucky's largest fine art museums, the **Owensboro Museum of Fine Art** (901 Frederica Street; 270–685–3181; www.omfa.us) has an impressive permanent collection of works from 18th-, 19th-, and 20th-century American, English, and French masters and a decorative arts collection of American, European, and Asian objects from the 15th to the 19th centuries. The museum has completed a $1.6 million expansion, which includes a new Exhibitions Wing; an Atrium Sculpture Court; a restored Civil War–era mansion; the Kentucky Spirit Galleries, featuring rotating exhibitions of Kentucky folk art and crafts; and the Yellowbanks Gallery, for works by regional artists. One highlight is an early-20th-century German stained glass collection displayed dramatically in 25-foot towers in an atrium gallery. The Mezzanine Gallery contains religious art. Hours are Tuesday through Friday from 10 A.M. to 4 P.M. and weekends from 1 to 4 P.M. Admission is free, but donations of $2 per adult and $1 per child are suggested.

There are times when rest can be found in activity. Do tennis (indoor and out), racquetball, swimming, horseback riding, fishing, canoeing, and weight lifting strike you as heavy labor? Joan Ramey, owner of Ramey Sports and Fitness Center and Ramey Riding Stables, has opened **Friendly Farms Bed & Breakfast** to all appreciative visitors. Several cottages are now available for bed-and-breakfast lodging at $85 per night; this includes Ms. Ramey's athlete's breakfast. The cottages are 3 miles east of Owensboro on Highway 56. Call (270) 771–5590 or fax (270) 771–4723 or visit www.rameycamps.com.

Weatherberry Bed and Breakfast, at 2731 West Second Street, offers country-style lodging very close to town. For $50 to $70 a night, depending on the size of the room, you get a private bath and a grand Kentucky-style breakfast or a more moderate "healthful" repast. The

trueblue

In addition to an official state song ("My Old Kentucky Home" by Stephen C. Foster), Kentucky also has an official bluegrass song, "Blue Moon of Kentucky" by Rosine, Kentucky, native Bill Monroe.

previous residents of the impressive 1840 farmhouse had a vineyard and collected weather information for the National Weather Bureau, hence the name Weatherberry. Call (270) 684–8760 for reservations.

In all cultures, people set time aside to take retreats, quiet time for contemplation away from the bustle of everyday life. Whether or not you are Catholic or connected to any church or creed in any way, **_Mount Saint Joseph Center and Community of Ursuline Sisters_** offers a quiet, respectful atmosphere to those of us yearning for space and time to absorb (or forget) life. Aside from retreats, the center offers all kinds of religious, cultural, and social programs. Call (270) 229–4103 for information or check www.msjcenter.org. To get there, take Parrish Avenue (Highway 81) west out of town until it turns due south; take Highway 56 to West Louisville, turn right (west) on Highway 815, and look for the sign within 2 miles.

Go in the Maple Mount Farm entrance, find the Mother House, and ask to see the museum. Artifacts range from desks of the founders to gifts from foreign missions, musical instruments, religious articles, books, and displays, such as *The Madonna Room*, which houses a collection of reproductions of famous European Madonna paintings. The non-Catholic visitor learns that reliquaries are saints' shrines of all sizes that can be displayed anywhere from behind an altar in a massive gold frame to behind a pendant in a tiny glass locket. The idea of wearing a first-degree relic, usually a chip of a saint's bone hidden in the back of a ring, has endless implications.

From Mount Saint Joseph take an eastward drive on Highway 56 for 2 miles to the **_Diamond Lake Resort and Campground._** Statewide catfish farming is on the rise because reclaimed surface mines are required to have settling ponds, which are appropriate places for raising fish. This farm is a successful, sophisticated business whose owners are more than happy to show people around. The resort has 270 campsites and 10 motel rooms for those who don't want to "rough it." Facilities include a pay fishing lake, pedal boats, go-carts, paint ball, laundry, grocery store, arcade, lakeside restaurant and grill. Open daily year-round 7 A.M. to 10 P.M. Call (270) 229–4900 or go to www.diamondlakeresort.net.

After the fish farm tour, you may be curious to know how the product tastes. The **_Windy Hollow, Raceway Park, Restaurant and Museum_** (270–785–4088) has a famous catfish buffet Friday and Saturday from 5 to 8:30 P.M. (and a big country-ham breakfast buffet on Sunday from 7 A.M. to 1:30 P.M. if fish isn't your dish). Every day is your lucky day at the pay lakes, and you don't even need a fishing license! Windy Hollow wins the contest for having the most going on at once: drag racing, water sliding, camping, pay-lake fishing, barbecuing, golf, and even old western movie viewing while you eat. Don't miss the cowboy museum. Yee-haw! From Owensboro follow Highway 81 south to Old 81 and exit west. Follow the signs.

Although the third weekend in October is the best time to visit **_Reid's Orchard,_** because it hosts a two-day harvest festival, any time during apple season in the fall is a good time to pick your own of whatever is ripe at that moment. The farm store offers cider, relishes, produce, and whatever else

A Soldier's Story

An unusual and thought-provoking legacy of World War II is preserved at the *James D. Veatch Camp Breckinridge Museum and Arts Center* near the Western Kentucky community of Morganfield. In the 1940s this was a huge military training center. It was also the location of a United States prisoner of war camp, and among the prisoners was a young Czechoslovakian named Daniel Mayer, who had been conscripted into the German army and captured in Tunisia. Homesick, this self-taught artist began painting murals of his homeland on the walls of the prisoners' quarters. The scenes were so beautiful that Erick Zychowski, who was in charge of the camp's Officers Club, asked Mayer to paint murals to decorate the club's walls. It is thought that he painted more than one hundred scenes in buildings throughout the camp. Though most of Camp Breckinridge was torn down after the military vacated it in the 1960s, a local citizens group worked to save the Officers Club building. Today owned by the county, it features numerous displays of World War II artifacts as well as plaques and memorials to United States veterans. But the most striking artifacts line the main hall—more than 40 huge pastoral murals painted by Mayer between May 1943 and his death of pneumonia at the camp in July 1945. You can learn more about this fascinating wartime legacy by visiting Camp Breckinridge. Museum hours are 10 A.M. to 3 P.M. Tuesday through Friday, 10 A.M. to 4 P.M. Saturday, and 1 to 4 P.M. Sunday. Admission is $3 for adults, $1 for children. Call (270) 389–4420 for more information' www.breckinridge-arts.org. Camp Breckinridge is located near Morganfield at the intersection of the U.S. Highway 60 Bypass and Highway 2091 S.

these industrious folks decide to make and sell. The orchard is located at 4818 Highway 144, off US 60, and is open spring through December with seasonal products. Call ahead (270–685–2444) for hours and information.

The *John James Audubon State Park* is about 20 miles west of Owensboro, along US 41 north of Henderson. Although Audubon is the most famous American painter of birds, he was a failure as a business executive. While he lived in this area, from 1810 to 1820, Audubon got involved in several entrepreneurial projects, all of which failed because instead of working, he spent his days in search of rare birds. With nothing left but his portfolio of bird paintings, his talent, and an idea, Audubon dragged his poor family all over the South while he painted and searched for a publisher. Eventually he found an engraver in London, England, who printed his 435 hand-colored plates as *The Birds of America*. A complete bound set of the original folios and numerous individual prints are on display in the Audubon Memorial and Nature Museum, as is the largest collection of Audubon memorabilia in existence, including many of his original paintings, journals, correspondence, and personal items. Another treasure in the museum is a rare 3-by-5-inch daguerreotype of the elderly Audubon taken by the famous early photographer Matthew Brady.

The whole northern half of the park was donated as a nature preserve, with the stipulation that it be treated as a bird sanctuary and that the old growth beech and sugar maple woods be preserved. Ask the park naturalist what wild and amazing flora and fauna can be seen. The park also sponsors spring and fall migration bird walks.

Adjacent to the museum is the Nature Center, which features a glass enclosed Nature Observatory and a Discovery Center with exhibits on bird biology and psychology. Daily programs are offered in the summer, and special events are sprinkled throughout the rest of the year. Museum hours are 10 A.M. to 5 P.M. daily. Admission to the museum and Nature Center is $4 for adults, $3 for children ages six to twelve, or a family charge of $10. The park is open daily, sunrise to sunset. Call (270) 826–2247 for more information (http://parks.ky.gov/findparks/recparks/au).

More Good Lodging in Western Kentucky

BENTON

Aire Castle Inn & Stained Glass Art
435 Salem Chapel Road North
(270) 354–5004 or
(866) 403–2473
www.airecastle.com
Near Kentucky Lake; country setting with in-ground pool. $75 guest room, $125 suites.

CADIZ

Lake Barkley State Resort Park
off U.S. Highway 68
(270) 924–1131
Two lodges and cottages; golf and fitness center. $60 to $170.

DAWSON SPRINGS

Pennyrile Forest State Resort Park
Highway 109
(270) 797–3421
Lodge and cottages. $70 to $120.

GILBERTSVILLE

Kentucky Dam Village State Resort Park
U.S. Highway 62 at U.S. Highway 641 on Kentucky Lake
(270) 362–4271
Lodge and cottages; golf course. $60 to $215.

GRAND RIVERS

Grand Rivers Inn
1949 JH OBryan Avenue
(270) 362–4487
www.grandriverinn.com
Rooms and cottages; ¼ mile from lake. $42 to $54.

HENDERSON

John James Audubon State Park
3100 Highway 41 North
(270) 826–2247
Lakeside cottages with fireplaces. $75 to $115.

L&N Bed and Breakfast
327 North Main Street
(270) 831–1100
www.inbbky.com
Historic home overlooking the river. $85.

Victorian Quarters Bed & Breakfast
109 Clay Street
(270) 831–2778
www.victorianquartersbb.com
Scenic mansion overlooking the Ohio River. Three rooms; $95.

MAYFIELD

Super 8 Motel
1100 Links Lane
(270) 247–8899
$60 and up.

Susan B. Seay's Magnolia Manor
401 South Seventh
(270) 247–4108
Bed-and-breakfast in a
1900 Greek Revival-style
mansion.

MURRAY

Baymont Inn
1210 North Twelfth Street
(270) 759–5910
www.baymontinn.com $79
and up.

Holiday Inn Express
U.S. Highway 641 North
(270) 759–4449
$95 and up.

Fairfield Inn
800 Salem Road
(270) 688–8887
$99 and up.

Helton House Bed and Breakfast
103 East Twenty-third
Street
(270) 926–7117
www.bbonline.com/ky/
helton
Mission-style home in a
tree-lined neighborhood.
$60 to $85.

PADUCAH

1857's
127 Market House Square
(270) 444–3960 or
(800) 264–5607
A three-story brick lodging
on the National Register of
Historic Places. Some pets
and children allowed. Pool
table and hot tub.

Rosewood Inn Bed & Breakfast
2740 South Friendship
Road
(270) 554–6632 or
(800) 548–3840
www.bbonline.com/ky/
rosewood
Two guest rooms and two
suites in a country farm-
house. $75 to $115.

More Fun Places to Eat in Western Kentucky

BENTON

Catfish Kitchen
136 Teal Run Circle
(270) 362–7306
Lakeside dining; great
seafood and homemade
desserts.

CADIZ

Ferrell's
2021 Main Street
(270) 522–3418
Hamburger-and-fries joint.

Lake Barkley State Resort Park
off U.S. Highway 68
(270) 924–1131
Spacious dining room
with fireplace; regional
specialties.

GRAND RIVERS

Dockers Grille Turtle Bay Resort
overlooking Lake Barkley
(270) 362–8364
Breakfast and lunch; try the
"turtle burger."

Knoth's Bar-B-Que
728 U.S. Highway 62
(270) 362–8580
Lunch and dinner with—
guess what—barbecue.
Notable sauce. If inclined,
you can buy a whole pork
shoulder to take home.

Miss Scarlett's Restaurant
708 Complex Drive
(270) 928–3126
Traditional Southern and
regional fare, with home-
made breads and soups.

HENDERSON

Wolf's Restaurant and Tavern
31 North Green Street
(270) 826–0980
Henderson's local hang-
out since the late 1800s;
famous for its bean soup
and corn bread.

HOPKINSVILLE

Woodshed Pit Bar-B-Que
1821 West Seventh Street
(270) 885–8144
Barbecue and other American fare.

KUTTAWA

Kuttawa Harbor Marina
1709 Lake Barkley Drive
(270) 388–9563
Famous for its "Rudyburger," indoor and outdoor dining.

MAYFIELD

Hill's Bar-B-Que
1002 Cuba Road
(Highway 303)
(270) 247–9121
Open every day all day except Sunday.

MURRAY

Sammon's Bakery
874 Chestnut Street
(270) 753–5434
Cheeseburgers on homemade buns, doughnuts, and pastries.

OWENSBORO

Old Hickory Pit
338 Washington Avenue
(270) 926–9000
Smoked mutton and great desserts.

Ole South Barbeque
3523 Highway 54
(270) 926–6464
More barbecue and accoutrements.

PADUCAH

BB Whiskers
2701 Irvin Cobb Drive
(270) 443–7076
Catfish and Western Kentucky–style barbecue.

C. C. Cohen Restaurant and Bar
103 Broadway
(270) 442–6391
Steaks and seafood with weekend entertainment.

Flamingo Row West
2100 Broadway
(270) 442–0460
Famous for more than 20 varieties of "stuffed bread." You can't miss the superbright building facade made of handmade tiles. Outdoor dining.

Jeremiah's Restaurant and Brew Pub
225 Broadway
(270) 443–3991
Twenty-ounce steaks and a large selection of ales.

Index

About the Author

Zoé Strecker is an artist and writer who lives with her husband and daughters on a farm near the Kentucky River.

About the Editor

An award-winning journalist and photographer, Jackie Sheckler Finch has covered a wide array of topics, from birth to death, with all the joy and sorrow in between. She has written half a dozen books and had articles published in numerous newspapers and magazines. She has been named the Mark Twain Travel Writer of the Year by Midwest Travel Writers Association a record four times—in 1998, 2001, 2003 and 2007—and is a member of The Society of American Travel Writers. Jackie shares her home with Pepper, resident guard dog and entertainer. One of her greatest joys is taking to the road to find the fascinating people and places that wait over the hill and around the next bend.